PROFILES OF OHIO WOMEN

1803 – 2003

PROFILES OF

OHIO WOMEN

1 8 0 3 – 2 0 0 3

JACQUELINE JONES ROYSTER

OHIO UNIVERSITY PRESS   ATHENS

Ohio University Press, Athens, Ohio 45701
© 2003 by Ohio University Press

11 10 09 08 07 06 05 04 03   5 4 3 2 1

Photos on jacket front from left, top to bottom. First column: Ethel G. Swanbeck, courtesy of the Ohio Historical Society; Frances Dana Gage; Farida Anna Wiley, courtesy Shelby County Historical Society. Second column: Toni Morrison, courtesy Toni Morrison; (Elizabeth) Anne O'Hare McCormick; Ruby Dee; (Geraldine) Jerrie L. Fredritz Mock, courtesy Jerrie Mock. Third column: Betty Zane; Karen Nussbaum; Hallie Quinn Brown. Fourth column: Tracy Chapman; Alice Schille; Farah Moavenzadeh Walters; V. Lanna Samaniego. Fifth column: Annie Oakley, courtesy of the Garst Museum; Dorothy L. Kazel, O.S.U.; Maude Charles Collins. *Unless otherwise noted, photos are courtesy Ohio Women's Hall of Fame.*

Library of Congress Cataloging-in-Publication Data

Royster, Jacqueline Jones.
    Profiles of Ohio women, 1803–2003 / Jacqueline Jones Royster.
        p. cm.
Includes bibliographical references and index.
    ISBN 0-8214-1508-5 (alk. paper)
     1. Women—Ohio—Biography. 2. Ohio—History. I. Title.

CT3260.R69 2003
920.72'09771—dc22

2003017285

This publication is dedicated to the untold numbers of Ohio women who have formed the fabric of life in this state and in the nation, but whose names and achievements are neither acknowledged nor celebrated in our history books. Although *Profiles of Ohio Women, 1803–2003* will not remedy these many omissions, it does symbolize new opportunities for women's active participation and leadership to be recognized, honored, and inscribed in their rightful places of respect and celebration as Ohio moves into its third century of success. We present this collection, therefore, during the bicentennial celebration as the tip of an iceberg, as a bold and concrete statement in acknowledgment of generations of remarkable women who helped to build the State of Ohio and the United States of America.

CONTENTS

Profiles of Two Hundred Ohio Women

Appendices

FOREWORD

THIS YEAR BRINGS us to our great state's bicentennial celebration and to a celebration of the contributions and achievements of Ohio women. *Profiles of Ohio Women, 1803–2003* chronicles the lives of two hundred remarkable women whose accomplishments have shaped and changed the face of Ohio, the nation, and the world.

These women come from every walk of life. They all shared an extraordinary commitment to excellence, achievement, and service to others. Their triumphs stand as a public record and hold the power to inspire all Ohioans, especially future generations.

During Ohio's 2003 bicentennial celebration we should all take the opportunity to recognize women leaders from the past, the present, and the future. The women featured in *Profiles of Ohio Women, 1803–2003* have left a testament to Ohio's great history and a legacy of the contributions and achievement of Ohio women.

First Lady Hope Taft
December 2002

INTRODUCTION

ON BEHALF OF the state of Ohio and the Ohio Bicentennial Commission, the Ohio Women's Advisory Council commissioned this publication, *Profiles of Ohio Women, 1803–2003,* in collaboration with the Ohioana Library Association. The members of the Women's Advisory Council and the staff of the Ohioana Library are listed in appendix 1.

The Ohioana Library Association is dedicated to encouraging and recognizing literary and other creative accomplishments of Ohioans, including women, and to maintaining and preserving a permanent collection of books and music by and about Ohioans. *Profiles of Ohio Women, 1803–2003* is a project that fits well within this mission. It recognizes two hundred remarkable Ohio women selected from a very large number of candidates who, through their contributions and achievements, have shaped history both within and beyond the borders of Ohio. This publication provides a record of their accomplishments that will enrich the history of the state and the nation and that will inspire all Ohioans to dream incredible dreams, to reach unknown heights, and to achieve beyond what any of us living today might predict. This book, therefore, is a celebration.

The legacies of leadership from Ohio women are varied and rich. For this bicentennial year we chose to highlight just two hundred of them, one for each year of Ohio history. Our purpose was twofold. On the one hand, we sought to showcase leadership statewide. On the other, we sought simultaneously to depict a range of achievements demonstrating the multiple pathways by which women, typically as unsung heroines, have shared their visions, time, and talents, often against incredible odds. The book is organized, therefore, into seventeen categories recognizing both the paid and voluntary contributions of these women.

To select the women who would actually be profiled in this book, the Bicentennial Commission issued a public announcement and a call for nominations on March 2, 2001. The call affirmed the commission's view of the importance of the project. Quoting Ellen Nasner of the Advisory Council, the announcement stated, "If we do not create an historical legacy of Ohio women for Ohio's Bicentennial, we have missed our opportunity for generations to follow. Women have played an invaluable role and made contributions that many people don't know about." With this statement, the Bicentennial Commission proclaimed women to be vital contributors deserving of high praise in the observance of two centuries of history and cultural and economic development.

Nominations were also sought from sixteen hundred historical organizations, libraries, and women's groups from around the state. The nomination form asked nominators to follow four basic guidelines:

1. To show that the nominee was born in Ohio, met a five-year residency requirement, or made extraordinary contributions to the state of Ohio.

2. To list the nominee's significant contributions.

3. To explain the significance of the uniqueness of the nominee's contribution to the course of history and how the nominee provided an example to others.

4. To explain how the achievements were unprecedented, a first for women, or an inspiration to others.

The process resulted in a master list of 562 names, all of which are included—for the record—in this publication. Two hundred are profiled, and the remaining 362 (plus two duplications, as explained below) are listed in appendix 4: Other Notable Ohio Women. The list of notable Ohio women includes both women who were nominated for the publication and women who have served as first ladies of Ohio and of the United States of America. From the first ladies list, the advisory council chose two representatives to be profiled, Lucy Webb Ware Hayes (as first lady of Ohio and of the United States) and Martha Kinney Cooper (Ohio); Hayes and Cooper are the only women who are profiled and whose names appear on the list of other notable Ohio women.

In selecting the final 200 women to be profiled from the list of 562 (minus the overlapping names), the decision was difficult. The selection subcommittee of the advisory council balanced the list on several principles:

1. Chronology—the call for nominations stated a desire to have one hundred women per century.

2. Geography—the advisory council wanted the two hundred women to be broadly representative of the state.

3. Contribution—the advisory council wanted a broad distribution of achievements across walks of life.

4. Race and ethnicity—the advisory council wanted the profiles to indicate in demographic terms, to the extent possible, the varied origins of the women who have shaped and developed the state.

The profiles that follow demonstrate these principles. There are women included from the eighteenth century (1), the nineteenth century (51), and the twentieth century (148). All regions of the state are represented. The women's contributions are organized into seventeen categories of achievements, as indicated by the table of contents. These categories emerged organically as we reviewed the list of nominations and paid attention to the pattern of achievements among them. Included are women diverse in race, ethnicity, and cultural heritage, but the group is just the tip of an iceberg in documenting jobs well done and services well rendered.

In developing the profiles, I acknowledge the invaluable assistance of:

1. My five research assistants, Kalenda C. Eaton, Pamela Y. Martin, Elizabeth Miglin, Nicole Rencher, and Na'im Tyson. All were relentless in helping me to locate photographs and to find the details that would make these profiles as substantive and as accurate as possible.

2. Molly Ryan, program coordinator of the Ohio Bicentennial Commission, who gave so generously of her time in scanning the photographs from the Ohio Women's Hall of Fame into usable images for the publication.

3. The staff of Humanities Information Systems at the Ohio State University, especially Scott Sprague and Paul Kotheimer, and Christopher J. Kinney of the McKinley Museum in Canton, Ohio, all of whom also provided technological support for the photographs.

4. Barbara Meister, Cynthia Sweet Bard, and Kathleen Hipes, who helped to pull files and gather other information at Ohioana Library.

5. Denise Mason of the College of Humanities staff, Rebecca M. Royster, and Giles Royster, who provided technical assistance with the database.

6. Several of the women profiled, the friends and family of many of them, and the staffs at libraries and museums statewide and nationwide, who helped to provide vital information and photographs.

7. Robin E. Rice, director of the Ohio Women's Hall of Fame, and Carolyn Casper-Duvall, manager, Women Making History Essay Contest, without whose cooperation in sharing photographs and information from the Hall of Fame files, this book would not have been possible.

8. Linda Hengst, director of the Ohioana Library Association, and Ellen Nasner, Ohio Reads, Department of Education, State of Ohio, for the critical work that they both did in developing the proposal for the book, getting the necessary endorsements for the project, working so closely with me in selecting the women to be profiled, and providing guidance and direction during the writing process. They are a formidable team of dedicated Ohio women, and it has been a pleasure to see that so many state records of Ohio women have been and are in such good and caring hands. Without their professionalism and expertise, this project would have failed.

9. The staff at Ohio University Press, including director David Sanders; editors Nancy Basmajian, Ricky S. Huard, and Sharon Rose; and production manager Beth Pratt.

Unless otherwise noted, all photographs are courtesy of the Ohio Women's Hall of Fame. Note also that the symbol shown below indicates that the woman profiled is a member of the Ohio Women's Hall of Fame.

Profiles of Ohio Women, 1803–2003 has been a remarkable collaboration that stands in tribute to the vital roles that the women of Ohio have played in the development of their communities, the state, and the nation. Their talents have made a difference in many fields, but the real difference has come from their dreams of a better world, their desires for adventure, their commitments to use their talents well, and the indomitable force that is generated by people who are willing to work tirelessly, not only in their own interests, but in the interest of others. The State of Ohio gratefully acknowledges the steady flow of high-achieving women who are our mothers, sisters, daughters, mentors, and friends. They have inspired and continue to inspire us as we look toward another two hundred years of success and leadership.

PROFILES OF TWO HUNDRED

OHIO WOMEN

BUSINESS

AND

FINANCE

EVEN TODAY, AS WE ENTER THE THIRD CENTURY of Ohio statehood, business and finance are envisioned largely as the high-powered world of men. We have come to understand that there are some exceptional women, but we still see them as going against the grain of expectations. Certainly, this was the case in the nineteenth century, which left little evidence to suggest that women were there. In Ohio, however, women *were* there and they managed not only to survive but to thrive. As documented by the profiles that follow, Ohio women were on Wall Street by 1870, managing highly profitable companies by 1896, developing cities by 1897, running banks by 1911, and much, much more. These torchbearers lighted the way for others, so that subsequent generations could blaze bolder, wider trails—and indeed they have. In 2003 we have a full spectrum of women in business and finance, and they are clearly helping the nation to reenvision both what and how this world should be.

DAEIDA HARTELL WILCOX BEVERIDGE

G. MAXINE HAXTON CARNAHAN

CORA BELL CLARK

NORMA B. CRADEN

LUCILLE G. FORD

LOUISE MCCARREN HERRING

ROSABETH MOSS KANTER

CHERYL KRUEGER-HORN

CAROL HILKIRK LATHAM

TAMI LONGABERGER

FARAH B. MOAVENZADELI MAJIDZADEH

FLORENCE SPURGEON ZACKS MELTON

KAREN NUSSBAUM

DARLENE M. OWENS

MURIEL SIEBERT

JULIA CURRY MONTGOMERY WALSH

VICTORIA CLAFLIN WOODHULL

NANNIE (SCOTT HONSHELL) KELLY WRIGHT

Daeida Hartell Wilcox
BEVERIDGE

1862–1914

DEFIANCE COUNTY

D AEIDA HARTELL WILCOX BEVERIDGE was born in Hicksville, Ohio, in 1862. She attended private school there and later went to a public school in Canton, Ohio. In 1883, having married Harvey Henderson Wilcox from Kansas, she moved to Los Angeles, California. Three years later the Wilcoxes purchased 120 acres nearby, with the intention of making the area a business investment. Harvey Wilcox divided the property into lots and laid out streets; Beveridge took on the task of landscaping and naming of the streets, some based on the natural beauty, others after friends in Ohio. The object of this work was to appeal to buyers who were purchasing the lots for $1000 each, a considerable mark-up from the $150 per acre initial purchase price. On a train trip back to Ohio, Beveridge met a woman whose description of her summer home near Chicago was the inspiration to name the Wilcox subdivision Hollywood.

In 1891, Harvey Wilcox died, leaving the development of the subdivision in the hands of Beveridge. An astute businesswoman and community leader, she increased the value of the property exponentially, turning Hollywood into a thriving city that beckoned residents, businesses, artists, and the newly emerging film industry. She donated land for three churches, a library, city hall, park, primary school, police station, post office, and theatrical playhouse. She built the Hollywood National and Citizen's Savings Bank and installed the city's first sidewalks.

In 1894, she married Philo Judson Beveridge, son of the governor of California, who shared her vision of community development. Together, they continued their philanthropic and civic-minded work until Beveridge's death on August 14, 1914.

3

Business and Finance

OHIO
WOMEN'S
HALL OF
FAME

G. Maxine Haxton CARNAHAN

1922–

COSHOCTON COUNTY

G. MAXINE HAXTON CARNAHAN, born on July 21, 1922, entered the work force during World War II, as many women did, to support the war effort and to keep the economy going. At the end of the war, like many of these same women, she left her job as a quality inspector in a munitions plant to work at home. After raising five children, Carnahan returned to the world of paid work and in 1975 became the first woman president of the United Paperworkers International Union in Coshocton, Ohio. In this position, Carnahan set many precedents for women's achievements, especially with regard to nontraditional work roles and the securing of benefits for workers. In addition, she served on the Coshocton Trades and Labor Council and on the City of Coshocton Zoning Board of Appeals.

In 1986, Carnahan retired, but she took the leadership skills that she had developed and honed at work and brought them into the community as an active volunteer in many organizations. From 1987 to 2001, she managed a travel club at the Coshocton Senior Center, providing a critical service for senior citizens who rarely traveled. She escorted seniors on trips to Mexico, the Panama Canal, Central America, Colombia, Aruba, Puerto Rico, and Nova Scotia. In 1998, she spearheaded a campaign to pass a levy to support home-delivered meals for seniors and the maintenance of programs at the senior center. In addition, she tutored in the Kraft Program at a middle school; volunteered at bingo games, the funds from which were used to offset the expenses of the senior center; and served for eight years on the board of trustees for the Area Agency on Aging.

In 1996, Carnahan was elected Senior Queen representing Roscoe Village Canal Days, where her responsibilities were to promote Roscoe Village as a tourist site. In 1999, she received the YWCA/BPW (Business and Professional Women) Award in the Tribute to Women of Achievement in Volunteerism.

4

LIVING THE LEGACY
OHIO
WOMEN'S
HALL OF
FAME

Cora Bell CLARK

1867–1939

LICKING COUNTY

Cora Bell Clark was born in Utica, Ohio, in 1867. As a child, she worked in the dining room of her parents' hotel, but by age 15 she was working at the town bank, which had been founded in 1871 by Abel J. Wilson, the man who would become her brother-in-law. She worked first as a copyist, then as a bookkeeper, and ultimately as a teller and assistant cashier. Acquiring this latter position made her the first woman cashier of a national bank in the United States.

In 1910 Wilson died, but before his death he named Clark his successor as owner of this private bank. This was an unprecedented move because women during this era rarely worked outside of the home or if they did, they were restaurant workers, sales clerks, seamstresses, domestic servants, or factory workers. Clark, however, was elected president of the bank on February 9, 1911, making her the first woman to hold this position as well. She presided over the business of the bank, making decisions about assets and income and giving investment advice and other financial guidance to farmers, businessmen, and would-be homeowners, many of whom did not realize that the "C. B." with whom they communicated in writing was a woman. Clark participated in American Bankers Association conventions and was quite a curiosity in her male-dominated field. She built an excellent reputation as an astute businesswoman and a compassionate community leader.

Among her many accomplishments as a banker was her success during the famous 1929 Bank Holiday, when banks across the nation were closed to prevent panic runs by depositors as the Great Depression took hold of the U.S. economy. Clark and her cashier, Roy Mantonya, traveled to Cleveland and successfully convinced officials that the Utica bank was solvent enough to remain open, to the great relief to her depositors.

In addition to presiding over the bank, Clark also owned a fourteen-acre truck farm. She raised fruits and vegetables, and was known by her neighbors and clientele to spend her days off pondering financial problems as she sorted beans and strawberries.

Norma B. CRADEN

1919–1992

LUCAS COUNTY

NORMA B. CRADEN was born in 1919 in Toronto, Ontario, but immigrated to Ohio and became a U.S. citizen. In Lucas County she was involved in the labor movement for fifty years, building a distinguished career as a union leader. She was the first female president of a United Auto Workers local in northwestern Ohio, and she was among the first in her community to become involved in the Coalition of Labor Union Women. Craden also served as president of the Communication Workers of America (CWA), AFL-CIO Local 4315, for eighteen years and attended eighteen of its national conventions.

In 1978, Craden retired from the Ohio Bell Telephone Company and stepped down as president of Local 4315 of the CWA. In retirement, she served as the Toledo-area AFL-CIO council's labor liaison to the United Way until 1985. In 1987, however, Craden was brought out of retirement by the unprecedented request that she run for president of Local 4315 to fill a six-month term in the aftermath of an internal dispute. She won the election, served the six months, and was then encouraged to seek a full three-year term. She campaigned and won, demonstrating the tremendous respect and support that she had garnered as a member of the union, even though she was retired rather than actively working.

Through the decades of her leadership, Craden fulfilled many important roles. She lobbied for legislation in both Columbus and Washington, D.C., to better conditions for workers. She was appointed by Mayor Kessler of Toledo to the Toledo Board of Community Relations and by Governor Rhodes to the Women's Advisory Committee of the Ohio Bureau of Employment Services. She served on the Ohio AFL-CIO Civil Rights Committee, the Toledo Port Council AFL-CIO, and the Advisory Board of Health and Human Services.

In addition to her long years of activism as a union member, Craden also volunteered with several community organizations, including the United Way and the Lucas County Children's Board.

6

OHIO
WOMEN'S
HALL OF
FAME

Lucille G. FORD

1921–

ASHLAND COUNTY

Lucille G. Ford was born on December 31, 1921. She graduated from Northwestern University with an M.B.A. at a time when few women were reaching such goals and later received a Ph.D. from Case Western Reserve University. She came to Ashland College in 1967 as a professor of economics. Over the next three decades, she helped transform a struggling college into a university with eighty major fields of study, thriving graduate and undergraduate programs, continuing education programs, and special programs at nineteen teaching locations throughout the state. As a professor, Ford encouraged in her students their thirst for knowledge and pushed them to live up to the high standards that she set both inside and outside the classroom. She was instrumental in creating the Gill Center for Business and Economic Education and was named its director in 1974. In addition to directing the center, she went on to fill other administrative roles as dean of the School of Business and Economics and as vice-president and provost of the university.

Ford has also had an impact outside the academic arena. In the 1960s she was the first and only woman to serve on the Ohio Edison Company board of directors and the first to be appointed to serve on the board of National City Bank. In 1972, she was listed among the American Men of Social Science. But perhaps her most notable first was in 1978, when she campaigned for the post of lieutenant governor as the running mate of Charles Kurfess, becoming the first woman to participate in an Ohio primary gubernatorial race.

In addition to these achievements, in 1980 Ford earned the designation of certified financial planner, and sixteen years later she received an M.A. in pastoral counseling and psychology from Ashland Theological Seminary. After retiring from Ashland University, Ford became the founding president of the Ashland County Community Foundation and continues to serve as a leader in this organization.

Business and Finance

Louise McCarren HERRING

1909–1987

CLINTON COUNTY

Louise McCarren Herring, born in 1909 in Clinton County, graduated from the University of Cincinnati in 1932 with a degree in commercial engineering. Although she was well prepared to be a company manager, Ohio in the 1930s was not ready for women in business leadership positions. Herring took a job instead at the Kroger Company as director of women's personnel. In this position, she was aware of the difficulties that employees had in saving money and getting low-interest loans and she became intrigued by the idea of credit unions espoused by Edward Filene, the Boston department store tycoon. Herring had a vision that people could live better lives through cooperative efforts and was pleased to represent the Kroger Company at an organizational meeting for the Credit Union National Association (CUNA) in Estes Park, Colorado. As a charter member of CUNA, Herring's enthusiasm was instrumental in starting Kemba (Kroger Employees Mutual Benefits Association), but her passion for the potential of credit unions also led her to leave Kroger to work with Filene in promoting credit unions nationwide.

In the 1930s, Herring led a three-year campaign for the passage of state legislation permitting the establishment and operation of credit unions in Ohio. After the law was approved, she helped create the credit union section in the state's Division of Securities and she became the first managing director of the Ohio Credit Union League. Over the next fifty years, Herring helped organize more than five hundred credit unions around the country, including, for example, those established at U.S. Steel, International Harvester, the NAACP, and the Columbus Police Department. Herring retired in 1945 to raise her family but returned in 1958, when she agreed to help consolidate credit unions in the merger of two newspapers in Cincinnati. She served as president of the Cincinnati Communicating Arts Credit Union until her death in 1987.

In 1983, Herring was inducted into the Cooperative Hall of Fame by the National Cooperative Business Association, only the second woman to be chosen. In addition, service awards in credit unions across the nation are named in her honor.

8

Rosabeth Moss KANTER

1943–

CUYAHOGA COUNTY

Rosabeth Moss Kanter, born in Cleveland, Ohio, on March 15, 1943, graduated with honors in 1964 from Bryn Mawr College and went on to complete an M.A. (1965) and a Ph.D. (1967) in sociology at the University of Michigan. Kanter is now the Ernest L. Arbuckle Professor of Business Administration at Harvard Business School, having left Yale University where she was on the faculty from 1977 to 1986. Kanter is an internationally known business leader, award-winning author, and expert on strategy, innovation, and the management of change.

Kanter, a prominent business speaker, has delivered addresses to hundreds of trade associations, civic groups, and national conventions in nearly every state in the United States and in more than twenty other countries. She has shared the stage with world leaders, including presidents, prime ministers, and leaders of business and industry. Kanter has authored or coauthored fifteen books, the most recent being *Evolve!: Succeeding in the Digital Culture of Tomorrow* (2001). Several of her earlier publications have been bestsellers, including *Men and Women of the Corporation* (1977), *Change Masters* (1983), *When Giants Learn to Dance* (1989), and *Rosabeth Moss Kanter on the Frontiers of Management* (1997). As a consultant, she cofounded Goodmeasure, Inc., and advises some of the world's most prominent companies. For example, she is a senior adviser to IBM's Reinventing Education initiative, which is currently active in twenty-one sites in the United States and in eight other countries.

Kanter has received twenty-one honorary degrees from distinguished universities nationwide and innumerable other awards. Among her most prestigious honors, she was named one of the one hundred most important women in America by *Ladies' Home Journal* and one of the fifty most powerful women in the world by the *Times* of London, and in 2001 she received the Academy of Management's Scholarly Contribution to Management Award, the highest award for scholarly contributions in her field.

9

Business and Finance

Cheryl KRUEGER-HORN

1952–

FRANKLIN COUNTY

CHERYL KRUEGER-HORN, born on January 1, 1952, graduated from Bowling Green State University in 1974 with a degree in home economics and business. She began her career as a buyer with Burdines department store. In 1976, she moved to The Limited Stores, Inc., as a merchandise manager, leaving in 1981 to become vice-president at Bernard Chaus, Inc., in New York City. Also in 1981, Krueger-Horn began her own company in Columbus, Cheryl's Cookies, with an old-fashioned cookie recipe passed down from her grandmother Elsie. The company grew quickly, and in 1985 Krueger-Horn was able to leave Chaus and devote full time to her own enterprise. By 1988, Krueger-Horn had diversified her product line to include other gourmet foods and gifts. To reflect this growth, she changed the name of the company to Cheryl&Co. It has continued to grow and is now one of the top five hundred women-owned businesses in the country.

Krueger-Horn takes pride in running a company that is highly successful, very supportive of finding ways to help employees integrate work and family, and greatly involved in the community. In addition to flexible scheduling, Cheryl&Co. offers several programs for professional development and an awards program for excellence in job performance. Equally conscientious is Krueger-Horn's commitment to philanthropic programs. She began, for example, a school-to-work program called C.C.H.I.P. (Cheryl&Co. Hometown Integrated Project) designed to provide hands-on business experience to high school students, and also Cookies for As, a program that encourages good grades among all students. In addition, she sends baked goods each week to a local food bank and distributes food items to nearby homeless shelters.

Krueger-Horn serves on several advisory boards, including the board of directors of the Federal Reserve Bank for the Fourth Federal Reserve District, the board of trustees of the Ohio State University's James Cancer Hospital, and the board of trustees for Columbus Academy. She has received many honors and awards. In 1987, she became the youngest woman ever to receive the Woman of Achievement Award from the YWCA (1987), and she was recognized also by the *Working Woman* magazine's Entrepreneurial Excellence Award for General Excellence.

10

OHIO
WOMEN'S
HALL OF
FAME

Profiles of Two Hundred Ohio Women

Carol Hilkirk LATHAM

1939⁻

CUYAHOGA COUNTY

CAROL HILKIRK LATHAM was born in Cuyahoga County on August 30, 1939, and graduated from Ohio Wesleyan University with a degree in chemistry. She spent the years immediately after graduation working at Sohio. After marrying and starting a family, however, she spent the next two decades as a homemaker and community volunteer with the Cleveland Orchestra, the Cleveland Ballet, the Cleveland Music School Settlement, the Koch School of Music, and the Lakewood and Lake Ridge Academy school systems. After a divorce in 1981, Latham again joined Sohio (which by that time had become BP America) in their research and development center, working on projects involving electronics. There she had an idea to help manage the heat in electronic applications, but she was not taken seriously; so in 1992, Latham left BP to start her own business as a custom manufacturer.

Especially interested in making research useful, Latham used her creativity to develop a unique technology for producing high-thermal-conductivity materials. She focused on making high-performance heat transfer materials for electronic components for computers and communications, transportation, and medical equipment. Although she had no prior experience in business, manufacturing, or sales, Latham's talents and ingenuity—and the timeliness of her products—prevailed. Thermagon, Inc. grew quickly in national and international markets. Thermagon has been showcased in the *Wall Street Journal* and has placed eighth in *Inc.* magazine's top one hundred fastest-growing, privately held companies, the only company to place in the top ten on this list for three consecutive years.

Latham has won several awards, including being named Cleveland Business Woman of the Year by *Inside Business* magazine (2000).

Business and Finance

11

Tami LONGABERGER

1964–

MUSKINGUM COUNTY

Tami Longaberger, born and raised in Dresden, Ohio, is president and CEO of The Longaberger Company, a family-owned national direct selling company founded by her father, Dave Longaberger, in 1973. The company is recognized as one of the five hundred largest privately held companies in the United States. It is the premier maker of handcrafted baskets, the original part of the family business begun by her grandfather J. W. Longaberger and her great-grandfather, both of whom had been full-time basket makers in Dresden.

In 1984, she graduated from the Ohio State University with a B.S. in marketing, becoming the first Longaberger in the business to have a college degree. She had worked at the company since she was fourteen years old, but in her new official capacity she appointed herself head of customer service. Longaberger instituted several innovative services, including the Longaberger Collectors Club (1996) and the opening of the Homestead, a resort with five restaurants, a retail center, craft demonstrations, and an eighteen-hole golf course that attracts five hundred thousand visitors a year. In 1994, Longaberger was named president of the company, taking the helm during a period of unprecedented growth, product diversification, and technological development. In 1998, she assumed the role of chief executive officer, and the company was recognized by *Working Woman* magazine as the eighteenth-largest woman-owned company in the United States.

Longaberger also serves as a board member of the Ohio State University, the John Glenn Institute for Public Service and Public Policy, and Battelle for Kids, and she has chaired the board of directors of the Direct Selling Association (1993–94), becoming the third woman and the youngest chair ever in the association's eighty-three-year history. In 1999, Longaberger was honored at the Martin Luther King, Jr., Prayer Breakfast as one of five women who have positively influenced her local area; she was presented the Business Award for entrepreneurship by the Ohio Federation of Business and Professional Women; and in 1999, she was recognized by Newman's Own, Inc., and *George* magazine for leading one of the top ten most generous companies in America.

12

OHIO
WOMEN'S
HALL OF
FAME

Profiles of Two Hundred Ohio Women

Farah B. Moavenzadeh
MAJIDZADEH

1938–

FRANKLIN COUNTY

ARAH B. MOAVENZADEH MAJIDZADEH, born in Tehran, Iran, in 1938, immigrated to the United States in 1960 after receiving a degree from the School of Nursing and Homeopathic Medicine in London, England, and taking courses in business management and marketing. Focused on raising her family in Columbus, she became fascinated by her husband Kamran's research as an engineering professor at the Ohio State University on revolutionary equipment that could be used to collect data on the durability of roads. In 1973, she founded her own business in her home to market technology applications for the road-building industry. As chief executive officer and chairperson of the board, Majidzadeh built Resource International, Inc., into a multinational, broad-based, multidisciplinary professional engineering consulting firm that specializes in construction management, information technology, and planning and design of buildings and infrastructure projects.

Majidzadeh is one of the few pioneering women who has successfully met the challenges of operating within a male-dominated area. Her success in business is illustrated, for example, by her being elected in 1984 as the first woman on the board of directors of the International Road Federation (IRF), a nonprofit global organization. She has served also as the vice-president of the International Road Educational Foundation, an organization that provides training, mentoring, and fellowship to transportation engineers from developing countries, and in 1990, she was elected executive director. Majidzadeh has been active also in the Columbus community, especially with programs that serve children, education, and women. She has served, for example, as a committee member with the Children's Defense Fund, the Columbus Coalition against Family Violence, and the Columbus Women Executives Committee.

Among the many honors and awards that Majidzadeh has received are the Executive Order of the Ohio Commodore for her commitment to international trade and the Ellis Island Medal of Honor (awarded earlier to her sister, Farah M. Walters, who also appears in this volume) created to pay homage to "remarkable Americans who exemplify outstanding qualities in both their personal and professional lives, while continuing to preserve the richness of their particular heritage."

13

Business and Finance

LIVING THE LEGACY
OHIO
WOMEN'S
HALL OF
FAME

Florence Spurgeon Zacks MELTON

1911–

FLORENCE SPURGEON ZACKS MELTON was born in Philadelphia, Pennsylvania, on November 6, 1911. She came to Columbus in 1941 with her first husband, Aaron Zacks. In 1946, the couple cofounded the R. G. Barry Company, which makes shoes and insulated goods. She first gained recognition as the inventor of removable washable shoulder pads, a line of chair pads, adjustable car seat covers, and neck pillows, thus securing her a place of honor in product development in the business world. After World War II, Melton developed foam-soled slippers, which revolutionized the foot-wear industry, and her company became the largest manufacturer of washable foam-soled slippers in the world.

Although Melton had to quit high school three months before graduation to help her family, she now holds two honorary doctorates and has been honored for her leadership in business as well as for her support of numerous community, religious, and charitable organizations. Among her awards are Woman of the Year, Community Service Award by the National Council of Jewish Women, Columbus, 1986; YWCA Woman of Achievement Award, 1988; Columbus Jewish Foundation Honoree, 1994; National Foundation for Jewish Culture Patronage Award, 1995; University Distinguished Service Award from the Ohio State University, 1997.

Her long list of honors and awards pays tribute not only to her achievements in business but also to her remarkable achievements in community service. Melton is a pioneer in Jewish education for adults. She proposed a new approach, developed at the Melton Centre for Jewish Education in the Diaspora, Hebrew University, Jerusalem. Currently, the Melton Adult Mini-School (supported by Melton and her second husband Samuel) operates in over sixty sites in the United States, Canada, the United Kingdom, and Australia. Melton has also been involved in other services. She established a foundation to provide prosthetics to needy children (1959); started the Meals on Wheels program with Gladys Lamb (1960s); organized the first women's division for fundraising for the United Jewish Appeal (1973); and initiated with the National Council of Jewish Women the Kids in Crisis Program to develop a directory of services available to teenagers (1986).

Melton remains an avid reader in the areas of religion, business news, world affairs, the arts, and education, and she continues to be active in meeting the needs of others.

14

Profiles of Two Hundred Ohio Women

Karen NUSSBAUM

1950–

CUYAHOGA COUNTY

KAREN NUSSBAUM, born in Chicago on April 25, 1950, graduated with a B.S. from Goddard College in 1975. In 1984, she was named the first director of the Working Women's Department of the AFL-CIO, a position which permitted her to bring a lifetime of commitment to working women into the labor movement and to serve as a tireless national spokesperson for women in the work force. Before assuming this position, Nussbaum was known for her work as a founder and executive director of 9to5, the National Association of Working Women (headquartered in Cleveland), with which she was associated for twenty years. This organization is active in more than 250 cities and was the inspiration for the popular movie *9 to 5,* starring Jane Fonda, Lily Tomlin, and Dolly Parton. In 1981, Nussbaum also became president of District 925 of the Service Employees International Union (SEIU), serving on the executive board and leading the union's 170,000-member Office Workers Division. A former office worker herself, she helped found the first local group of office workers in Boston in 1973, building on her own experiences as a clerical worker at Harvard University.

In 1993, during the Clinton administration, Nussbaum was nominated by the president to become the thirteenth director of the Women's Bureau of the U.S. Department of Labor, which was founded in 1920 to promote opportunities and improve conditions for women in the U.S. work force. In this position, she served as policy advisor to the secretary of labor and as the chief advocate for America's fifty-eight million working women.

Nussbaum is the co-author with John Sweeney of *Solutions for the New Work Force: Policies for a New Social Contract,* and with Ellen Cassedy of *9 to 5: The Working Woman's Guide to Office Survival.* She has been recognized as a leading activist by the *Wall Street Journal, Newsweek,* and *Ms.* magazine. She has appeared on national television programs, testified before Congress as an authority on the problems of working women, and addressed many audiences on the subject of women and work.

15

Business and Finance

OHIO WOMEN'S HALL OF FAME

Darlene M. OWENS

1947–2000

CUYAHOGA COUNTY

Women can do anything they set their minds to do.

—Darlene M. Owens

DARLENE M. OWENS was born and grew up in Cleveland, Ohio. In 1979, she participated in the Cleveland Hometown Program, which at that time was recruiting minorities for the building trades. She had trained as a welder at a local trade school, so she signed up for slots in the pipefitters, plumbers, and electricians unions. The pipefitters had the first opening, and Owens became the first woman pipefitter in Ohio, reaching ultimately the journey level of experience and expertise.

At the same time that Owens was entering the Pipefitters Union and becoming active in her Local #120, Hard Hatted Women was forming as an organization in which women in the trades could meet, share experiences, and offer each other advice in their male-dominated professions. Owens soon joined the group. Through this organization, she quickly became a role model for other women, especially African American women. She served as the group's board president and developed strategies with each new opportunity—for example, with the building of the BP America Building on Public Square—to assure a place for women.

When she became a pipefitter, Owens walked into a very difficult situation for women, but she was able to demonstrate clearly her skills and expertise. She was tireless in her efforts to bring about changes in both attitudes and practices for new generations of women who might follow her path. As a single parent who raised three children and achieved success in a nontraditional area for women, she was well positioned on both the personal and professional front to offer encouragement and support for those who might lack confidence. She set a pace for activism and advocacy for herself and others and provided leadership for women in her profession who have been compelled to fight and struggle still for their rights.

16

Profiles of Two Hundred Ohio Women

Muriel SIEBERT

1932–

CUYAHOGA COUNTY

MURIEL SIEBERT, born in Cleveland, Ohio, in 1932, attended Case Western Reserve University. Although she never graduated from college, after a distinguished career in business she has received honorary degrees from eight colleges and has served as a visiting professor or lecturer at numerous schools, including the Harvard Business School.

When Siebert started her career as a financial analyst in 1954, she faced stereotypical attitudes toward women in business but succeeded in becoming a partner with a leading Wall Street brokerage firm. In 1967, she started her own company, Muriel Siebert & Company, Inc., and in that same year became the first woman to buy her own seat on the New York Stock Exchange. In 1977, she took a leave from her firm to serve five years as the first woman Superintendent of Banking for the State of New York. During those troubling times for banks nationwide, Siebert made bold and often controversial moves in launching protective measures—including taking over the management of one floundering bank herself—so that banks in New York would not collapse. None did. In 1982, when Siebert returned to take control of her company, she discovered that she faced the critical challenge of rebuilding. She was successful, refusing to sell and recommitting herself to the responsibility of being the only woman owner of a New York Stock Exchange firm.

Siebert is also an advocate for women and women's issues. For example, she was a founding member of and currently serves as president of the International Women's Forum and also a founding member of the WISH (Women in the Senate and House) List, a political action group that supports pro-choice Republican women candidates. In addition, she is CEO, president, and chairwoman of the Women's Financial Network, a web site dedicated to educating women about investing, and she is widely recognized for her leadership on many advisory boards including both community organizations, such as the United Way, as well as those related to her profession.

Siebert's list of honors and awards is long and prestigious. It includes the White House Conference on Small Business Award for Entrepreneurial Excellence presented by President Reagan (1986) and the Benjamin Botwinick Prize in Business Ethics awarded by the Columbia Business School (1992).

17

Business and Finance

Julia Curry Montgomery WALSH

1923–

SUMMIT COUNTY

JULIA CURRY MONTGOMERY WALSH, born on March 29, 1923, in Akron, Ohio, attended Kent State University, where she became the first woman president of the student body and in 1945 was the first woman to receive a degree in business. Inspired by Eleanor Roosevelt, Walsh entered the Foreign Service, serving as a personnel officer for the American Consulate General in Munich and later as director of the Fulbright program in Turkey. After marriage, Walsh left the Foreign Service (as was then required) and returned to the United States. She began taking graduate courses at Washington University and became an unpaid intern with Ferris & Company, an investment firm. In 1957, her husband was killed in a military accident. At the age of thirty-four, she was left a widow with four small children. Interested in building a career in the financial world, Walsh remained with Ferris & Company for twenty-two years. By 1959, she had become a partner; by 1971, vice-president; and by 1973, vice-chairman.

Among numerous other accomplishments during these years, Walsh was the first woman accepted at the Advanced Management Program of the Harvard Business School Executive Education Program (1962). In 1963, she earned the highest income of any woman in the nation's capital. In 1965, she became the first woman to gain entry into the American Stock Exchange and in 1969 was the first from the securities industry to serve on the board of a major stock exchange. In 1977, she left Ferris & Company to start J. M. Walsh & Sons with three of her sons and a stepson. With Walsh as president, the company became one of the most successful stock brokerage firms in Washington, D.C.

Walsh's honors and awards are manifold, including being named in 1997 Alumnus of the Year by the College of Business Administration and Graduate School of Management at Kent State University. In 1996, she coauthored a memoir with Anne Conover Carson, *Risks and Rewards*.

18

Victoria Claflin WOODHULL

1838–1927

LICKING COUNTY

*Courtesy of Ohioana
Library Association*

Victoria Claflin Woodhull was born on September 23, 1838, in Homer, Ohio. She received very little formal education as a child, spending most of her time traveling with her family's medicine show, telling fortunes, selling patent medicines, and performing a spiritualist act with her sister Tennessee Claflin. By age fifteen, she was married to Canning Woodhull, whom she divorced in 1864. Two years later she married Colonel James Harvey Blood. In 1868, she moved with her sister to New York City. In New York, she became friends with millionaire railroad magnate Cornelius Vanderbilt, who helped the enterprising sisters to become the first women to establish a brokerage firm on Wall Street: Woodhull, Claflin & Company.

Woodhull and Claflin were successful in their business ventures, which enabled them to publish their own journal, *Woodhull and Claflin's Weekly,* for six years. The journal was noted for addressing controversial topics, such as woman suffrage, labor relations, and issues of personal and social freedoms. Woodhull was a leader in the New York section of the International Workingman's Association, the National American Woman Suffrage Association, and the free love movement.

On April 2, 1870, however, Woodhull made her most radical move: She announced her plans in the *New York Herald* to run for president of the United States in the election of 1872, the first woman to do so. Woodhull understood that although women could not vote at the time, there was no law to prevent them from running for office. She was nominated by the Equal Rights Party, and Frederick Douglass (famous orator and African American abolitionist) was nominated as her vice-presidential running mate, although he later declined the nomination. Woodhull ran on a platform of political and social reform. Her campaign faced many obstacles, however, ranging from a smear campaign to discredit her personally (which through various lawsuits depleted her income and other resources, including her ability to continue publishing her newspaper), to difficulties in securing adequate financial backing, to the fact that she was also several months below the required age of thirty-five. Woodhull lost to Ulysses S. Grant.

In 1878, Woodhull, known by that point as "Wicked Woodhull," moved to England, married John Bidbulph, a retired banker, and died there on June 9, 1927.

Nannie (Scott Honshell) Kelly WRIGHT
1856–1946

LAWRENCE COUNTY

NANNIE (SCOTT HONSHELL) KELLY WRIGHT was born on September 8, 1856, in Catlettsburg, Kentucky, and moved to Ironton, Ohio, in 1879, following her marriage to Lindsey Kelly, who managed the family-owned Centre Furnace at Superior in Lawrence County. During the economic depression that followed the Panic of 1873, the iron industry suffered, and by 1891, when the Kelly patriarch died, Centre Furnace and the other Kelly holdings in real estate and finance were in distress and eventually went into receivership. In 1896 and 1898, Wright resourcefully gathered her own finances and purchased at auction both the furnace and ten thousand acres of land. She learned the iron business, opened the mines, renovated the furnace and the company houses provided for the employees, and began hiring workers when many in the nation were out of work. In addition, she brought in community resources, such as a physician for the families, churches, schools, and a post office. The community of Superior thrived, with Wright working alongside her employees in the factory whenever it was necessary. Wright's Centre Furnace prospered, becoming, for example, one of the first companies to produce and ship iron by rail during the Spanish American War. In the rebuilding of the business, Wright demonstrated that she was a clever businesswoman, and she also gained the reputation of being one of the wealthiest women in Ohio.

With the deaths of her husband in 1903 and her son in 1904, Wright began to travel frequently and left the business in other hands for a while. In 1908, she married D. Gregory Wright, whom she divorced in 1919. During these years, Wright kept her stocks in Centre Furnace and other family holdings, but in 1923 she decided to sell many of them. She invested the profits but lost her home and most of her wealth in the stock market crash of 1929. Despite such great losses, Wright was still able to lead a comfortable lifestyle. She moved into the Marting Hotel in Ironton and by selling off personal assets (for example, her jewelry and art) managed to support herself until her death on September 12, 1946.

Courtesy of Briggs Lawrence County Public Library

COMMUNICATIONS

ON SOME VERY BASIC LEVEL, OUR TWENTY-FIRST-century sensibilities might suggest that women have always been perceived to be well suited for the area of communications. Current stereotypes portray women as socially conditioned to listen, responsive, and able to manage several activities at once. Although such talents are useful in the world of communications, this discipline is also a place where ideas are articulated and claimed, where power is negotiated, and where history—especially the lives of men and the actions of nations—is chronicled. Such a world, then, has historically been presumed not to be a "natural" one for women. Ohio women have defied that presumption, however. In newspapers and magazines, on television, and even on the cartoon page, Ohio women have broken new ground, mastered these enterprises, and excelled well beyond the expectations engendered by earlier stereotypes.

ERMA FISTE BOMBECK

CHRISTINE BRENNAN

ZELL PATTI SMITH HART DEMING

DOROTHY (DORA SCHNELL) FULDHEIM

CATHY GUISEWITE

RUTH REEVES LYONS

AUDREY MACKIEWICZ

(ELIZABETH) ANNE O'HARE MCCORMICK

MARJORIE B. PARHAM

LUDEL BODEN SAUVAGEOT

GLORIA STEINEM

HELEN E. WEINER ZELKOWITZ

Erma Fiste BOMBECK

1927–1996

MONTGOMERY COUNTY

Courtesy of William L. Bombeck; Rod Moyer, photographer

Erma Fiste Bombeck, born in Dayton, Ohio, on February 21, 1927, demonstrated early in her life a talent for humor, writing, and social criticism. At Patterson Vocational High School in Dayton, she wrote for the school paper and participated in a cooperative work program as a copygirl for the *Dayton Herald*. After finishing high school, she enrolled first at Ohio University and then at the University of Dayton, where she wrote for the student newspaper and magazine, graduating in 1949 with a B.A. in English. After graduation, she became a reporter at the *Dayton Journal Herald*, preparing radio listings, writing obituaries, and authoring feature articles for the women's page. On August 13, 1949, she married fellow journalist William Lawrence Bombeck, and after their first child was born, she became a suburban housewife.

In Ellen Goodman's eulogy for Bombeck, she related that Bombeck once wrote, "I hid my dreams in the back of my mind—it was the only safe place in the house. From time to time I would get them out and play with them, not daring to reveal them to anyone else because they were fragile and might get broken." In 1963, Bombeck allowed her dreams to resurface and started writing a weekly column from home for the *Kettering-Oakwood Times*. In 1965, she began writing two columns a week for the *Journal Herald*. In those early days of the modern women's movement, her humor and insight helped break open the prevailing stereotypes of the housewife happily cleaning in heels and pearls. Ultimately, her humorous critiques of middle-class domestic life appeared in nine hundred newspapers and established her securely among the most widely syndicated humorists of the twentieth century. By 1975, Bombeck was also appearing frequently on television programs, including eleven years as a commentator on ABC's *Good Morning America*.

Bombeck's first book, *At Wit's End* (1967), would be followed by eleven others. Nine made the *New York Times* Best Sellers List, including *I Want to Grow Hair. I Want to Grow Up. I Want to Go to Boise.* (1989). All proceeds from this book were donated to cancer research. In 1990, Bombeck was awarded the American Cancer Society's Medal of Honor. *Forever, Erma* (1996), a collection of her best-loved columns, was published after her death from complications of a kidney transplant.

Communications

OHIO WOMEN'S HALL OF FAME

Christine BRENNAN

1958–

WOOD COUNTY

CHRISTINE BRENNAN, born on May 14, 1958, in Toledo, Ohio, received a B.A. (1980) and an M.A. (1981) in journalism from Northwestern University. Since then, she has fashioned a remarkable career as a pioneering sports columnist, television sports analyst, and author of three books.

In 1981, Brennan accepted a position as staff writer at the *Miami Herald* and became their first sports writer for women's sports. In 1984, she went to the *Washington Post,* where she became the first woman to cover the Washington Redskins. Most notably during her tenure at the *Post* from 1984 to 1996, she covered all of the Olympic Games, six consecutive Super Bowls, and five national championship college football bowl games. Her specialty, however, was writing about the Olympics and international sports. In 1997, Brennan joined the staff of *USA Today,* which has established her as one of the country's most widely read sports writers and a prominent voice in Olympic coverage. She was elected in 1988 as the first president of the Association for Women in Sports Media. Under her leadership, the organization established a scholarship-internship program for college women, and Brennan became a major voice for women's issues.

As a sports analyst, Brennan has appeared on ABC, NBC, and CNN, and she was ESPN's reporter at the 1998 Olympic Games. Among other programs, she has appeared on *Nightline,* the *Today Show,* and *Meet the Press,* and she appears regularly on ESPN Radio and on WMAL Radio in Washington, D.C. In addition, Brennan is a best-selling author of three books on figure skating, starting with her controversial publication, *Inside Edge* (1996) in which she wrote a hard-hitting and intimate portrayal of the lives of figure skaters, highlighting issues such as homosexuality, AIDS, and overbearing parents.

In 1993, Brennan was named Capital Press Women's Woman of Achievement, and she has also won national awards from the Women's Sports Foundation (1990, 1993).

24

Zell Patti Smith Hart
DEMING

C. 1868–1936

TRUMBULL COUNTY

*Courtesy of the Harriet Taylor Upton
Association*

*Her success in publishing a thoroughly good social newspaper which respected and practiced
the finest principles in American journalism made her famous from coast to coast . . . She
was capable of writing an editorial or news article, operating the business office, managing
advertising, circulation or even the mechanical department.*

—Marlen Pew, *Editor and Publisher*

ZELL PATTI SMITH HART DEMING was born around 1868 in Warren, Ohio. Immediately after high school graduation, she married Frank Hart, also of Warren, and moved to Chicago. After two years there, Deming was widowed and returned home with an infant daughter in 1893. On her own as a single parent, Deming began work at the Warren *Tribune* as a society reporter. With hard work and dedication, she became proficient in both the editorial and the business sides of newspaper operations and built a noteworthy career, rising in the ranks at the paper to become secretary and treasurer, president, general manager, and controlling stockholder.

In 1907, having already acquired a controlling interest in the paper, she married William C. Deming, who was the publisher of the *Cheyenne Tribune* (Wyoming) and a stockholder in the *Warren Tribune*. Deming lived and worked in Cheyenne until she was divorced in 1918 and again returned to Warren. She resumed work at the *Warren Tribune* as manager, and under her guidance the paper grew from a four-page daily with modest circulation to become one of the few papers in the country that went into virtually every home in the city. In 1921 she constructed a new building for the paper and filled it with the latest equipment, making the plant a showplace visited by many major figures in the publishing industry. In 1923, she expanded her holdings to include the *Warren Daily Chronicle,* the second-oldest paper in Ohio (known earlier as the *Trump of Fame*). In 1924, she became president and general manager of the paper.

With her position as a leader in local business, industry, and civic growth well secured, Deming also rose to prominence in the national arena. In 1923, she was elected to the central advisory board of the Associated Press, becoming the first woman to hold this position. She was also a member of the American Society of Newspaper Editors.

Communications

LIVING THE LEGACY
OHIO
WOMEN'S
HALL OF
FAME

Dorothy (Dora Schnell) FULDHEIM

1893-1989

CUYAHOGA COUNTY

Dorothy (Dora Schnell) Fuldheim, was born in Passaic, New Jersey, on June 26, 1893. She grew up in Milwaukee, Wisconsin, graduated from Milwaukee College with a degree in English, and began a career as a teacher. After marriage, she moved to Cleveland, Ohio, where she began working with the newly established WTAM radio station. Her responsibilities included news reporting, a local historical biography series, and a weekly editorial, all of which served to launch a distinctive career in broadcast media during an era in which women in this field were very unusual.

In 1947, after retiring from teaching, Fuldheim joined the staff at the WEWS television station, the first television station in the state of Ohio, two months before it went on the air. She was originally signed to a thirteen-week contract with the expectation that she would be replaced, presumably by a male. Fuldheim, however, remained at the station for thirty-seven years. She became the first woman in the country with her own news show, combining news summaries with commentaries and interviews for the next seventeen years. From 1957 to 1964 she also hosted the *One O'Clock Club,* which followed a talk-variety show format.

During her decades in broadcast media, Fuldheim developed a distinctive style of interviewing that was straightforward and provocative. Over the course of her long career she traveled the world and conducted an estimated fifteen thousand interviews, among them interviews with Adolph Hitler, all of the presidents of the United States of the day, the Duke of Windsor, Helen Keller, Wilt Chamberlain, and innumerable others. Fuldheim also published four books, including three autobiographies/memoirs: *I Laughed, I Cried, I Loved: A News Analyst's Love Affair with the World* (1966); *A Thousand Friends* (1974); and *Three and a Half Husbands* (1976).

Fuldheim won numerous awards including several United Press International awards for editorial excellence, an Overseas Press Club of America award, being named one of America's most admired women by a Gallup poll, and being included among the charter members of the Cleveland Journalism Hall of Fame. Fuldheim died on November 3, 1989.

Courtesy of WEWS News, Cleveland

26

Cathy GUISEWITE

1950–

MONTGOMERY COUNTY

CATHY GUISEWITE was born in Dayton, Ohio, on September 5, 1950, and grew up in Midland, Michigan. She graduated from the University of Michigan in 1972 with a degree in English and began her career in an advertising agency in Detroit as a copywriter. In 1976, with the encouragement of her mother, she sent to Universal Press Syndicate a collection of drawings and text and began her career as the author of the comic strip *Cathy*. She was immediately successful and by 1980 she had moved to California and made the transition to full-time cartoonist.

Cathy is now syndicated in more than five hundred newspapers, and *Cathy* products are available in gift, card, and department stores nationwide. In 1978, Guisewite began publishing humor books featuring collections of *Cathy* comic strips, including *I'd Scream Except I Look So Fabulous* (1999) and *Cathy 2004* (2003); she also began writing animated *Cathy* specials for CBS. Guisewite has appeared frequently on talk shows and television magazine shows, including *The Tonight Show, CBS Morning News, Today, Entertainment Tonight, PM Magazine,* and *Sally Jessy Raphael.* She has been featured as well in print magazine publications, including *Life, People, Newsweek, Glamour,* and *USA Today.*

Guisewite has received many honors and awards, including three honorary degrees from colleges and universities, the Outstanding Communicator of the Year Award from Los Angeles Advertising Women (1982), and the Distinguished Women's Award from Northwood University (1984). In 1992 she won the Cartoonist of the Year Award from the National Cartoonist Society, and she has won an Emmy for Outstanding Animated Program for *Cathy.*

27

Ruth Reeves LYONS

1905–1988

CUYAHOGA COUNTY

R UTH REEVES LYONS, born in Cincinnati, Ohio, in 1905, came
of age with the ratification of the Nineteenth Amendment,
which gave women the right to vote in national elections, a cause
that her grandmother Mary Hirst Reeves had championed through
the Women's Christian Temperance Union. This historic event inspired Lyons to activism and leadership in her community and
high school, which in turn led to her long and prestigious career in radio and television broadcasting, a field that in her day included very few women.

Lyons has been called the "Mother of the TV Talk Show" and described herself
as a housewife who did a daily television show just for the fun of it, but neither of
these images adequately captures her media personality or her achievements as an
astute businesswoman. Lyons first appeared on air on a WSAI program in 1925 as a
piano accompanist for Howard Hafford. When Hafford became musical director of
WKRC Radio, he recruited Lyons as his assistant. A few months later, she had the
opportunity to sit in at *The Woman's Hour,* when the regular host was ill. She kept
the job and by 1937 she was one of Cincinnati's most popular radio personalities.
Lyons used her shows both for entertainment and for advocacy of causes that she
supported, for example, the Ruth Lyons Children's Fund that she established in 1939,
a charity that continues to thrive as one of her most lasting legacies.

Over the next several years, Lyons moved to the Crosley Broadcasting Company
(WSAI and WLW) and hosted *Petticoat Partyline, Morning Matinee, Collect Calls
from Lowenthal's,* and *The Fifty Club.* Between 1948 and 1949, she moved the *Fifty
Club* to WLWT television where it became the *Fifty-Fifty Club* and also the first local
program to be broadcast in color. Lyons retired from the show in 1967 and spent the
next two years writing her memoir, *Remember with Me.* In 1983, the Cincinnati City
Council named a downtown street in her honor, and in 1986 she was given a Great
Living Cincinnatian Award by the Cincinnati Chamber of Commerce. Lyons died on
November 7, 1988.

28

Audrey MACKIEWICZ

1924–

ERIE COUNTY

AUDREY MACKIEWICZ, born in Huron, Ohio, on August 24, 1924, enlisted in the U.S. Coast Guard Women's Reserve (SPARs) and served during World War II as a yeoman assigned to interview servicemen who were mentally and physically injured in battle and scheduled for discharge from the hospital. She coordinated their return home and counseled and worked with families to ease the transition back into a nonmilitary world. Mackiewicz has worked for more than fifty-two years as an advocate for veterans on the local, state, and national levels. She was the first woman to serve on the Erie County Veterans Service Commission. She was also the first woman to serve on the board of trustees of the Ohio Veterans Home (OVH) and was instrumental in the 1969 decision to allow female veterans admission to the OVH. Mackiewicz has always sought to ensure that all veterans receive the benefits that they deserve and to be a strong advocate for women, encouraging them to seek appointments in traditionally male-dominated areas. For these services and more, Mackiewicz was inducted into the Ohio Veterans Hall of Fame in 1995.

Mackiewicz's contributions were not limited to advocacy for veterans, however. In 1961, she began a career in journalism that spanned twenty-six years, ending with her position as special features editor for the *Sandusky Register*. In 1972, in response to requests by farmers for their own paper, she initiated the *Firelands Farmer*, an agricultural publication serving a primarily rural five-county area and providing a central resource for literature and information to agriculturalists. Mackiewicz became the first female member of the Newspaper Farm Editors of America (now the North American Agricultural Journalists) and the first woman president of this association. Over the course of her career, she interviewed four U.S. presidents, penned countless human-interest articles, coauthored the history of Huron with Lee Miesele, and wrote an award-winning series of articles in 1977 based on her own experiences with breast cancer.

Among her many achievements, Mackiewicz has received two United Press International awards for general excellence (1978 and 1983); two J. S. Russell Memorial Awards from the North American Agricultural Journalists (1982 and 1996); and the Huron Sesquicentennial Award.

29

Communications

OHIO
WOMEN'S
HALL OF
FAME

(Elizabeth) Anne O'Hare McCORMICK

1880-1954

FRANKLIN COUNTY

(E LIZABETH) ANNE O'HARE McCORMICK was born in Great Britain on May 16, 1880, but grew up in Columbus, Ohio. Her only formal education was at Saint Mary of the Springs Academy , from which she graduated as valedictorian in 1898. When she and her family moved to Cleveland, McCormick began a career in journalism with the *Catholic Universe Bulletin.* After her marriage to Francis J. McCormick, she moved to Dayton where she free-lanced for *Catholic World, Christian Reader,* and the *New York Times.* During these early years, she often traveled to Europe with her husband, who was an engineer and importer, and wrote pieces for the *New York Times Magazine.* In 1921, the *Times* managing editor, Carr V. Van Anda, asked her to send dispatches from abroad. She sent analyses of the social, political, and economic events of post–World War I Europe that Van Anda liked very much; he then hired her as the first foreign-affairs columnist in the history of the *Times.*

McCormick's column was first called "In Europe," then "Abroad" from 1936 onward. Over the thirty-two years that she wrote for the *Times,* she wrote two editorials and three columns per week while traveling. She interviewed world leaders—such as Roosevelt, Churchill, Hitler, Mussolini, Stalin, and Popes Pius XI and Pius XII—and many other prominent figures, but she also wrote about how ordinary people were affected by foreign affairs. In 1937, she became the first woman to win a Pulitzer Prize in journalism. In addition, in 1936, McCormick became the first woman to sit on the editorial board of the *Times.*

30

In the 1940s, McCormick went on to exert considerable influence in her field. She was named to the Advisory Committee on Post-War Foreign Policy and she served as a delegate to UNESCO conferences. She received honorary degrees from seventeen institutions, including Ohio Dominican University, the Ohio State University, and Columbia University. She was also named woman of the year by several women's organizations, including the National Federation of Press Women (1939).

At the time of her death in 1954, McCormick was hailed as one of the greatest women journalists of all time.

Marjorie B. PARHAM

1918–

HAMILTON COUNTY

M ARJORIE B. PARHAM, born on February 12, 1918, in
Batavia, Ohio, attended Wilberforce University,
graduated from the University of Cincinnati, and received
additional training at the Chase School of Business. In 1955,
Parham's husband Gerald Porter founded a weekly news-
paper, the *Cincinnati Herald,* and a short while later a second paper in Dayton, the
Dayton Tribune. Parham became the business manager at the *Tribune.* In fact, she
was also reporter, copyeditor, editor-in-chief, and advertising representative, and
began shuttling back and forth between Dayton and Cincinnati, where she and her
family lived.

During that era, the early days of the modern Civil Rights movement, the African
American press was critically important. Not only did it showcase news about the
African American community, which was not given any attention at all in "main-
stream" presses, it was also a critical source for the interpretation of local, national,
and world events, and was a forum for actively engaging in critical discourses about
issues and concerns that affected the community. Among her many other responsibilities as business manager, Parham had the important task of generating the advertising income necessary for the papers to thrive, and with determination and
persistence, she fulfilled this responsibility.

After the tragic loss of her husband in an automobile accident, Parham faced the
challenge of managing both papers. She took the helm as publisher and did not miss
a single issue. Eventually, the *Dayton Tribune* closed, but the *Cincinnati Herald* continued under her control until 1978, when she sold it to SESH Communications.

Among Parham's many awards are Business Woman of the Year, Iota Phi Lambda
(1970); Outstanding Woman in Communications, Women in Communications
(1973); YWCA Woman of Achievement (1988); Trail Blazer Award, given by the
National Association of Black Journalists (1993); the Governor's Award, Outstanding
Journalism (1994); Lifetime Achiever, *Applause!* magazine (1994); and induction into
the Society of Professional Journalists Hall of Fame (1999).

Communications

OHIO
WOMEN'S
HALL OF
FAME

Ludel Boden SAUVAGEOT

1906–1996

SUMMIT COUNTY

Ludel Boden Sauvageot, born in 1906 in Athens, Ohio, was the first female journalism graduate of Ohio University. Her first jobs out of college were at newspapers in Ohio and Illinois. She then accepted a position handling public relations for a large Methodist Church mission group in Philadelphia, a job that took her to the slums of Cuba as well as to the hills of Appalachia. While in Philadelphia, she met and married Paul Sauvageot, a cardiologist. In the 1930s, they moved to Akron and began raising their two boys. During World War II, just as Sauvageot had decided to return to work, her husband was commissioned in the armed forces and stationed in Oregon. Instead of becoming a writer with the *Akron Beacon Journal,* she began working with public relations with the United States Air Force. At the end of the war, Sauvageot and her family returned to Akron, where Sauvageot was hired by Akron General Medical Center to establish the first public relations department in any Akron hospital. During her years at Akron General, Sauvageot and her husband often spoke publicly together—both locally and nationally—about two-career marriages and how to make them work.

Sauvageot left Akron General in the 1950s to become secretary of the International Council of Industrial Editors and to set up their first international office. In 1967, she returned to Akron General and remained there until 1976, when she retired at the age of seventy. Thirty days later, she returned to serve as a public relations consultant. She also taught journalism at Kent State University as a part-time instructor.

Much of her time, however, was spent traveling, raising money for charities, and mentoring others in the field. Sauvageot also wrote four books. Her first book, *Service for All: The Story of Akron General Medical Center, 1914–1977* (1977) was followed by an update, *Service for All: The Story of Akron General Medical Center, 1914–1986* (1986); *Partners in History: The Story of Ohio Hospitals and the Ohio Hospital Association* (1992); and *A Matter of Heart: The History of the American Heart Association in Akron, Ohio from Its Founding in 1950 through May 1995* (1995).

Gloria STEINEM

1934–

WOOD COUNTY

GLORIA STEINEM was born in Toledo, Ohio, on March 25, 1934. Despite a difficult childhood, she excelled in school, graduating Phi Beta Kappa from Smith College in 1956. In college, Steinem became very politically active, volunteering for the Adlai Stevenson presidential campaign, writing for the college newspaper, and discovering the activist roots in her own family. Steinem's grandmother, Pauline Perlmutter Steinem (1863–1940), was a social activist in Toledo. She was the first president of the Toledo District Council of Jewish Women (1899), president of the Toledo Federation of Women's Clubs (1901), the first woman elected to the Toledo School Board (1904), and president of the Ohio Woman Suffrage Association (1908–11). Before marriage and the onset of a lifelong bout with depression, Steinem's mother Ruth was a successful journalist in Toledo. This knowledge influenced not only Steinem's understanding of her own family, but also her perception of the history and politics of women's lives.

After graduation, Steinem received a fellowship to study in India for two years. She returned to the United States with a new understanding of poverty and oppression, and was inspired to write. She entered the field of journalism during an era when women were not taken seriously as political reporters. Her first position with *Help!* magazine placed her in professional circles with prominent journalists. Through this network, she began writing free-lance articles and by 1963 had embarked on a full-time free-lance career, which included writing for the television show *That Was the Week That Was*. Steinem used her celebrity status as one of a small number of women television writers to cover Senator George McGovern's campaign for the presidency and to become a founding editor of *New York* magazine. This position enabled her to become a political columnist, covering national events and establishing herself as a leader during the 1970s in the women's liberation movement.

Steinem's accomplishments are many, as are the honors and awards she has garnered. Together with Dorothy Pitman Hughes, she cofounded the Women's Action Alliance and *Ms.* magazine, where she continues to serve as contributing editor. Many of her articles have been widely anthologized, and she is the author of several books, including *Revolution from Within: A Book of Self-Esteem* (1992) and *Outrageous Acts and Everyday Rebellions* (1983). In 1993, Steinem was inducted into the National Women's Hall of Fame in Seneca Falls, New York.

Communications

Helen E. Weiner
ZELKOWITZ

1911–

KNOX COUNTY

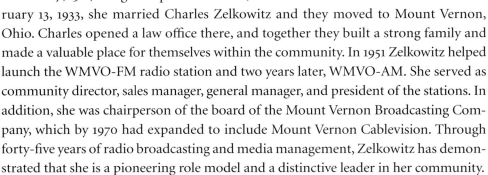

HELEN E. WEINER ZELKOWITZ was born on November 7, 1911, and grew up in Columbus, Ohio. On February 13, 1933, she married Charles Zelkowitz and they moved to Mount Vernon, Ohio. Charles opened a law office there, and together they built a strong family and made a valuable place for themselves within the community. In 1951 Zelkowitz helped launch the WMVO-FM radio station and two years later, WMVO-AM. She served as community director, sales manager, general manager, and president of the stations. In addition, she was chairperson of the board of the Mount Vernon Broadcasting Company, which by 1970 had expanded to include Mount Vernon Cablevision. Through forty-five years of radio broadcasting and media management, Zelkowitz has demonstrated that she is a pioneering role model and a distinctive leader in her community.

For forty-four years at the radio station, Zelkowitz hosted *Coffee Cup*. Through this program and the general management of the station, she created strong ties between the station and the community. She constantly showed her respect and appreciation of the people of the community and her desire to keep them informed with insight, wit, and humor. In an interview with Judy Divelbiss, city editor of the *Mount Vernon News*, Zelkowitz highlighted one of her most striking memories at the station. She recalled that during a flood, the station continued operating for three days straight. The station served as the primary clearinghouse for information for families wanting to know whether other family members were safe. Individuals called the station with questions or information, and the radio staff delivered messages on the air.

Zelkowitz was also active in professional and community organizations. For example, she was the president of the American Women in Radio and Television Education Foundation, the first woman to chair the United Way of Knox County, a member of the Governor's Comprehensive Mental Health Committee, a volunteer with the American Red Cross, the Kidney Foundation, and other organizations. Her many awards include being named Woman of the Year by the Mount Vernon Area Chamber of Commerce and being the first to be named Woman Broadcaster of the Year by the Ohio Association of Broadcasters.

34

Profiles of Two Hundred Ohio Women

COMMUNITY

SERVICE

IN NO FIELD HAVE WOMEN BEEN MORE PROMINENT than in community service. They have often labored, however, under a certain stereotype: that women have deep desires to nurture and care for others and that their contributions are merely a continuation of work in the home extended into the community, a metaphoric greater home. The accomplishments of these women certainly offer evidence of a nurturing and caring heart. What we sometimes do not acknowledge, however, is that with this nurture and care come also demonstrations of noteworthy leadership abilities. Throughout the history of Ohio, women have come to vital community needs with the insight to perceive the problems to be addressed, with the talents and skills to draw together critical resources, and with the capacity to get the work done. The women showcased in this section have established a commanding presence as community leaders who have worked quite ingeniously and effectively to manage and rearrange the world in response to the critical needs of those around them.

MARTHA KINNEY COOPER

JESSIE STEPHENS GLOVER

AURORA GONZALEZ

LUCY WARE WEBB HAYES

MARIWYN DWYER HEATH

SYLVIA LEWIS

ADA M. HOWE MARTIN

NANCY C. REYNOLDS OAKLEY

MARGARET ARLINE WEBB PRATT

V. LANNA SAMANIEGO

LOUELLA THOMPSON

IMOGEN DAVENPORT TROLANDER

GEORGETA BLEBEA WASHINGTON

GRAYCE EDWARDS WILLIAMS

Martha Kinney COOPER

1874–1964

HAMILTON COUNTY

As long as we have authors, poets and musicians, I trust that we shall be able to supply a suitable home for their splendid works, providing also a means to give them the publicity and thanks they so rightly deserve.

—Martha Kinney Cooper

Courtesy of Ohioana Library Association

MARTHA KINNEY COOPER was born on January 12, 1874, in Cincinnati, Ohio. She was a musician and a volunteer in many civic, literary, and cultural organizations. She was particularly active in the Ohio Federation of Women's Clubs and in the Daughters of the American Revolution. Much of her time, however, was devoted to supporting her husband, Myers Y. Cooper, whom she had married on December 15, 1897. He was a Cincinnati businessman who had political aspirations, and on January 14, 1929, he became the governor of Ohio.

When Cooper moved into the Governor's Mansion, she found that there were no books by Ohio authors in the mansion library and realized that Ohio had done very little to honor its writers, musicians, and artists. With the advice of Florence Roberts Head, a member of the state library staff, she began implementing the idea that Ohio should have a library for Ohioans and about Ohio. On October 5, 1929, she invited twenty-one Ohioans who had distinguished themselves in various fields to the Governor's Mansion, and thirteen of them attended the initial meeting. Out of this meeting grew the organization that is now known as the Martha Kinney Cooper Ohioana Library.

In its early days, the library consisted of bookshelves in the solarium of the Governor's Mansion, stocked with volumes that Cooper had collected through direct solicitation from the authors themselves. In 1935, the collection outgrew the solarium and moved to 65 S. Front Street in Columbus. In January 2001, it moved again, along with the State Library of Ohio, to 274 E. First Avenue. The collection is extensive, containing thousands of books, musical compositions, radio scripts, and other artifacts related to Ohio and its history and culture.

With her foresight, Cooper set in motion a living legacy that is an invaluable resource for the state and for the nation.

37

Community Service

Jessie Stephens GLOVER

1882–1966

FRANKLIN COUNTY

JESSIE STEPHENS GLOVER was born in 1882 in Columbus, Ohio, the daughter of former slaves who taught her to believe that all things are possible through hard work and perseverance. It came as no surprise, then, that Glover attended the Ohio State University and graduated in 1905 with a B.A. in modern languages, the first African American woman to graduate from this institution. After leaving Ohio State, Glover moved to Tallahassee, Florida, where she began to teach German and English at Florida Agricultural and Mechanical College for Negroes (now Florida A&M University). During World War I, she moved to Virginia to teach at Virginia Normal and Collegiate Institute (now Virginia State University). She continued to teach German and English but added to this repertoire French as well.

After a few years, Glover returned to Columbus, married Edward E. Glover, began raising her two daughters and devoting herself mainly to community service. In the 1930s, she was a volunteer probation officer with the Franklin County Domestic Relations Court and was later hired in that capacity as a full-time professional to counsel juvenile offenders. Glover worked vigorously and continuously with the YWCA, the NAACP, the National Association of Colored Women's Clubs, and St. Philip's Episcopal Church. She was particularly influential in building the local chapter of Alpha Kappa Alpha Sorority, Inc., and in guiding this organization toward greater involvement in the life and affairs of the local African American community, including helping bring about the establishment of a system of public playgrounds in Columbus.

Glover died in Columbus in 1966 at the age of 83.

Courtesy of Aleta Sunico

Aurora GONZALEZ

1924–1991

LUCAS COUNTY

Courtesy of Toledo Blade

AURORA GONZALEZ was born on February 24, 1924, in Bird Island, Minnesota. Her family was among the first Hispanic families to immigrate to this area from Mexico. During the 1930s, they moved first to a farm near Fremont, Ohio, and then to Toledo, where Gonzalez graduated from Central Catholic High School. She then attended the University of Toledo from 1951 to 1953 and took short courses at Davis Business College. After high school graduation Gonzalez was employed by the Community Chest for two years before she moved to the Libbey-Owens-Ford glass company (LOF), where she spent the next fifteen years in the finance department. At that point, she applied for and was appointed to the position of secretary to the board of directors at LOF, where she remained until her retirement in 1979.

After retiring, Gonzalez turned her energy to her growing concerns about community affairs. In the 1970s, she had participated in an effort to establish a neighborhood recreation center in South Toledo, where many Hispanics had settled. Gonzalez rose as a leader in this cause, and the group became known as La Voz del Barrio (The Voice of the Neighborhood). With the advocacy of this organization, the center was indeed placed in South Toledo and was named Centro Unico. After this success, La Voz del Barrio continued to serve as an active and effective force in the Hispanic community, enabling community development through peaceful mechanisms, supporting political action, and advocating for the economic development of the area. Gonzalez became the coordinator of the La Voz/Midwest Voter Registration Education Project coalition and gained broad recognition for her dedication and consistent achievements. In 1980, she was honored by the Guadalupe Community Center for her outstanding contributions to the Hispanic community.

On October 8, 1991, Gonzalez was involved in a car accident and died at the age of 67. Her family received a memorial tribute from the General Assembly of the State of Ohio for her exceptional humanitarian concerns and insights and for her tireless efforts "to better the world around her." In 1992, the Centro Unico was renamed in her honor, and in 1993 the intersection of South Avenue and the Anthony Wayne Trail was renamed Aurora Gonzalez Drive.

39

Community Service

LIVING THE LEGACY

OHIO
WOMEN'S
HALL OF
FAME

Lucy Ware Webb HAYES

1831–1889

ROSS COUNTY

Lucy Ware Webb Hayes, first lady of Ohio and later of the United States of America, was born on August 28, 1831, in Chillicothe, Ohio. She attended the preparatory department of Ohio Wesleyan University, becoming the first woman to receive academic credit from this institution. In 1850, she graduated from Wesleyan Female College in Cincinnati, making her the first of Ohio's "first ladies" to earn a college degree. She met Rutherford B. Hayes while she was a student at Ohio Wesleyan. They were married on December 30, 1852. She became the first lady of Ohio from 1868 to 1872 and from 1876 to 1877 and later the first lady of the United States from 1878 to 1881.

Unlikely to have the opportunity to hold her own public office, given the gendered expectation and stereotypes of her day, Hayes regarded her husband's political career as their joint career. When her husband was city solicitor for Cincinnati, Hayes's staunch abolitionist views influenced him to make himself available at all hours for legal aid to enslaved African Americans detained while seeking their freedom. During the Civil War, she spent time in military camps where he was major to the Twenty-Third Ohio Volunteer Infantry, ministering to the wounded, comforting the dying, and encouraging the living, work that gave her the name "Mother Lucy." As the first lady of Ohio, her interests in politics led her to influence legislation behind the scenes, most notably the establishment of the Ohio Soldiers' and Sailors' Orphans Home in Xenia and other legislation in support of children and family affairs.

Nationally, Hayes was the first presidential wife known to be referred to as "first lady" in print. In this role, Hayes started the first restoration of the White House, the first significant White House art collection, and the Easter Egg Roll on the White House lawn. She also added the eagle to the White House stationery. She supported temperance but, despite her apparent personal interests, she did not openly support the more politically contentious woman suffrage movement. In 1881, when Hayes and her husband returned to their home in Fremont, Ohio, she became the national president of the Woman's Home Missionary Society of the Methodist Episcopal Church. Hayes died on June 25, 1889, in Fremont, and was survived by her husband. Both are buried on the grounds of Spiegel Grove where their home and the first presidential library are open for touring.

Profiles of Two Hundred Ohio Women

Mariwyn Dwyer HEATH

1935–

MONTGOMERY COUNTY

Courtesy of Mariwyn D. Heath

Mariwyn Dwyer Heath was born on May 1, 1935, in Chicago, Illinois. She attended Webster College in St. Louis, Missouri, and the University of Missouri, where she became the first woman to receive a degree in journalism. Having been mentored by a politically active mother, Heath demonstrated leadership skills early. For example, while still in college she volunteered in the Foreign Student Advisor's Office and served as a board member, officer, and ultimately president of the university's Cosmopolitan Club. She was also active in the Inter-American Club and the YWCA.

Heath married after college and moved to Elmira, New York, where she was employed as managing editor of *Chemung Valley Reporter* in Horseheads, New York (1956–58), and began working as a free-lance speech writer, an occupation that continued to involve her in political campaigns for the next two decades. During her New York years, Heath was an officer in the Business and Professional Women (BPW) organization and in Theta Sigma Phi, a national journalism honorary society that later changed its name to the Association for Women in Communications. In 1960, she and her family moved to Lancaster, Ohio, and then to Dayton in 1963. From 1964 to 1982, she held both regional and national appointments in the Association for Women in Communications; from 1967 to 1969, she became president of BPW/Dayton; from 1968 to 1972, she held local and state positions with the American Association of University Women; and from 1969 to 1974, she held leadership positions with the Dayton Area YWCA. By 1974, all of Heath's activism was focused on women's issues and the participation of women in the political process. Most notably, she was named Equal Rights Amendment (ERA) coordinator for BPW/USA; she chaired the Number One Imperative Committee (to eliminate institutional racism by any means possible) for the national YWCA; and she was an active platform speaker and lobbyist for BPW for the ERA in the Ohio Statehouse, in Congress, and in fifteen states that had not ratified the ERA between 1968 and 1982.

Heath has served since then on various committees and commissions for five Ohio governors and in several national roles related particularly to women's causes. She has been honored by many groups, including Soroptimist International, which named her one of the Ten Outstanding Women of the World. Heath and her husband currently own a consulting firm, Heath Associates.

Community Service

41

OHIO WOMEN'S HALL OF FAME

Sylvia LEWIS

1927–

SUMMIT COUNTY

If you want your children to follow in your footsteps, be very careful where you put your feet.
—Sylvia Lewis

SYLVIA LEWIS, born on April 28, 1927, has spent her life in Akron, Ohio, and dedicated herself to serving her community. In 1966, she was one of fifteen women selected to participate in a Na'amat (which translates as "working women and volunteers") Young Leadership Seminar. Na'amat is the largest Jewish women's organization in the world with chapters in sixteen countries. It fights for women's rights, civil rights, child welfare, and social justice in Israel and in the United States. In 1993, Lewis was elected national president of Na'amat USA.

In her leadership roles, Lewis has been a delegate to the World Zionist Congress in Israel three times. In 1992, she was elected to Zionist General Council of the World Zionist Organization. She is also on several advisory boards, including the United Israel Appeal, the Jewish National Fund, the American Zionist Movement, the National Committee for Labor Israel, and the Habonim Dror Foundation. Lewis has provided leadership to the Akron community as well. For example, she was president of the Jerome Lippman Jewish Community Day School, chairperson of the education committee of the Akron Jewish Community Federation; an Akron delegate on the government affairs committee of Ohio Jewish Communities; chairperson of the Akron Jewish Community High School; and a volunteer with the Akron Area Interfaith Council, Head Start, and the Blossom Music Center.

Lewis is the recipient of numerous honors and awards. In 1985, she was honored by the Akron chapter of Na'amat USA as a Woman Who Makes a Difference. In 1994 she received the JC Penney Golden Rule Award. In 1997, she was named one of northern Ohio's top professional women by *Northern Ohio Live* magazine, and in 1999 she was selected as a Woman of Achievement by the YWCA of Summit County.

OHIO
WOMEN'S
HALL OF
FAME

Ada M. Howe MARTIN

1949–2000

FRANKLIN COUNTY

She didn't care how dirty you were or what you had . . . . I used to tell people, "Ada is an angel. I just don't know where she hides her wings."
—Barbara Myers, Take It to the Streets

Courtesy of Rhonda Martin-Cage

ADA M. HOWE MARTIN, born on March 23, 1949, and her husband Harold started the Take It to the Streets Foundation with an act of kindness in 1982. They and their two children, Rhonda and Sabrina, were skating on a Saturday afternoon when Harold observed a homeless man stealing a pair of shoes that belonged to someone who was skating in the rink. When the man was caught, Harold convinced him to return the shoes in exchange for his own shoes, socks, and coat. From that moment, Martin and her family's commitment to the homeless people of Columbus began.

The Take It to the Streets Foundation started as a grass-roots, community-based organization dedicated to helping an estimated one thousand men, women, and children who call the streets of Columbus home, including those addicted to drugs and alcohol. The Martins regularly provided food, clothing, blankets, spiritual support, and occasionally a shower and a place to sleep in their own home. Over the years, Martin inspired dozens of volunteers and corporate sponsors to help in this noble cause, for example, the preparation of a full Thanksgiving meal with as many as twenty turkeys donated by the Kroger corporation. Much of the support that they provided, however, especially during the early years, came from the Martins' own resources.

43

When Martin and her family first started this philanthropic work, she was employed by the Ohio Department of Rehabilitation and Correction. However, in 1994 —the year in which the foundation received its nonprofit status—she was diagnosed with a rare disease, sarcoidosis. Her health had been fragile for many years, but this diagnosis meant that she had to take a medical retirement from her job. Although this news was quite a blow, it did not deter her commitment to the homeless. She continued her passionate efforts until her death at fifty-one years of age on July 29, 2000.

The tributes from the homeless and others across the city were filled with love and appreciation for her dedicated service, and her legacy lives on. Despite the deep loss of her presence, the Martin family continues the work of the foundation and its much-needed ministry to the homeless.

Community Service

OHIO
WOMEN'S
HALL OF
FAME

Nancy C. Reynolds OAKLEY

1933⁻

CUYAHOGA COUNTY

NANCY C. REYNOLDS OAKLEY, born on January 2, 1933, in Rossford, Ohio, is a passionate educational advocate. In 1974, she launched Project: LEARN. It was designed to be a local site for Laubach Literacy Action, a national literacy movement that trains volunteers to teach adults in one-to-one relationships. The project is directed specifically toward adults in correctional institutions, those in workplace environments, and those studying English as a second language. In 1990, in recognition of the importance of Oakley's work, First Lady Barbara Bush visited the project, gave a public speech, and praised the achievements of the organization.

Although Oakley has retired from Project: LEARN, she remains involved in literacy education. She tutors adult immigrants in English and she now serves as a member of the Friends of Project: LEARN. With this group, she helps raise funds in support of the ongoing work of the organization. In addition, Oakley is also a member of the Friends of the Valley View School, a public elementary school in Cleveland. This small but dedicated group has raised over ten thousand dollars to provide teachers, students, and staff with materials that can help to improve the quality of the educational experiences that the children receive.

44

OHIO
WOMEN'S
HALL OF
FAME

Margaret Arline Webb PRATT

1872-1966

STARK COUNTY

Margaret Arline Webb Pratt was born in 1872 in Massillon, Ohio. On an evening in 1930, she was traveling on the cruise ship HMS *Carinthia* of the Cunard Line out of New York Harbor. She expressed to her traveling companion Grace Merwin her dismay at not being able to see the Statue of Liberty in the dark as they steamed out of port.

Pratt enlisted the help of the captain of the ship and its cruise director, who assisted the two Massillon women in finding others on the ship who might be interested in action. Pratt and Merwin were a part of a group of twenty-five members of the Daughters of the American Revolution (DAR). While they were still on board the ship, Pratt formed an impromptu group and developed a resolution expressing the need to illuminate this striking symbol of the nation. The resolution's purpose, as recorded in the ship's log, was "to memorialize our government to inaugurate a suitable system of illumination of the Statue of Liberty to the end that it shall constantly proclaim the great principles it symbolizes." The resolution was signed by Mrs. Edward U. Pratt, chairman, and Mrs. E. C. Merwin, secretary, and it was to be taken to the DAR local, state, and national organizations.

Upon her return to Massillon, Pratt enlisted the support of Harry Ross, the head of the Ohio Public Service Company, the local utility company. Ross took the request to the Chicago headquarters of City Service Company. It took several months for Pratt to reach her goal, but she did succeed. The Statue of Liberty shines today, in day and in night, as a national beacon for freedom. Credit for this feat went to the DAR, but the momentum for action came from Arline Pratt and Grace Merwin of Massillon, Ohio.

45

Community Service

V. Lanna SAMANIEGO

1943−

MERCER COUNTY

V. LANNA SAMANIEGO, of Eastern Cherokee ancestry, was born on March 3, 1943, and raised in Ohio. Her long record of community activism began in 1975, when she served on the Governor's Health Council. She advocated improvement of the living conditions for migrant farm workers in state migrant camps. During this period, Samaniego served on local clinic boards to provide better health care to migrants and she was instrumental in opening both the first migrant day care center and the first migrant service center in Mercer County.

In 1979, Samaniego began working with Ohio's Native American population through the North American Indian Cultural Center, where she has served in several capacities for more than twenty years, including her current position as executive director. Samaniego has been a passionate activist for Ohio's Native Americans and has worked to improve lives and conditions through education, employment, and advocacy. For example, she has helped educate agencies and the larger Ohio community about the needs and issues of Ohio's Native American population and she has worked with the Ohio Commission on Minority Health and the Ohio Department of Mental Health to identify issues and needs and to develop responsive programs. She coordinates the Mercer County Ministerial Association's food pantry and supportive services program, and she mentors Native American children through the Black Swamp Singers and Dancers, a Native American alcohol and drug abuse prevention program.

Samaniego is active with many local, state, and regional organizations, serving currently, for example, on the Summit/Portage Area Health Education Network, the Committee for Native American Reburial and Repatriation of the Ohio Center for Native American Affairs, and the Ohio State University Multicultural Affairs Committee. Still, she finds the time and energy to be an author. She has received an Award of Excellence from the International Poetry Society for two of her published poems. Currently, she is writing books for children of color to help them with the challenges of prejudice and adversity.

Louella THOMPSON

BUTLER COUNTY

Louella Thompson, born April 30, 1925, has spent more than four decades in Middletown, Ohio. While working as a lay minister and beautician, she had the idea that she could feed the hungry in her community. In September 1987, she began a project to prepare and serve meals to people who were needy, lonely, disabled, and shut-in. She started with fifteen dollars and an unshakable faith that she could accomplish her goal. As she began to visit people in need, she realized that food was not enough. As the weather became colder, she saw that both the adults and children needed warm clothing. Thompson, however, was not deterred. She forged ahead with the help of a well-organized crew of volunteers, and her Feed the Hungry Project, which provided both food and clothing, was well underway.

The Feed the Hungry Project provides carryout meals the fourth Saturday of each month and a daily breakfast. Relying completely on donations and volunteers, she received support from businesses, students, individuals, churches, inmates, and civic groups. As the project grew, she set up a board of advisers, received tax-exempt status, and obtained a license from the local health department. In 1992, after working for five years and raising more than one hundred thousand dollars, Thompson purchased land for a new kitchen and dining facility and watched what had been an optimistic dream turn into a reality.

Thompson has received many honors and awards, including the JC Penney Golden Rule Award and the Outstanding Women of the Year Achievement Award from the YWCA of Hamilton in 1990.

47

Community Service

Imogen Davenport TROLANDER
1924–2000

GREENE COUNTY

Courtesy of Joan Ackerman

IMOGEN DAVENPORT TROLANDER was born on September 13, 1924, in Detroit, Michigan, to a family that was active in organizing the United Auto Workers and in other progressive causes. In 1944, she came to Antioch College with the intention of becoming a labor organizer. At Antioch, however, she met and married Hardy Trolander and determined that teaching was a more practical career choice.

After graduation, Trolander taught at the Antioch School, the college's alternative demonstration primary school, until she began taking care of her family full time. During her fifteen years as a homemaker, she volunteered with the local Democratic Party, the Community Children's Center, the Head Start program, the Yellow Springs Library Association, and the public schools. In 1970, she returned to teaching in the Xenia Community Schools while completing an M.A. in education at the Antioch/Putney Graduate School of Education. In 1974, after a devastating tornado in the area, Trolander served her community in yet another way, organizing a twenty-four-hour day care center. Later, she would become the director of the Day Care Home Mothers Program at Sinclair Community College in Dayton.

Throughout these years, Trolander did not leave her activist commitments behind, as illustrated by her early membership in the National Organization for Women and her activities with this group, and most clearly by her leadership in founding three local projects. In 1974, she cofounded Women, Inc., an organization dedicated to studying and acting on issues of concern to women. In the spring of 1998, the Ohio Women's Policy and Research Commission honored the project with a Making a Difference Award. In 1992, Trolander initiated the Women's History Project of Greene County with the mission of promoting an awareness of women's contributions to life in Greene County. This group published *Women of Greene County* in 1994. In 1997, she organized a committee to plan the Women's Park of Yellow Springs to counter the fact that all the public buildings, parks, schools, and streets in the town had been named to honor men. In 1999, Trolander published a book, *Celebrating Women: The Women's Park of Yellow Springs* which contained narratives about many of the five hundred women honored in the park.

On March 18, 2000, Trolander died, leaving behind a legacy of activism and service.

Profiles of Two Hundred Ohio Women

Georgeta Blebea WASHINGTON

CUYAHOGA COUNTY

GEORGETA BLEBEA WASHINGTON was born in a small village in Transylvania, Romania, on January 20, 1953. She immigrated to the United States at the age of twelve and was raised in Alliance, Ohio. Washington attended both Cleveland State University and the Ohio State University before entering the Fairview General Hospital School of Nursing and becoming a registered nurse in 1989. Washington's mark on the world is being made in another way, however, as she establishes herself as a dynamic leader and cultural advocate for Americans of Romanian ancestry.

Throughout her childhood, Washington participated with her family in Romanian American activities at the local, state, and national levels, demonstrating a commitment to social and cultural activities that have helped to maintain this ethnic heritage. In 1998, her leadership was rewarded when she was elected as the first woman president of the Union and League of Romanian Societies of America, the largest and oldest fraternal organization of American Romanians.

Washington served as the first woman editor of the oldest continuously run Romanian newspaper outside of Romania, *Americai;* she also authored two books on Romanian history in the United States. Washington has represented the interests of Romanians in Washington, D.C., advocating for Romania's entry into NATO and the EU and for economic aid. From 1998 to 2000, she spearheaded a program for donation of funds and supplies to Romanian hospitals. For her contributions, three universities in Romania have awarded her honorary degrees.

On a local level, Washington campaigned successfully for the establishment of December first of each year as Romanian National Day, recognizing Romania's over-

49

throw of the communist dictatorship and the reestablishment of democracy on December 1, 1989, and the contributions of Romanian Americans to Ohio. In addition, she has been a volunteer teacher of English as a foreign language in the Alliance Public Schools and is collaborating with Cleveland's TV Channel 8 on a documentary on Romania.

Now in her second term as president of the Union and League of Romanian Societies of America, her success as a leader has been an inspiration and an example for others.

Community Service

OHIO
WOMEN'S
HALL OF
FAME

Grayce Edwards WILLIAMS

1919−2002

FRANKLIN COUNTY

Grayce Edwards Williams was born in Williamson, West Virginia, in 1919. While a student in the segregated school system of her hometown, she was inspired by her study of African American history to make her own significant contributions to society. By the age of seventeen, when she refused to move to the back of a bus in North Carolina, she had already begun to set her mark in what would be a lifelong commitment to justice, equality, and the well-being of others.

Williams moved to Columbus, Ohio, in 1943 and took a job lubricating train engines. She became ill from the oil, however, and had to be reassigned to a dining car, where she met her husband, Howard Williams. During her first year in Columbus, she joined the YWCA and remained a volunteer in the organization until her death in 2002. She served as a member of the YWCA board of directors, and in 1973 she was elected board president, becoming the first African American to occupy this position.

Williams was a visible leader in the YWCA at the state level, as well, serving as vice-president and later as president of the Council of Ohio YWCAs. Through this group, she worked in Ohio to encourage the YWCA's organizational services to implement its national mission to empower women. She provided leadership for many teen programs, reaching out especially to mentor young women from the inner city, and she represented the council at a briefing at the White House on issues of concern to women. For these efforts, the YWCA honored her with a Woman of Achievement Award.

Williams's community activism extended beyond the YWCA, however. In 1972, Williams became a volunteer with A Better Chance, a program that sent gifted urban students to boarding schools around the country, and in 1976, she helped to found the Action Ohio Coalition for Battered Women, a statewide resource for victims of domestic abuse. In addition, she volunteered with the Metropolitan Columbus Schools Committee, the Columbus Public Schools Superintendent's Advisory Committee, United Way, Church Women United, the Franklin County Extension Services 4-H Program, Ohio Women, Inc., and the League against Child Abuse.

50

OHIO
WOMEN'S
HALL OF
FAME

Profiles of Two Hundred Ohio Women

EDUCATION

IN EDUCATION—LONG CONSIDERED A TRADITIONAL
work arena for women—Ohio women have been shining stars. In
public schools, private schools, colleges and universities, as well as in
community-based organizations, women have been tireless in both
their leadership and their facilitation of educational quality and excellence. They have founded schools, raised money to support them,
developed and implemented innovative curricula, and garnered the
goodwill of patrons. Most of all, however, they have touched hearts
and minds—not only those of the students who are forever changed
because of the presence of these women in their lives, but also those of
the communities in which they have worked. Women have provided
priceless educational services as central players in a state noted worldwide for early and long-standing commitments to educational opportunity and achievement.

MARY BEAUMONT, O.S.U.

HALLIE QUINN BROWN

CAROL A. CARTWRIGHT

FRANCES MARION (FANNY) JACKSON COPPIN

RUTH L. DAVIS

ELECTRA COLLINS DOREN

SARAH JANE WOODSON EARLY

ESTHER M. GREISHEIMER

JOAN C. HEIDELBERG

CAROL S. KELLY

JENNIE MANNHEIMER

NORMA SNIPES MARCERE

MARY ANDREW MATESICH

WILLA B. PLAYER

JENNIE DAVIS PORTER

LORLE PORTER

PHEBE TEMPERANCE SUTLIFF

VIRGINIA MacMILLAN VARGA

Mary BEAUMONT, O.S.U.

1818–1881

CUYAHOGA COUNTY

Whatever you have, graciously share it with others.

—Mother Mary of the Annunciation

Mary Beaumont (Mother Mary of the Annunciation) was thirty-two years old in 1850 when she came to Cleveland with four other religious women from Boulogne-sur-Mer in France to found the Order of Saint Ursula in Cleveland. In 1871, this order founded Ursuline College, the first chartered college for women in the state of Ohio.

Mother Mary was an energetic woman with educational insight who envisioned a place of leadership for women. During a century when there was nothing at all automatic about the possibility of education—and especially higher education—for women, she pushed to the forefront to assure that there was more than hope, but expectation. As the number of congregants in the parish grew, the order also grew and spread its influence throughout northern Ohio, establishing academies for girls in Toledo, Tiffin, and Youngstown. The sisters' concern for the poor and for immigrants was legendary, and they dedicated themselves to educational support at all levels.

Over the years, graduates of Ursuline College have been at the forefront in providing responsible and caring leaders. Many graduates have taught in schools located

in trouble-ridden communities; others have become nurses in hospitals across the state; others have become leaders in the arts, sciences, and social work. All of these contributions are attributable to the wisdom and commitment of Mary Beaumont and her sisters who dared to do what no one in the state had done before, to found a school for women.

53

Education

Hallie Quinn BROWN

c. 1845-1949

GREENE COUNTY

Hallie Quinn Brown, the daughter of former slaves, was born in Pittsburgh, Pennsylvania, on March 10, 1845, and raised in Chatham, Ontario. Her parents successfully educated all six of their children, moving their family in 1870 to Wilberforce, Ohio, where Brown and her brother could attend Wilberforce University, from which she graduated in 1873.

Brown began a career as a teacher of both adults and children in South Carolina, Mississippi, and Georgia in the aftermath of the Civil War. In 1875, she returned to Ohio to teach in the Dayton Public Schools. In 1885, she was named dean of women at Allen University in Columbia, South Carolina, where she also administered a night school for adults. From 1892 to 1893, she served as dean of women at Tuskegee Institute, under the leadership of Booker T. Washington. In 1893, she returned to Ohio as professor of elocution at Wilberforce University, where she retained her connection for the rest of her life.

Early in her career, Brown earned a reputation as a passionate advocate for education and as an excellent public speaker, a talent that she would use as a social activist throughout her life. In 1894, for example, she began a five-year stint as lecturer for the British Woman's Temperance Association and was made a member of the Royal Scottish Geographical Society. She returned to teach at Wilberforce in 1906, but by then her work as an activist equaled her work as an educator. She was a highly respected leader in the African American Episcopal Church, women's organizations, and the Republican Party; her other leadership positions included founder of the Neighborhood Club in Wilberforce, president of the Ohio Federation of Colored Women's Clubs (1905–12) and the National Association of Colored Women (1920–24), a speaker for state, local, and national political campaigns in Ohio, Pennsylvania, Illinois, and Missouri, and vice-president of the Ohio Council of Republican Women, speaking in 1924 at the Republican National Convention in Cleveland.

During this period, Brown also authored seven books, the best known of which were *Bits and Odds: A Choice Selection of Recitations* (1880) and *Homespun Heroines and Other Women of Distinction* (1926). Brown died on September 16, 1949, in Wilberforce, where two buildings now stand as memorials to her.

Carol A. CARTWRIGHT

1941–

PORTAGE COUNTY

CAROL A. CARTWRIGHT, born on June 19, 1941, in Sioux City, Iowa, earned a B.A. from the University of Wisconsin–Whitewater and an M.A. and Ph.D. from the University of Pittsburgh. She was vice-chancellor for academic affairs at the University of California–Davis, and dean for undergraduate programs and vice-provost at Pennsylvania State University. In March 1991, however, Cartwright made history when she became the first woman president of a public university in the state of Ohio.

Highly respected for her academic vision and her advocacy for women and cultural diversity, Cartwright has helped establish Kent State University as an institution that balances high-quality undergraduate programs and innovative research in selected areas. Cartwright has championed Kent State's commitment to regional development, demonstrating her own active engagement through the many organizations with which she is involved. In addition to serving on the boards of directors of several local companies, she has served as president of the Akron Roundtable board of trustees and on the board of directors of the Ohio Division of the American Cancer Society. She is a member of the Greater Akron Chamber, the Greater Cleveland Roundtable, Cleveland Tomorrow, and the Northeast Ohio Council on Higher Education.

Cartwright has also been at the educational forefront on a national level, having chaired the board of directors of the American Association for Higher Education and having served as well on the boards of the American Council on Education and the National Association of State Universities and Land Grant Colleges. Her other lead-

ership positions include service on the boards of directors of the National Collegiate Athletic Association and the National First Ladies' Library, on the steering committee of the national education initiatives America Reads and America Counts, and on the board of trustees of the Woodrow Wilson International Center for Scholars. In other words, Cartwright is highly visible and greatly involved in the community, the state, and the nation, and she serves as a dynamic model of academic leadership for others.

Education

OHIO WOMEN'S HALL OF FAME

Frances Marion (Fanny) Jackson COPPIN

1837–1913

LORAIN COUNTY

Frances Marion (Fanny) Jackson Coppin, born in Washington, D.C., in 1837, spent most of her life in Philadelphia, Pennsylvania, but from 1860 to 1865 she lived in Oberlin, Ohio. Born a slave, Coppin's freedom was bought by a devoted aunt, Sarah Orr. After living, working, and studying in New Bedford, Massachusetts, and Newport, Rhode Island, she enrolled in 1860 in the Ladies' Department of Oberlin College, and in 1865, she became the second African American woman in the United States to be awarded a B.A. In *The Three Sarahs: Documents of Antebellum Black College Women* (1984), Ellen NicKenzie Lawson described Coppin as "Oberlin's most distinguished antebellum Black graduate."

Upon graduation from Oberlin, Coppin was appointed principal of the female department at the Institute for Colored Youth in Philadelphia, becoming principal of the entire institute in 1889, a position that she would hold until her retirement in 1902. In the 1880s, Coppin campaigned to establish an industrial department at the institute to provide African Americans with the much-needed opportunity to compete for a growing number of technical and industrial jobs. This department opened in January 1889, making it the first trade school for African Americans in Philadelphia.

In addition to being a leader in education, Coppin was also politically active throughout her life. She often spoke at political rallies, usually as the only woman on the program. She was among the founding members of the National Association of Colored Women (1896), a coalition of African American women's clubs that was highly successful in forwarding an agenda in support of African American causes. She wrote children's stories and a woman's column for the *Christian Recorder,* the newspaper of the African Methodist Episcopal (AME) Church. She was president of the local Women's Mite Missionary Society and later national president of the Women's Home and Foreign Missionary Society of the AME Church. Coppin also traveled extensively both nationally and internationally with her husband, who was a minister and eventually a bishop in the church.

Coppin died on January 21, 1913, in Philadephia. A girls' dormitory is named for her at Wilberforce Institute in Cape Town, South Africa, and Coppin State College in Baltimore, Maryland, is named for her as well.

Courtesy of Oberlin College Archives

Profiles of Two Hundred Ohio Women

56

Ruth L. DAVIS

1910−

LUCAS COUNTY

Ruth L. Davis was born on March 24, 1910, in Toledo, Ohio. In 1948, she became the third generation of the Davis family—and the first woman—to assume the role of president of Davis College, the oldest proprietary school in Ohio. Under Davis's leadership, the college grew and prospered. She dedicated herself to instilling high expectations in her students and others around her, especially women. She encouraged women to be leaders and provided them a bold example. As a teacher, academic professional, and community leader, Davis supported both educational and leadership advancement for almost sixty years.

Over the course of her long career, Davis spent many hours with students, recognizing that teaching often happens outside of the classroom. She tells stories of students who came to Davis College with little more than a dream. She enrolled them in classes, bought them clothes, and assured them that they could be professionals in the world of work. They graduated from Davis with knowledge and also with confidence and pride.

In addition to her work on the campus, Davis viewed service to professional and community organizations as a vital extension of her position. She assumed leadership roles as president of the International Association of Personnel Women; treasurer, vice-president, and president of the Toledo chapter of Zonta International; president and area director of the Administrative Management Society; and president of the Ohio Business School Association. She has served also on the board of directors of the American Society for Training and Development, Mid-American Bank, the Future Business Leaders of America, and the Ohio Council of Private Colleges and Schools.

Davis has received proclamations from the mayor of Toledo and the Ohio State House of Representatives; she has been named the Outstanding Business School Educator by Phi Theta Pi; and she has received the Distinguished Citizenship Award from the International Business Institute at the University of Toledo.

Education

Electra Collins DOREN

1861–1927

MONTGOMERY COUNTY

Eʟᴇᴄᴛʀᴀ Cᴏʟʟɪɴs Dᴏʀᴇɴ, born in 1861 near Cincinnati, graduated from Cooper Female Seminary in Dayton and spent a year studying at the Library School of Albany, New York. In 1896, she began working for the Dayton Public Library and soon became chief librarian. Significant among her contributions was the reorganization of the library by the Dewey decimal system, which facilitated the opening of the collection to public use and allowed library patrons to browse and select their own books for the first time. She initiated a book wagon service, the first in the nation, which took books to outlying areas of the community and she formed a school library department, which sent selections of juvenile literature to public schools for use by children and teachers.

In addition, Doren established a library training school—only the second of its kind in the United States—which was housed at the library. In 1905, she moved to Cleveland to become the first director of the School of Library Science at Case Western Reserve University. A few years later, however, she returned to Dayton in the face of a devastating flood to lead library staff and volunteers in an effort to salvage thousands of items that were damaged by the waters. Through all of these years, Doren collected various and sundry materials related to the Ohio woman suffrage movement. This collection now forms the core of the Dayton Metro Library's Women's Suffrage Collection, the largest collection of suffrage materials in the United States.

Doren was also active in professional organizations. She helped found and served

as president of the Ohio Library Association (now the Ohio Library Council). She held leadership positions in the American Library Association (ALA) and worked with the ALA War Service Committee to establish field libraries overseas during World War I.

In 1928, the city of Dayton dedicated the E. C. Doren Branch Library, located in the Old North Dayton area, and in 1997, inducted her into the Dayton Walk of Fame.

58

OHIO
WOMEN'S
HALL OF
FAME

Profiles of Two Hundred Ohio Women

Sarah Jane Woodson EARLY

1825–1907

ROSS COUNTY

Courtesy of the Schomburg Center for Research in Black Culture, New York Public Library

S ARAH JANE WOODSON EARLY, born on November 15, 1825, in Chillicothe, Ohio, was the granddaughter of Sally Hemings and possibly of Hemings's slave master, former United States president Thomas Jefferson. She was a pioneering educator and social activist in the African Methodist Episcopal (AME) Church and in the early women's movement. When Early was still a young child, her family joined others in Chillicothe to form the first AME Church west of the Allegheny Mountains. Her brother Lewis founded the African Education and Benefit Society of Chillicothe and a similar society in Pittsburgh, where one of his most well-known students was Martin Delaney, who later became nationally renowned as a physician, writer, and black nationalist. Early grew up, therefore, surrounded by activists and leaders who believed in political action, self-determination, temperance, hard work, and education.

In 1856, Early graduated from Oberlin College with a literary degree, becoming one of the first African American women to complete a four-year college-level program. She began her career, while still in college, as a teacher in several African American communities in Ohio and served as principal of the African American public school in Xenia. In 1858, she was appointed preceptress of English and Latin and lady principal and matron at Wilberforce University, becoming the first African American woman to serve on the faculty of an American university. In 1868, Early left Wilberforce to go South after the Civil War to teach in a girls' school in Hillsboro, North Carolina. After her marriage to Jordan Winston Early, an AME minister, Early moved to Tennessee where she taught and assumed numerous leadership roles in the AME Church until the couple retired in 1888.

Early rose to national prominence when she became superintendent of the colored division of the Women's Christian Temperance Union from 1888 to 1892 and served also as spokesperson for the Prohibition Party in Tennessee. Throughout this period, Early lectured broadly as an advocate for temperance, self-help, and the elevation of both her race and gender. In 1893, she was selected a Representative Woman of the World at the Women's Congress of the Chicago World's Fair. Early died in 1907.

59

Education

Esther M. GREISHEIMER

1891–1982

ROSS COUNTY

Esther M. Greisheimer was born on October 31, 1891, in Chillicothe, Ohio. In 1914, she received a B.A. in education from Ohio University. She also received an M.A. in general physiology from Clark University in Massachusetts in 1916; a Ph.D. in human physiology and biochemistry from the University of Chicago in 1919; and an M.D. from the University of Minnesota in 1923. In 1924, she was licensed to practice medicine and surgery.

Greisheimer spent the next fifty years holding academic positions. She spent eighteen years at the University of Minnesota, eight years at the Medical College of Pennsylvania, and twenty-five years at the Temple University School of Medicine. Over the course of her career, she authored more than one hundred fifty articles published in various medical and scientific journals. She is most noted, however, for her book *Physiology and Anatomy*. It has been widely used as a textbook and is now in its ninth edition.

Greisheimer was elected to membership in the honorary medical societies Sigma Xi and Alpha Omega Alpha, and she was awarded the Ohio University Medal of Merit in recognition of her pioneering contributions to medical education.

Profiles of Two Hundred Ohio Women

OHIO
WOMEN'S
HALL OF
FAME

Joan C. HEIDELBERG

1932–

MIAMI COUNTY

JOAN C. HEIDELBERG was born on October 27, 1932, in Alabama. She received a B.A. from Samford University in biology, chemistry, and physics, and an M.A. from Rice University in biology. In 1953, she began her career as a teacher in Cullman, Alabama, but in 1955 she moved to Cincinnati, Ohio, and accepted a position as a health physics assistant with the General Electric Company in the aircraft nuclear propulsion department. She moved to Houston, Texas, and worked as a supervisor in a radioisotope laboratory at the Anderson Hospital and Tumor Institute from 1956 to 1962. In 1963, she moved back to Ohio and began raising a family and volunteering with the Dayton Museum of Natural History. With these activities, she developed new interests that ultimately shifted her career path.

In 1973, Heidelberg became the administrative director of the Brukner Nature Center in Troy, Ohio, where she began building the environmental education center into a nationally recognized institution. The Institute for Museum Services named it one of the top three natural history museums in the United States. Under her leadership, the center has grown into a private nonprofit organization that draws thousands of visitors annually. It provides outreach programs, environmental workshops for educators, wildlife rehabilitation, and animal therapy programs. With Heidelberg's guidance, the center has served over two hundred thousand students from Miami County and ten other surrounding counties through organized programs and activities with the schools. Thousands of adults have participated in nature hikes and stargazing, and many groups have journeyed with Heidelberg on natural history trips to places such as Alaska, the Galapagos Islands, Kenya, New Zealand, and Australia. Hundreds of hospitalized residents have been visited by animals from the animal therapy program. Heidelberg has succeeded in orchestrating new understandings of natural history for people in her area and well beyond, particularly through the publication, *The Brukner Nature Center: The Primer of Wildlife Care and Rehabilitation* (authored by Patti L. Raley in 1992) for which she served as technical consultant.

In recognition of her achievements, Heidelberg was the recipient of the North American Association for Environmental Education's Walter E. Jeske Award for her outstanding contributions to environmental education.

Education

Carol S. KELLY

1939–

FRANKLIN COUNTY

CAROL S. KELLY, born on May 15, 1939, graduated from the Ohio State University, where she was a member of the women's basketball team, hockey team, concert band, Women's Self-Government Association, and president of several campus organizations. Kelly has spent most of her career on the faculty of California State University at Northridge and is now professor emerita. As an educator, she is internationally recognized for her leadership in developing and implementing an innovative interdisciplinary major in child and adolescent development. She has taught, counseled, and mentored students from diverse racial and cultural backgrounds, but particularly students with disabilities.

Kelly organized a peace exposition that encompassed more than sixty community agencies and campus organizations and drew more than five thousand participants. In 1993, she served as senior consultant to the United Nations in Vienna for its International Year of the Family effort. She has also been the U.S. representative to the International Federation of Educative Communities, which focuses on institutionalized children and youth, and she has presented symposia at the 1996 Convention on the Rights of the Child in Romania, the 1995 International Child and Youth Care Conference in South Africa, the XXIII Interamerican Congress of Psychology in Costa Rica, and a 1990 Family Life Education for Peace event in Costa Rica. In addition, Kelly has produced a videotape on creating careers, which has been viewed at three international conferences, and she has also written and produced television programs, including *Families: Understanding Deaf Culture* for public access television. Kelly is coauthor of *Careers with Children and Youth: An Invitation to explore Personal and Professional Potentials* (1996) and she has also facilitated the success of hundreds of women who have earned scholarships, grants, awards, and fellowships.

Kelly's awards include a Distinguished Teaching Award from the California State University at Northridge, a merit award from the San Fernando Valley chapter of the United Nations Association, and a medallion of appreciation from the Romanian International Federation of Educative Communities.

Jennie MANNHEIMER

1872–1943

HAMILTON COUNTY

J ENNIE MANNHEIMER (who later changed her name to Jane Manner) was born in New York on January 9, 1872. When she was a child, her family moved to Cincinnati, where she was educated. She was one of the first two women to receive a B.A. in the field of Hebrew letters from Hebrew Union College in Cincinnati in 1892; she later earned a B.A. from the University of Cincinnati as well.

Mannheimer's teaching career began when she accepted a position as a teacher and director of the drama department of the Cincinnati College of Music (now the College-Conservatory of Music) at the University of Cincinnati, where she remained until 1907. Believing that Americans did not take the time to pay attention to correct and proper language and that success was very much tied to careful speech, she founded her own school, the Cincinnati School of Expression, where she served as director until 1912.

Mannheimer's focus was on the interpretation of literature and the teaching of speech. In 1913, however, she began a series of modern drama readings that were presented at the Cincinnati Women's Club. With the success of these performances, Mannheimer presented a similar series at the Plaza Hotel in New York. Later she moved to New York to continue her career as reader and teacher, and as director of the Jane Manner Drama Studio. As she had done in Cincinnati, Mannheimer gave numerous recitals and readings and she directed many plays. She performed at Carnegie Hall, the Brooklyn Institute of Arts and Sciences, and the Waldorf Astoria, where she gave recitals for seven consecutive years. Over the course of her career, Mannheimer taught many students who went on to distinguished careers on stage, screen, and radio. She also published books on drama and speech, including *The Silver Treasury, Prose and Verse for Every Mood* (1934), which dealt with the teaching and interpretation of literature. Mannheimer died on May 26, 1943.

Courtesy of the Jacob Rader Marcus Center of the American Jewish Archives, Cincinnati, Ohio

Education

Norma Snipes MARCERE

1908–

STARK COUNTY

Norma Snipes Marcere was born in 1908 in Canton, Ohio. After finishing high school, she worked to pay for her college education at Kent State University, where she received a teaching certificate in 1929 and went on to earn a B.A. in education and an M.A. in counseling. Her first teaching position was for Massillon City Schools as an English teacher at Edmund A. Jones Junior High School; later she went to the Akron Public Schools, where she became the first African American guidance counselor and the first African American school psychologist for the district. Although Marcere had wanted to teach in her hometown, these desires were dashed by a superintendent who swore that he would not hire a "colored teacher" and that she should go south to teach. This incident and others like it strengthened her resolve to fulfill all her aspirations and to build a remarkable career as a pioneering advocate for civil rights, a feminist educator, and a leader in Stark County.

In addition to working in the school system, Marcere also provided complementary services in the larger community. When she saw that many students were not achieving as she thought that they should and could, she founded Project Academic Exellence (PAX), a Saturday school for inner-city youths at St. Mary's Church of the Immaculate Conception in Canton. In addition to helping students with their school work, Marcere also focused on enhancing their self-esteem and helping them plan careers. The program became a landmark for support and educational development for children in her community.

64

Marcere retired from the Akron Public Schools in 1976, but her work continued. She has authored two autobiographies, 'Round the Dining Room Table (1985) and The Fences Between (1989). The two books formed the basis of a play written and directed by Lois DiGiacomo, The Fences Between, that was performed for the first time in 1994 at the Cultural Center for the Arts in Canton. Marcere has also received a Woman of the Year Award from the Junior League and is the recipient of an honorary degree from Walsh College.

Courtesy Dr. Norma Marcere

Profiles of Two Hundred Ohio Women

Mary Andrew MATESICH

1939−

FRANKLIN COUNTY

MARY ANDREW MATESICH, a member of the Dominican Sisters of St. Mary of the Springs since her senior year in high school, was born on May 5, 1939, in Zanesville, Ohio. She graduated summa cum laude in 1962 from Ohio Dominican University with a degree in chemistry. She received a National Science Foundation Graduate Fellowship to attend the University of California at Berkeley, where she received both a master's degree and a Ph.D. in chemistry. In 1965, while Matesich was still completing her doctorate, she began teaching chemistry at her alma mater. In 1966, she joined the faculty as a full-time member and in 1967, she was appointed chair of the natural science department. Matesich continued to rise through the ranks: By 1973, she had been named executive vice-president and academic dean, a position that she held until 1978 when she was named president.

Under Matesich's leadership, college enrollment has grown and its mission to provide an excellent academic experience and to serve disadvantaged and underserved populations has expanded and flourished. She has created opportunities for working adults to earn college degrees through programs such as Weekend College, Learning Enhanced Adult Degree (LEAD), PATRIOTS (for veterans), and Operation Second Chance (for those who dropped out of college before obtaining a degree).

Matesich is also active in professional and community organizations. She has been a member of the National Association of Independent Colleges and Universities and she has served on the advisory boards of the Council of Independent Colleges and the Association of Independent Colleges and Universities of Ohio. In addition, she has participated actively with the United Way of Central Ohio, Columbus Together 2000, the Greater Columbus Promise for Youth governing committee, the Zivili Dance Company, and the Columbus Rotary and Torch Clubs.

In recognition of excellence and service, Matesich has received a YWCA Outstanding Woman of Achievement Award, a salute from the Columbus Foundation, the Anti-Defamation League's Jack Resler Award, the Henry Paley Award, and honorary degrees from several colleges and universities.

65

Education

Willa B. PLAYER

1909–

SUMMIT COUNTY

Willa B. Player, born on August 9, 1909, in Jackson, Mississippi, moved at the age of seven with her family to Akron, Ohio. She graduated from Ohio Wesleyan University in 1929; received an M.A. from Oberlin in 1930; received the Certificat d'Etudes in French from the University of Grenoble (France) in 1935; and earned a Ph.D. from Columbia University in 1948. In 1930, Player was appointed to the faculty at Bennett College, a historically African American college for women in Greensboro, North Carolina. Over the next fifteen years, she held several administrative positions at this institution and in 1955 she made history by being named the first woman president of the college, a position that she held until her retirement in 1966. With this title, she became the first African American woman to be appointed president of a four-year women's college.

Player's rise to the presidency of Bennett occurred during the era of the Civil Rights movement. Not only was she responsible for providing an enlightened academic vision and a core of opportunities for intellectual and personal development for young African American women at Bennett, she also served as a stabilizing force for a remarkable generation of young women who were determined to be active participants in sit-ins and other nonviolent protests. Player considered their activism to be important, but rather than suggesting to the women that they join the protests, she instead told them, "You will be expected to practice what you've learned." Her role, then, was to support all who were involved, to be vigilant in letting their parents know that they were safe, and to encourage them to learn how to stay out of jail so that their views could be articulated and understood.

After retiring in 1966, Player continued to provide critical leadership through her work with the U.S. Office of Education, Bureau of Higher Education, where she served as director of the Division of College Support. In this position she provided leadership in funding historically African American colleges and universities and other institutions that served the minority population. She retired from that position in 1977. In addition to several honorary degrees, Player has received many other awards, including the Superior Service Award and the Distinguished Service Award from the former U.S. Department of Health, Education, and Welfare.

66

Profiles of Two Hundred Ohio Women

Jennie Davis PORTER

1876–1936

HAMILTON COUNTY

JENNIE DAVIS PORTER was born in Cincinnati, Ohio, in 1876. After graduating from the University of Cincinnati, she began teaching African American children in that city's public schools in 1897. From that point forward, she used her professional talents in the interest of the education of children and the welfare of her community.

After a flood struck the area in 1913, Porter worked with flood relief teams; as a result of this work in the community, she discovered 147 African American children between eight and fourteen years of age who were not attending school. Concerned about their opportunities, she opened a summer school in the vacant Hughes Building. Believing that there were advantages in having separate educational opportunities for African Americans, she supported the experimental effort to hold classes in the Hughes Building. Enrollment in the program grew rapidly to 350 students, making the experiment a success. In the 1914–15 academic year, the school system established the program as a separate school and named it in honor of Harriet Beecher Stowe (see entry under Literature). Porter became the principal, establishing her as the first African American woman to be named to such a post in the Cincinnati school system. With the huge influx of African American families from the rural South who were migrating northward, the Stowe school quickly grew to twenty-eight hundred students by 1925.

The school was a prototype for vocational education, as well as a school that encouraged high standards, academic achievement, and preparation for higher education. Porter, in fact, was determined to provide opportunities for African American children that were not offered to them at other schools. She brought in speakers of national renown and organized both teachers and children into glee clubs, bands, and orchestras that played at local sites, and also engaged in a vibrant campaign "to mould public sentiment favorably." With the success of her principalship securely in place, Porter enrolled in the University of Cincinnati's College of Education at the age of forty-two. She completed the program, and in 1928 she became the first African American to be granted a Ph.D.

Porter also supported many community activities and organizations. She served as a trustee of Wilberforce University, and, most notably, she participated in the black clubwomen's movement.

Education

Lorle PORTER

MUSKINGUM COUNTY

She has a magic touch in gathering the dust of Ohio history and shaping it into a living breathing entity.

> —Jo Anne Libert, past president of the Fairfield County Heritage Association

LORLE PORTER was born on April 7, 1938, in Mount Vernon, Ohio. She received a B.A. from Notre Dame College (1960), an M.A. from Boston College (1961), and a Ph.D. from the University of New Mexico (1965). Upon completion of her doctorate, she was appointed to the faculty at Muskingum College, becoming the first woman to be hired in the social science division and, later, the first to chair a department and the first to serve as coordinator of a division. Porter spent her full career at Muskingum, retiring in 1998, but she assumed a new position as regional historian in residence at the college "in recognition of her continuing dedicated service to the region and her visionary interpretation and enthusiasm for Southeastern Ohio history."

While active on the faculty at Muskingum, Porter provided valuable leadership as an administrator and as a teacher, as demonstrated by the teaching awards that she received: the Phi Theta Beta Educational Honorary's Outstanding Teacher Award (1980), the Outstanding Teaching Award from the Ohio Academy of History (1998), and the William Oxley Thompson Award for Excellence in Teaching (1989). Even more distinctive is her record of scholarship. Porter has written seven books—the most recent *Sara's Table: "Keeping House" in Ohio, 1800–1950* (2001)—which have established

her as an expert in Ohio history and a well-known proponent for heritage tourism and heritage education in southeastern Ohio. In 1996, she was recognized by the American Association for State and Local History for her contributions to the understanding of southeastern Ohio history.

As a retiree, Porter is even more actively involved in the history and heritage of Ohio. She is a member of the Ohio Arts Council and a trustee of the Ohio Civil War Trail Commission, and is working on a Civil War museum in Harrison County.

OHIO WOMEN'S HALL OF FAME

Profiles of Two Hundred Ohio Women

Phebe Temperance SUTLIFF

1859–1955

TRUMBULL COUNTY

P HEBE TEMPERANCE SUTLIFF was born on January 16, 1859 in Warren County, Ohio. In 1880, she graduated Phi Beta Kappa with a B.A. from Vassar College; in 1890 she earned an M.A. from Cornell; and in 1891, she received a graduate certificate from the University of Zurich in Switzerland in philosophy. Sutliff also attended the University of Chicago, where she studied U.S. constitutional history.

During the 1885–86 school year, Sutliff was lady principal at Hiram College. From 1887 to 1889, she was a professor of history and English at Rockford College in Illinois and was so highly regarded there that in 1896 she was named president. She was recognized as a brilliant scholar, a powerful lecturer, and a dynamic fundraiser. She was dedicated to raising the academic standing of the institution and succeeded in transforming Rockford from a seminary to an accredited college. In 1901, Sutliffe resigned to return to Ohio to care for her ill mother.

In Ohio, Sutliffe continued to excel. In 1914, in response to the rising numbers of European immigrants in the community, she organized a free evening school focused on the teaching of reading and writing. In 1923, she founded and became the first president of the Warren branch of the American Association of University Women. She helped organize the Warren Urban League to address the needs of African Americans in the community and served as its first president. She began and was president of the Warren Child Labor League. She was trustee of the Warren Public Volunteer Health Association and helped to initiate the local Visiting Nurses' Association to help especially with the health care needs of immigrant families. She was a trustee of the Warren Public Library for thirty-two years and a member of the executive committee of the Warren Community Fund Organization. All of these activities identified her as a leader in the state, which meant that she was called upon often by governors to provide services related to education and community development.

After women gained the right to vote, Sutliff was also active in the Democratic Party, and in 1924 she became the first woman to be unanimously nominated as Democratic candidate for Congress from the Nineteenth District. After many decades of service, Sutliff died on July 25, 1955.

Education

Virginia MacMillan VARGA

1929–

MONTGOMERY COUNTY

VIRGINIA MACMILLAN VARGA was born on June 19, 1929, in Dayton, Ohio. In 1951, she graduated from the University of Dayton with a degree in education and in 1961 she went on to become one of the first people in the United States to receive Montessori training from the International Montessori Association (IMA) and the American Montessori Society (AMS). The Montessori educational philosophy encourages children to learn through experience, and in 1962, Varga and her husband founded the first school in Dayton—and only the second in Ohio—embracing this approach, the Gloria Dei Montessori School. Over the next few years the school expanded, adding a toddler program in 1965 (the first offered in the United States). In 1967, the school added classes for six-to-nine-year-olds and eventually for nine-to-twelve-year-olds. Currently, the school serves approximately two hundred children between the ages of three months and twelve years, and Varga has opened a new school called the Montessori Educare of Kettering for infants and toddlers.

Varga's influence extends beyond Dayton, however. As an internationally known Montessori educator and expert, she has established or influenced hundreds of Montessori schools and day care centers around the globe, including Central America, Africa, China, Hong Kong, Japan, China, and Canada. In addition, she has served as chairperson of the AMS Teacher Section (1966–68); a school consultant (since 1966); regional director of consultation (1971–73); and a member of the AMS board (1969–77). In 1980, she instituted a teacher training program for infant and toddler

specialists for the Center for Montessori Teacher Education and in 1988, she created the first Montessori Accreditation Council for Teacher Education and Evaluation.

For her achievements, Varga received an honorary degree from the University of Dayton in 1999 and the American Montessori Society's Living Legacy Award in 1993.

EXPLORATION

AND

ADVENTURE

WEBSTER'S NEW WORLD DICTIONARY DEFINES AN explorer as "a person who explores an unknown or little-known region" and an adventurer as "a person who has or likes to have adventures." Adventure, in turn, is glossed as "the encountering of danger" or "an unusual, stirring experience, often of romantic nature." These, of course, are not images that are typically associated with women. Stereotypically, women do not go where others have not gone before; they stay home to be protected and to anchor others. When we look closely, however, at what Ohio women have actually done, we do see such images well in play. They have ventured into the unknown and many certainly have exhibited a desire for dangerous, soul-stirring adventures. Indeed, a great many women in this collection could have been placed in this category. We have chosen to highlight some of the boldest, most courageous, and most unusual among them.

MARY LEONORE JOBE AKELEY

RAE NATALIE PROSSER DE GOODALL

(GERALDINE) JERRIE L. FREDRITZ MOCK

ZOE DELL LANTIS NUTTER

JUDITH A. RESNIK

LAURETTA SCHIMMOLER

Mary Leonore Jobe AKELEY

1878–1966

HARRISON COUNTY

Courtesy of the Connecticut
Women's Hall of Fame

MARY LEONORE JOBE AKELEY, born on a farm in Tappan, Ohio, on January 29, 1878, built an illustrious career as a geographer, mountaineer, photographer, and writer. She graduated from Scio College (later merged into Mount Union College) in 1897, completed two years of graduate study at Bryn Mawr, and earned an M.A. in history and English from Columbia University in 1909. She taught at Temple College (later Temple University) and the Normal College of the City of New York (later Hunter College), where she remained until 1916.

Often described as fiercely independent, Akeley began her career as an explorer in 1909 by joining an exploration party in British Columbia. Her interest in the Canadian Rockies continued, and she made several journeys in subsequent years for botanical research, mountain climbing, and photography. The Canadian government commissioned her to explore and map the headwaters of the Fraser River, and she made two attempts to climb Mt. Sir Alexander, one of the highest then uncharted peaks in the Canadian Rockies. The Canadian government honored these accomplishments by naming another of the highest peaks Jobe. She was also nominated as a fellow of the Royal Geographical Society of London.

In 1924, she married noted explorer Carl Akeley and shifted her own explorational interests to the focus of his work, the continent of Africa. In 1926, she served as field assistant, safari manager, secretary, and photographer on her husband's expedition to what was then the Belgian Congo. Carl Akeley died suddenly of a fever, but Akeley continued the expedition. This journey was the first of many; Akeley went on to lead expeditions of her own, including several in southern Africa. This work in uncharted areas was deemed invaluable; King Albert I of Belgium honored her with the Croix de Chevalier de l'Ordre de la Couronne.

Akeley's interest in outdoor life also took her in another direction. In 1914, she purchased land in Mystic, Connecticut, to establish a camp for girls, which she ran from 1916 until the camp closed in 1930. Through this experience, the daughters of affluent families learned about outdoor living and met famous explorers. After she retired, Akeley built a home in Mystic and lived there until her death on July 19, 1966.

Exploration and Adventure

Rae Natalie Prosser de GOODALL

1935-

MORROW COUNTY

R AE NATALIE PROSSER DE GOODALL was born on April 13, 1935, on a small farm in Lexington, Ohio. She received a B.S. in education, biology, and art (1957) and an M.S. in biology (1959) from Kent State University. After graduation, she accepted a position as a teacher for Mobil Oil and went to Venezuela to begin her career in an oil camp. While traveling through South America, she was inspired by a book about Tierra del Fuego, the archipelago at South America's tip; she sought and received an invitation to visit Estancia Harberton, one of the oldest sheep ranches in this area. At Estancia Harberton, she met the Goodall family, including Thomas, who would become her husband in 1963. She lives there still, an Ohio-born woman who has spent her life as an adventurer facing the challenge of living and working in the southernmost permanently inhabited region of the earth.

After settling at the ranch, Goodall began studying, collecting, and illustrating the native flora of Tierra del Fuego. Her work resulted in a collection of over seven thousand herbarium specimens, seven scientific papers, the illustrations for the book *Flora of Tierra del Fuego,* a volume in the series *Flora Patagónica,* and one-woman shows and illustrations in the Hunt Botanical Library, Pittsburgh, Pennsylvania. In 1976, her interests turned toward stranded dolphins and whales. She began collecting beach-worn dolphin skulls and ultimately became a self-taught expert on southern South American cetaceans. Students from around the world have interned with her. She has worked with the International Whaling Commission; received numerous grants from the National Geographic Society; prepared multiple environmental reports on coastal birds and mammals for oil companies; and continued to publish books and papers.

In 1996, Goodall was named one of fifteen women in the seventy-one-year history of the Society of Woman Geographers to receive its Gold Medal award, the organization's highest honor, and she has also been honored by the Universidad Nacional de la Patagonia (1983) and the government of Tierra del Fuego (1994).

74

OHIO
WOMEN'S
HALL OF
FAME

Profiles of Two Hundred Ohio Women

(Geraldine) Jerrie L. Fredritz MOCK

1925–

LICKING COUNTY

Courtesy of Jerrie Mock

(G)ERALDINE) JERRIE L. FREDRITZ MOCK was born on November 22, 1925, in Newark, Ohio. She attended the Ohio State University, and became known first as "the flying housewife" and later the "flying grandmother," but these epithets do not do justice to this adventurous woman of great achievement in the field of aviation.

In 1964, Mock became the first woman to pilot an aircraft on a solo trip around the world. Twenty-seven years after Amelia Earhart's unsuccessful attempt, Mock accomplished this feat in a ten-year-old, custom-made 1953 Cessna 180 single-engine monoplane, the *Spirit of Columbus*. Mock departed from Columbus on her solo flight on April 17, 1964. Twenty-nine days, eleven hours, and fifty-nine minutes later, she arrived back home after flying 23,103 miles around the world. On May 4, 1964, President Lyndon B. Johnson awarded Mock the Federal Aviation Administration's Exceptional Service Decoration. After the flight, the Cessna Aircraft Corporation of Wichita, Kansas, exchanged Mock's plane for a new one; the company kept the record-making craft in its factory until 1975, when they donated it to the Smithsonian National Air and Space Museum.

Mock's accomplishments did not end there, however. In addition to setting a women's nonstop distance record of over forty-five hundred miles (Honolulu–Columbus) in thirty-one hours, Mock was also the first woman to fly from the United States to Africa via the Azores; across the Pacific in a single-engine plane; across the Pacific from west to east; across both the Atlantic and the Pacific; across the Pacific in both directions; and within Saudi Arabia. In addition, Mock was the producer and coordinator of *Youth Has Its Say,* the first youth talk series on television, which ran for five years. She was a writer and director for the *Opera Preludea* radio series and the author of several magazine articles and her own book *3–8 Charlie*.

Mock was also appointed vice-chairperson of the Women's Advisory Committee on Aviation, and she is the recipient of over a hundred honors, awards, and citations, including the Louis Bleriot Medal, the highest award of the Fédération Aéronautique Internationale to a pilot who overtakes an existing record in a light plane. She was the first woman and the first American to receive the award.

75

Exploration and Adventure

OHIO WOMEN'S HALL OF FAME

Zoe Dell Lantis NUTTER

1915–

GREENE COUNTY

Pursue your goals and dreams. If you are willing to work and keep trying, you will achieve them and might even surpass them.

—Zoe Dell Lantis Nutter

ZOE DELL LANTIS NUTTER, born on June 14, 1915, moved to Xenia, Ohio, in 1965. Throughout her life, she has been a staunch promoter of aviation both across the nation and in the state of Ohio. She was the first woman to serve as president of the National Aviation Hall of Fame and later was the first female chairperson of the board. In addition, Nutter served as co-chairperson for the dedication of the Wright Brothers Room at Wright State University. For more than twenty years, Nutter has given of her time, money, and influence as the moving force behind the success of the hall of fame, all with a generosity of spirit that modestly understates her own role in the field of aviation.

Nutter has logged more than two thousand hours as a commercial multi-instrument pilot and served as an officer in the Civil Air Patrol, for which she flew search and rescue missions. In 1939 and 1940, Nutter was the official hostess of the Golden Gate International Exposition on Treasure Island in San Francisco and was declared the "Most Photographed and Publicized Girl in the World" for 1938–39. In 1958, she was the official representative from the state of California to the Brussels World's Fair; in 1962 she was "Flying Ambassadress" to the Century 21 Exposition at Seattle; and in 1964 she held the same title for the New York World's Fair.

For her pioneering achievements as an aviator and her dedicated community service, Nutter has received many honors and awards, including the Tambourine Award from the Salvation Army of Greater Dayton (1982), the Aviation Trail's Trail Blazer Award (1985), and the Governor's Award for Volunteerism (1992). She was included in *Who's Who in American Women* (1993–94), and in 1999 she was named one of the year's Ten Top Women in the Miami Valley for unique and valuable contributions to her profession and the community.

76

Courtesy of Zoe Dell Lantis Nutter

OHIO
WOMEN'S
HALL OF
FAME

Judith A. RESNIK

1949-1986

SUMMIT COUNTY

Courtesy of the National Aeronautics and Space Administration

Judith A. Resnik was born in Akron, Ohio, on April 5, 1949. She graduated as valedictorian of Firestone High School in 1966, received a B.S. in electrical engineering from Carnegie-Mellon University in 1970 and a Ph.D. in electrical engineering from the University of Maryland in 1977. Her career in science and technology began after college, when she was hired by RCA as a design engineer. Her work in circuit design included the development of custom integrated circuitry for phased-array radar control systems. From 1974 to 1977 she was a biomedical engineer and staff fellow in the Laboratory of Neurophysiology of the National Institutes of Health, where she conducted biological research related to the physiology of visual systems. In 1978, she became a senior systems engineer in product development with Xerox Corporation. Later that year, however, Resnik was selected by NASA to become an astronaut, a member of the most elite team of explorers of the modern era.

Resnik completed NASA training in August 1979. As an astronaut, she worked on several projects in support of space shuttle orbiter development, including software development and training techniques. On August 30, 1984, she flew her first space mission as a mission specialist on the maiden flight of the orbiter *Discovery,* becoming the second American woman in space. Among their tasks, the team successfully removed hazardous ice particles using the remote manipulator system and gained the nickname "Icebusters." She completed 96 orbits of the earth, logging 144 hours and 57 minutes in space before landing at Edwards Air Force Base, California. She was awarded the NASA Space Flight Medal.

On January 28, 1986, Resnik was again mission specialist on her second space voyage. The seven-person crew launched from the Kennedy Space Center aboard the orbiter *Challenger.* The *Challenger* exploded shortly after launch and fell into the sea. All aboard perished. Resnik entered history as a heroine, one of two women space explorers (Christa McAuliffe was the other) who were lost that day in the line of duty.

Exploration and Adventure

OHIO WOMEN'S HALL OF FAME

Lauretta SCHIMMOLER

1900–1981

PUTNAM COUNTY

L̲AURETTA SCHIMMOLER, born in Fort Jennings, Ohio, on September 17, 1900, graduated with honors from Bliss Business College in Columbus. After graduation, Schimmoler took a job as an assistant to the court stenographer of Crawford County and studied law with Judge William J. Schwenck. Schimmoler decided not to pursue a career in law and instead became secretary to the Bucyrus Hatchery and ultimately the owner of her own poultry business. A turning point for Schimmoler, however, came in 1919, when she saw an altitude test flight in Dayton.

On August 10, 1929, Schimmoler received a student pilot's license and enrolled in flight school in Sycamore, Ohio, where she was hired by the owner to be his advertising manager. An astute business woman, Schimmoler convinced the owner to move his airport to Bucyrus, where in 1929 she became the first woman to establish and manage an airport. On September 8, 1930, she received her pilot's license and became one of only a few women pilots in Ohio and the nation. In 1932, the Bucyrus Municipal Airport was named the best small airport in the state of Ohio. In that same year, in recognition of her achievements in aviation, Schimmoler was inducted into the Ninety-Nines, the national organization of licensed women pilots, where she remained an active leader alongside other pioneering pilots such as Amelia Earhart.

Schimmoler's dream, however, was to start an organization of flight-ready nurses who could be flown quickly into areas of need. To accomplish this goal with little support, she took jobs in California with the U.S. Air Mail, Lockheed Aircraft, and the U.S. Weather Bureau in order to learn more about flying. In 1936, she and ten nurses established the Aerial Nurse Corps of America. This organization lasted for only fifteen years, but it provided a model for what became the U.S. Air Force Flight Nurse Corps and a nucleus of experienced women who went on to serve in air evacuation squadrons.

78

In 1942, Columbia Studios made a movie based on Schimmoler's life, *Parachute Nurse*. Starting as a technical director for the film, Schimmoler ended up playing the central role. In 1966, Schimmoler was honored by the Air Force for her pioneering contributions with the gold wings of the flight nurse.

Profiles of Two Hundred Ohio Women

HEALTH CARE

THE WOMEN HONORED IN THIS SECTION FOR THEIR work as doctors, nurses, administrators, medical researchers, and health care activists have been steadfast in ministering to health needs, whether for a local community, the state of Ohio, the nation, or the world. They have taken on the critical responsibilities of noticing and inquiring into medical needs, healing and keeping us well, and helping us to feel strong and more confident about our abilities to live healthy lives, even when we face physical challenges. These women have been and are angels of mercy, but they have also been leaders and innovators of the vital developments and practices by which our bodies have greatly benefited.

MILDRED MASON BAYER

ELIZABETH BLACKWELL

DOROTHY ALICE CORNELIUS

ANTOINETTE PARISI EATON

MARILYN HUGHES GASTON

MARY IGNATIA GAVIN, C.S.A.

BERNADINE HEALY

REBECCA D. JACKSON

BEATRICE LAMPKIN

HATTIE LENA GADD LARLHAM

NANCY LINENKUGEL, O.S.G.

IRENE DUHART LONG

JACQUELYN J. MAYER (TOWNSEND)

MARTHA J. PITUCH

EMMA ANN REYNOLDS

BARBARA ROSS-LEE

ELLA NORA PHILLIPS MYERS STEWART

LILLIAN D. WALD

FARAH MOAVANZADEH WALTERS

FAYE WATTLETON

Mildred Mason BAYER

1908–1990

WOOD COUNTY

MILDRED MASON BAYER, born in 1908 in Weston, Ohio, graduated from the St. Vincent Hospital School of Nursing in Toledo, Ohio. As the wife of a prominent physician, she could have lived a life of leisure without paying much attention at all to those in need. Bayer chose differently, dedicating her talents and resources to filling the critical health needs of others.

In 1960, Bayer played a significant role in the founding of two medical clinics in Lucas County for migrant workers. In 1967, she helped organize Mobile Meals of Toledo and served as its first volunteer coordinator. She also initiated the Friendly Visiting Program of the Toledo Education Association for the Aged and Chronically Ill in northwestern Ohio. In addition, she was instrumental in the passage of state legislation requiring nursing home operators to be licensed.

After the death of her husband in 1968, Bayer began a sixteen-month mission to Nigeria on behalf of St. Vincent Hospital's Grey Nuns in order to establish portable health clinics. The mission operated a ninety-bed hospital in the small village of Kabba, the only medical facility within twenty-eight hundred miles. Bayer adapted the portable system of Toledo's Mobile Meals to deliver health services and education, setting up two health care teams to treat people wherever they might be—in makeshift shelters, under a nearby shade tree, or even along the side of the road. Ultimately, Bayer returned six more times to oversee operations and to set up twenty-one more clinics.

Back in Toledo in 1984, Bayer founded Health Clinics International (HCI) to provide medical help and shelter for the homeless. A medical clinic staffed by volunteer doctors and nurses and a temporary shelter were started in St. Paul's Community Center. Later the clinic was expanded to include dental services. In 1985, the clinic had outgrown its space and moved into new quarters at 1604 Monroe Street with the help of Dr. Bob Maley.

In 1969, Bayer received the Outstanding Service Award from the Toledo Educational Association for the Aged and Chronically Ill and the Stella Maris Award from Mary Manse College. HCI was renamed the Mildred Bayer Health Clinic for the Homeless.

81

Health Care

Elizabeth BLACKWELL

1821–1910

HAMILTON COUNTY

Eᴌɪᴢᴀʙᴇᴛʜ Bʟᴀᴄᴋᴡᴇʟʟ, born in Counterslip Bristol, England, on February 3, 1821, immigrated to the United States at the age of eleven, settling ultimately with her family in Cincinnati, Ohio, in 1838. Her father died shortly after the move, and Blackwell helped support the family by teaching, but she was determined to become a physician. Blackwell applied without success to nearly thirty medical schools. In 1847, however, she was admitted to Geneva Medical College in New York, where she graduated in 1849 as the first woman to receive a degree from a medical college. Subsequently, she obtained further training at St. Bartholomew's Hospital in London and at La Maternité in Paris, where she contracted ophthalmia which resulted in blindness in one eye and prevented her from becoming a surgeon. In 1851, Blackwell returned to the United States and settled in New York City.

The gender biases prevalent during this era severely hampered Blackwell's ability to practice her profession. Finding no place in hospitals open to her and no one willing to rent her office space, she began giving lectures in her home on good hygiene for women, later published as *The Laws of Life: With Special Reference to the Physical Education of Girls* (1852). Slowly building a clientele, Blackwell opened a small dispensary to care for poor women. Three years later she was joined by her sister Emily, who had also become a physician, and others to form an all-female staff. By 1857, the dispensary had become a hospital, the New York Infirmary for Women and Children, that still exists today as the New York University Downtown Hospital.

82

Blackwell's dedication resulted in other distinctive achievements as well. During the Civil War, her advocacy with others for strict health measures in the army camps resulted in the establishment of the United States Sanitary Commission, the forerunner of the American Red Cross. In 1868, she opened the Women's Medical College of the New York Infirmary. Returning to England in 1869, she founded the National Health Society to promote hygiene and support other women doctors.

Blackwell retired in 1876, spending the remainder of her life writing books that advocated for social and moral reform. She died in Hastings, England, on May 31, 1910. The Elizabeth Blackwell Center at Riverside Hospital in Columbus was named for her.

OHIO
WOMEN'S
HALL OF
FAME

Profiles of Two Hundred Ohio Women

Dorothy Alice CORNELIUS

1918–1992

FRANKLIN COUNTY

Courtesy of the Mid-Ohio District Nurses Association

DOROTHY ALICE CORNELIUS was born on March 9, 1918, in Johnstown, Pennsylvania. In 1939, she received a degree in nursing from Conemaugh Valley Memorial Hospital, and in 1942, she graduated from the University of Pittsburgh School of Nursing. After graduation, she became director of nursing for the Tuberculosis Hospital in Pittsburgh, where she worked for the American Red Cross. She also served as chief nurse of the American Red Cross blood program in her hometown and in Cleveland. While in Cleveland, Cornelius was recruited to become executive director of the Ohio Nurses Association (ONA), headquartered in Columbus, where she served from 1957 to 1983.

With the Ohio Nurses Association, Cornelius provided stellar leadership and service to Ohio and the nation. She chaired the committee on the Ohio Girls' Industrial School and the Ohio Women's Civil Defense Council. She was secretary of the Ohio Cancer Coordinating Committee and a member of the Ohio Citizens' Council on Health and Welfare, and the Regional Advisory Committee of the Ohio State Regional Medical Program. At the national level, during World War II, Cornelius served in the U.S. Navy Nurse Corps; she served on numerous committees and commissions, receiving commendations from Presidents Eisenhower, Johnson, and Nixon; and she was elected in 1968 as president of the American Nurses Association (ANA).

In the community of Reynoldsburg where she lived, Cornelius served in a different way. In 1963, she was the first woman to run for the city council. In 1965, she was elected ward committeewoman and she chaired the Reynoldsburg Civil Service Commission. In 1973, she was a member of the Reynoldsburg Planning and Zoning Commission and after retiring from the ONA in 1983, she became president of her neighborhood civic association.

Cornelius received many honors and awards in recognition of her service, including the ONA Honorary Recognition Award (1969), American Red Cross National Award for outstanding service (1979); she was named a fellow in the American Academy of Nursing (1977); and the ONA headquarters building was named in her honor in 1977.

83

Health Care

Antoinette Parisi EATON

1931–

Antoinette Parisi Eaton, born on January 11, 1931, in Youngstown, Ohio, received a medical degree in 1956 from the Woman's Medical College of Pennsylvania and pediatric training at the Ohio State University and Children's Hospital in Columbus. Throughout her career, Eaton has been a leader in clinical practice, in public health administration, and in academic roles; she has demonstrated a lifelong commitment to the welfare of children and their families. She has testified before Congress on several occasions, and she is widely recognized for implementing innovative programs to address the complex needs of the community, as demonstrated by her work with Sudden Infant Death Syndrome, "drive-through" deliveries, and children with special needs.

Eaton has held many prestigious positions. At Children's Hospital in Columbus, she has served as assistant medical director (1962–66); chief of the Handicapped Children's Section and director of the Birth Defects Center (1967–74); associate medical director, Ambulatory Services (1980–89); and interim medical director (1994–95). She has also served as chief of the Division of Maternal and Child Health of the Ohio Department of Health (1974–80), now the Division of Family and Community Health Services. In addition, Eaton has been associated with the Ohio State University over the course of her career. She has served as assistant to the dean for public health and is currently professor emerita of pediatrics and preventive medicine.

Eaton was the first woman president of the American Academy of Pediatrics (1990), where she concentrated on the problem of children without health insurance. She has served in many other roles as well, including chairperson of the Department of Health and Human Services Advisory Committee on Infant Mortality and chairperson of the governor's Task Force on Adolescent Sexuality and Pregnancy.

Eaton is the recipient of many awards, including the Job Lewis Smith Award (1995) by the American Academy of Pediatrics; the 1997 Champion of Children by Columbus leaders; and the Martha May Eliot Award (2002) from the American Public Health Association for exceptional achievement in the field of maternal and child health.

84

Marilyn Hughes GASTON

1939–

HAMILTON COUNTY

MARILYN HUGHES GASTON, born on January 31, 1939, in Cincinnati, Ohio, graduated from Miami University of Ohio in 1960 with a degree in zoology and received a medical degree from the College of Medicine at the University of Cincinnati in 1964. Gaston's career has been dedicated to improving the health of children and their families, especially underprivileged and minority families. Her contributions have included clinical research, medical education, and health administration. She is nationally and internationally recognized for her leadership in combating sickle cell anemia, improving health care access, eliminating health disparities for vulnerable people; for her advocacy of African American women's health issues and the needs of the young; and as a former assistant surgeon general of the United States.

Early in her career, Gaston established the Comprehensive Sickle Cell Center at the University of Cincinnati Children's Hospital Medical Center, designed as a community health center serving a large African American, low-income population. She also served as its first director. From 1976 to 1989, she held various posts at the National Institutes of Health (NIH), including being appointed in 1988 acting chief of NIH's Sickle Cell Disease Branch of the National Heart, Lung, and Blood Institute, and acting national coordinator of the National Sickle Cell Program. In 1989, she joined the Health Resources and Services Administration (HRSA) as director of the Division of Medicine in the Bureau of Health Professions. In 1990, she was appointed director of the Bureau of Primary Health Care in HRSA, the first African American woman to be appointed. In addition, Gaston is a much sought after public speaker on health issues, and she has coauthored a book entitled *Prime Time: The African American Woman's Complete Guide to Midlife Health and Wellness* (2001) which helps African American women to address disparities in health care resources and opportunities.

Gaston's list of honors and awards includes several honorary degrees and awards, among them the Living Legend Award and the Scroll of Merit from the National Medical Association. The University of Cincinnati has established a four-year, full-tuition scholarship in her name, which is given annually to two students chosen from underprivileged and minority applicants. The first Gaston Scholars entered the College of Medicine in 1999.

85

Health Care

OHIO
WOMEN'S
HALL OF
FAME

Mary Ignatia GAVIN, C.S.A.

1889–1966

SUMMIT COUNTY

Mary Ignatia Gavin (Bridget Della Mary Gavin) was born on January 2, 1889, in Cleveland, Ohio. Before entering the convent of the Sisters of Charity of Saint Augustine at age twenty-five, she supported her parents by teaching piano, organ, voice, and violin. At the convent, she was the only musician in a community of women who were teachers and nurses. She pioneered a music school for children at Parmadale Orphanage in 1925. By 1927, she was overcome by exhaustion and personal problems and experienced a mental breakdown. Her recovery was long, and her solution was to leave behind her career in music. In 1928, she accepted a position as an admitting clerk in the Sisters' new St. Thomas Hospital in Akron and succeeded in changing the world.

Gavin was the first person to recognize and dignify the disease of addiction by admitting, without permission and at great personal risk, alcoholics and drug addicts to St. Thomas for medical care. She became a spiritual advisor to Dr. Bob Smith, a physician trying to reestablish his reputation after a long history of drinking, and to Bill Wilson, a recovering alcoholic from New York. In 1939, they published *Alcoholics Anonymous,* outlining their philosophy of recovery and their twelve-step program, and they set up the first alcoholic treatment center in the world with Gavin managing the hospital care. Her pioneering work became a model for all chemical dependency treatment, and she became known as the "angel of Alcoholics Anonymous."

Gavin salvaged more than five thousand alcoholics in Akron before transferring to Cleveland's St. Vincent Charity Hospital in 1952, where she saved another ten thousand lives before her own death in 1966. She was also the first to set up a family treatment program, to establish a women's ward, to treat alcoholic nuns and priests, to provide employee assistance services, and to establish Al-Anon, a support organization for family and friends of alcoholics in Ohio.

Gavin received numerous awards from the U.S. Congress, the Cleveland City Council, President John F. Kennedy, labor unions, colleges and universities, church organizations, and Alcoholics Anonymous, among them the 1954 Catherine of Sienna Award by the Theta Pi Alpha Sorority of National Catholic Women's Colleges given to Catholic women who most exemplify the qualities of the fourteenth-century reformer and saint.

86

Bernadine HEALY

1944−

CUYAHOGA COUNTY

B ERNADINE HEALY, born on August 2, 1944, in New York City, graduated summa cum laude from Vassar College in 1965 with a major in chemistry. She received an M.D., cum laude, in 1970 from Harvard University and underwent postgraduate training in internal medicine and cardiology at Johns Hopkins School of Medicine, where she later served as professor of medicine and cardiology, director of the coronary care unit, and assistant dean for postdoctoral programs and faculty development (1976–84). Healy has become a nationally recognized leader in medical education, biomedical research, and university and public administration.

In 1984, Healy was appointed by President Ronald Reagan as deputy director of the Office of Science and Technology Policy at the White House. In 1985, she was appointed chairperson of the Lerner Research Institute of the Cleveland Clinic Foundation, where she directed research programs of nine departments. In 1991 she was appointed director of the National Institutes of Health (NIH), where she established grants to foster creative and innovative approaches in biomedical research, created a major intramural laboratory for human genetics, and launched the NIH Women's Health Initiative, a $625 million effort to study the causes, prevention, and cures of diseases that affect women. In 1995, Healy was appointed dean of the College of Medicine and Public Health and professor of medicine at the Ohio State University, and in 1999 she became the president and chief executive officer of the American Red Cross.

Healy has also served as president of the American Heart Association, where she initiated a Women and Minorities Leadership Task Force and a Women and Heart Disease Program; served on numerous boards (for example, the American Board of Internal Medicine, the American Heart Association, and the Ohio Council on Research and Economic Development); and authored or coauthored more than two hundred manuscripts in cardiovascular research. These accomplishments have yielded numerous prestigious awards, among them the Charles A. Dana Foundation Distinguished Achievement Award (1992) for her exceptional leadership of NIH; Humanitarian of the Year (jointly with her husband, cardiologist Floyd D. Loop) by the American Red Cross (1997); the Democracy in Action Award from the League of Women Voters (1998); and the Women Making History Award from the National Women's History Museum (1998).

87

Health Care

OHIO
WOMEN'S
HALL OF
FAME

Rebecca D. JACKSON

1955–

FRANKLIN COUNTY

Courtesy of Rebecca D. Jackson

REBECCA D. JACKSON, born on August 18, 1955, in Columbus, Ohio, graduated from the Ohio State University (OSU) in 1975 with a degree in microbiology. Three years later, at the age of twenty-three, she earned an M.D. After graduation from OSU, she completed an internship and residency program at Johns Hopkins Hospital in Baltimore, Maryland. In 1981, she returned to OSU as a clinical instructor with a Kellogg National Fellowship (1982–85). In 1983, she became an assistant professor in the division of endocrinology in the department of medicine, where she has received the Clinical Associate Physician Award and the Physician Scientist Training Award, both from the National Institutes of Health (NIH).

Currently associate professor of internal medicine in the division of endocrinology, diabetes, and metabolism at OSU, Jackson has focused her career on clinical and translational research in the area of metabolic bone diseases and women's health. She was instrumental in developing the clinical trials office for the Comprehensive Cancer Center and served as its first director. She became the director of the endocrinology fellowship, a position that she still holds. She is principal investigator of the Columbus Clinical Center of the Women's Health Initiative (WHI) and serves as vice-chairperson of the WHI Steering Committee.

Jackson was one of the authors of the landmark study on the overall balance of risks and benefits of estrogen plus progestin therapy for postmenopausal women. She has received numerous grants, published more than sixty chapters and articles in prestigious publications, and made numerous presentations to scientific bodies and to the general public on osteoporosis and other women's health issues. Most recently, Jackson was awarded a new multimillion dollar, multiyear grant from NIH to determine the factors that contribute to the development and progression of knee osteoarthritis.

In addition to the awards cited above, Jackson has been named the Disabled Professional Woman of the Year by the Zonta Foundation, and she has also received a Simpson Research Award from the Ohio State University College of Medicine and Public Health and a YWCA Woman of Achievement Award.

88

Beatrice LAMPKIN

1934–

HAMILTON COUNTY

BEATRICE LAMPKIN was born on January 16, 1934, in Tuscaloosa, Alabama. She graduated from the Medical College of Alabama in 1960 and since that time has devoted her life to medical research with special attention to the diagnosis and treatment of children. In 1965, she joined the division of hematology/oncology at Children's Hospital Medical Center in Cincinnati as the only pediatric hematologist in the city. From this beginning, she built up the division and became its director in 1973, ultimately supervising more than eighty people and directing one of the best hematology/oncology divisions for children in the United States.

Lampkin's accomplishments during these years alone establish her as a pioneering leader. She has an excellent record of research related to leukemia in children—having published, for example, more than 125 articles—and an equally impressive record of health administration and educational services especially with regard to the numbers of people who trained under her leadership. Lampkin retired in 1991, but the end of one career was just the beginning of another. At age sixty-two, she became the volunteer president and founding member of GLAD (Giving Life a Dream) House, a substance abuse prevention and intervention program for children ages six to twelve whose mothers are undergoing treatment for drug and alcohol addiction. For this work and for her efforts with the recovery community, Lampkin was awarded the Kindred Spirit Award from the Center for Chemical Addiction Treatment in Cincinnati and the Weir Goodman Award from the Alcoholism Council of the Cincinnati Area in 1998.

Lampkin has received many other awards during her distinguished career, among them Outstanding Woman of the Year in Medicine from the Medical College of Pennsylvania in 1976; the Distinguished Career Award from the American Society of Pediatric Hematology/Oncology; the Daniel Drake Medal from the University of Cincinnati College of Medicine, the highest honor given by that college; the Founders Award from the Cincinnati Pediatric Society in 1991; and the Oscar Schmidt Public Service Award from the University of Cincinnati.

Currently, Lampkin remains president of the board of GLAD House and teaches in the division of pediatric hematology/oncology.

89

Health Care

OHIO
WOMEN'S
HALL OF
FAME

Hattie Lena Gadd
LARLHAM

1914-1996

PORTAGE COUNTY

Courtesy of Hattie Larlham

HATTIE LENA GADD LARLHAM was born in 1914 in Reader, West Virginia. After graduating as valedictorian of her high school class, Larlham moved to Ohio where she graduated from the Youngstown Hospital Association School of Nursing. Larlham began her work in a small county hospital in Ravenna, Ohio, where she met Richard R. Larlham. A year later, they were married.

During the next twenty-five years as a registered nurse, Larlham recognized the need for early intervention in the care of children with profound mental retardation or developmental disabilities. At that time, Ohio did not provide care for individuals with disabilities under the age of six. In 1961, after lengthy legislative petitioning, the state granted Larlham a license and the funding to open her home to children and infants who required constant medical attention. The Larlham household soon became a haven for the families of children with disabilities.

In 1964, with their home filled to capacity and over a hundred names on a waiting list, the Hattie Larlham Foundation (now Hattie Larlham) was formally established. In 1972, the organization secured funding for and built the 126-bed facility that would become the Hattie Larlham Center for Children with Disabilities on twenty-seven acres of family land in Mantua, Ohio.

Larlham acted as the organization's administrator until 1977. She also served as an advisor on mental retardation to the Carter, Reagan, and Bush administrations. She founded the Ohio Private Residential Association, and she served as a member of the American Nurses Association.

In recognition of her efforts, Larlham was inducted into the Ohio Women's Hall of Fame in 1980 and was awarded the Ohio Private Residential Association's Lifetime Achievement Award in 1994.

Larlham passed away on February 28, 1996, and is buried, according to her wishes, at the Hattie Larlham Center for Children with Disabilities. Today, the legacy of care that she began over forty years ago continues. Hattie Larlham (the foundation) has expanded to include six agencies, each dedicated to providing quality care through family care management, community homes, home and foster care services, and integrated day care services.

OHIO
WOMEN'S
HALL OF
FAME

Profiles of Two Hundred Ohio Women

Nancy LINENKUGEL, O.S.G.

ERIE COUNTY

Sister Nancy Linenkugel, born in Toledo, Ohio, on April 19, 1950, joined the Sisters of St. Francis of Sylvania in 1968. She received an A.A. from Lourdes Junior College in 1971; a B.A. in education from Mary Manse College in 1974; an M.A. in hospital and health administration from Xavier University of Ohio in 1980; and a doctorate in management from Case Western Reserve University in 1999. She began her career as a junior high school teacher at Catholic schools in Cincinnati and Rossford, Ohio. In 1980, however, she accepted a position as vice-president of support services at St. John Medical Center in Steubenville. This job change marked the beginning of an illustrious career in health care administration.

In 1986, Sister Nancy was appointed president and chief executive officer of Providence Hospital in Sandusky, where her accomplishments in meeting the health care needs of her community were manifold. She served as president of the Providence Properties; board chairperson of the Providence Fund, Providence Enterprises, and the Providence Professional Corporation; and board secretary of Providence Care Center. Through these organizational entities, Sister Nancy shepherded various health and educational services: the Jacquelyn Mayer Rehab and Nursing Facility (now the Firelands Therapy Program); Kiddie Korral Day Care Center; the area's only dedicated women's center for mammography and women's health services; and the Providence BirthPlace; the Providence Healthline, a telephone health information and referral service; the *Ask the Doctor* weekly radio program; and community outreach programs that connect health care to the community at local business sites. In addition,

Sister Nancy was also the first woman member of the Sandusky Rotary Club and its first woman president, and she served on many advisory boards. In 1992, she was named Businesswoman of the Year/Athena Award by the Erie County Chamber of Commerce.

Sister Nancy provided leadership for the Providence Health System for fifteen years before assuming the presidency in 2002 of Chatfield College, a private two-year college in St. Martin and Cincinnati, Ohio.

Health Care

OHIO
WOMEN'S
HALL OF
FAME

Irene Duhart LONG

1950–

CUYAHOGA COUNTY

IRENE DUHART LONG was born on November 16, 1950, in Cleveland, Ohio. She received a B.A. in pre-medicine and biology from Northwestern University in 1973 and an M.D. from the St. Louis University School of Medicine in 1977. She spent two years residency in general surgery at the Cleveland Clinic and the Mount Sinai Hospital of Cleveland, and she completed a three-year residency in aerospace medicine through Wright State University School of Medicine in Dayton, where she also received an M.S. in that discipline. Long's residency in aerospace medicine included rotations at the Ames Research Center (1981) and the Kennedy Space Center (1982). In 1982, Long was appointed to the Kennedy Space Center staff. Her contributions over two decades to the National Aeronautics and Space Administration (NASA) have been widely acknowledged, as she has provided specialized medical support in the space program.

Long is the first female to be named the Kennedy Space Center chief medical officer and the associate director of spaceport services. In this position, she is responsible for coordinating services related to occupational health, institutional safety, and environmental functions. She has been instrumental in NASA's employee development, educational outreach, and community service activities. She designed the Space Life Sciences Training Program, for example, to increase the number of women and minorities in science and related fields. Long coordinates medical support activities for space shuttle launch and landing; this includes services to astronauts, families, senior management, and the general public. In fact, she and her team have been personally involved with the launch and recovery of every space shuttle orbiter mission.

Long is also involved in community outreach activities, including the United Way, the Crosswinds Youth Shelter, two successful Kennedy Space Center bone marrow donor registration drives, and work with local teachers and students in the schools. Long has received the Kennedy Space Center Federal Woman of the Year Award (1986), the President's Special Award from the Society of NASA Flight Surgeons (1995), and the Women in Aerospace Outstanding Achievement Award (1998).

92

Jacquelyn J. MAYER (Townsend)

1942–

ERIE COUNTY

JACQUELYN J. MAYER (TOWNSEND), born in Sandusky, Ohio, on August 20, 1942, might have been best known as the winner of the title of Miss America in 1963. This accomplishment, although significant, pales in the light of the extraordinary impact that Mayer has had as a passionate voice for those who have suffered strokes and other neurological disorders.

In 1963, as a twenty-one-year-old student at Northwestern University, Mayer became Miss America. She fulfilled her duties admirably and anticipated a career as an actress. In 1970, however, at the age of twenty-eight, Mayer suffered a stroke that left her paralyzed and without speech. After seven long years of rehabilitating herself without recourse to organized therapy programs for stroke victims, Mayer courageously took the national stage again as an advocate for rehabilitation programs and stroke prevention and education. More than twenty years later, she has visited thousands of patients at hospitals and rehabilitation centers.

Mayer has served as the lay-spokesperson on stroke rehabilitation and prevention for the American Heart Association. She was a founding board member of the National Stroke Association. She has served on numerous advisory boards, among them the Advisory Council of the National Institute of Neurological Disorders and Stroke. She has appeared on local and national television and radio programs, including *Good Morning America* and *Geraldo*. She has completed four educational video programs on stroke rehabilitation. She authored "Jackie's Corner" from 1997 to 1998 for the National Stroke Association's bimonthly publication, *Be Stroke Smart*. Her story has been told in numerous newspapers and magazines across the nation.

Mayer's awards include the Award of Hope and Courage from the National Stroke Association (1985) and the Meritorious Service Award from the Ohio Hospital Association (2000). Most recently the state of Ohio added to this list by naming a highway in her honor.

93

Martha J. PITUCH

1932–

LUCAS COUNTY

MARTHA J. PITUCH was born on September 7, 1932, in Battle Creek, Michigan. She received a nursing diploma from W. A. Foote Memorial Hospital School of Nursing in Jackson, Michigan, and advanced degrees in nursing from Wayne State University. In 1969, she accepted a position at the University of Michigan as an assistant professor in public health nursing before joining the staff of the Medical College of Ohio (MCO) as an associate professor of nursing in 1977.

Pituch has focused her energies on improving access to health care and raising health standards for the medically underserved. In 1985, she founded a nursing clinic at MCO to provide primary care for homeless persons. She has also pioneered self-care support strategies and counseling services for persons with HIV/AIDS and their caregivers, created a model of self-care for battered women, and developed nationally recognized health and safety education materials for school-age children and a self-care program for children with asthma.

When Pituch established the clinic, MCO's nursing school became the first in the United States to have a primary facility for homeless individuals and to provide nursing students with an opportunity for clinical experience in public health and mental health nursing. Through the clinic, Pituch became an early participant in providing services for persons with HIV/AIDS and their caretakers, and she was a primary investigator for groundbreaking research on health and self-care relating to this devastating disease. Pituch was nominated for the prestigious Public Health Service Award for Nurses who have exhibited courage and compassion for persons with HIV/AIDS.

Pituch also received several other honors and awards, including an Outstanding Service Award from the American Lung Association of Ohio in 1983.

94

Emma Ann REYNOLDS

1862–1917

ROSS COUNTY

Emma Ann Reynolds was born near Frankfort, Kentucky, in 1862. She desired to attend nursing school in Chicago but was refused because of her race. She enrolled in Wilberforce University instead. Upon graduation, she moved to Kansas City, Missouri, where four of her brothers lived, and where she taught in the public schools for seven years. Agitated by the poor health conditions of African Americans during this era, Reynolds convinced one of her brothers, the pastor of an African Methodist Episcopal Church in Chicago, to join her in seeking social reforms to address these pressing needs. Her brother contacted Dr. Daniel Hale Williams, a prominent African American physician and surgeon. In 1890, Williams organized the first interracial hospital, Provident Hospital in Chicago, and opened a school of nursing. Reynolds was one of the first two graduates to complete the eighteen-month nursing program in 1892.

Reynolds went on to further training at the Northwestern University School of Medicine and became the first African American woman to receive an M.D. from that program. For the next seven years, she was a physician in Waco, Texas, and New Orleans, Louisiana, before returning to Ohio in 1902 because of ill health. After her recovery, Reynolds began practicing medicine in Ross County. She provided much-needed services to the rural residents of this area until her death in 1917.

For her achievements, Reynolds was inducted into the Chillicothe-Ross County Women's Hall of Fame in the field of medicine in 1991.

95

Barbara ROSS-LEE

1942–

ATHENS COUNTY

BARBARA ROSS-LEE was born on June 1, 1942, in Detroit, Michigan, the oldest of six children (among them, singer Diana Ross). Although Ross-Lee faced the hardships of poverty, she was determined to excel, graduating from Wayne State University with a degree in biology and chemistry and receiving a D.O. in 1973 from the Michigan State University College of Osteopathic Medicine. That year, she returned to inner-city Detroit and ran a bustling family practice for ten years, working tirelessly to address the health care needs of vulnerable populations, especially women, children, and minorities. At that point, Ross-Lee began pursuing an academic career, accepting a position as chairperson of the department of family medicine and associate dean for health policy at the Michigan State University College of Medicine. During these years, she was the first osteopathic physician to participate in the Robert Wood Johnson Health Policy Fellowships Program, where she served as legislative assistant for health to Senator Bill Bradley. She also served often as an adviser on primary care, medical education, minority health, women's health, and rural health care issues.

In 1993, Ross-Lee accepted a position as dean of the Ohio University College of Osteopathic Medicine and made history as the first African American woman to head a U.S. medical school. In 1997, she was selected by the Pew Charitable Trusts to serve on the national advisory board of its Americans Discuss Social Security program. She was a member of the National Advisory Committee on Rural Health of the U.S. Department of Health and Human Services, the board of governors of the American Association of Colleges of Osteopathic Medicine, the board of directors of the Association of Clinicians for the Underserved, and the Ohio Corporation for Health Information. In 2001, Ross-Lee left Ohio, accepting a position as dean of allied health and life sciences and vice-president for health sciences and medical affairs at the New York Institute of Technology.

Ross-Lee has received numerous honors and awards, including the Magnificent Seven Award from the Business and Professional Women/USA; the Patenge Medal of Public Service from the Michigan State University College of Osteopathic Medicine; and the Women's Health Award from Blackboard African American National Bestsellers.

96

Ella Nora Phillips Myers STEWART

1893–1987

LUCAS COUNTY

ELLA NORA PHILLIPS MYERS STEWART, born on March 6, 1893, in Berryville, Virginia, graduated from Storer College in Virginia, where she met and married Charles Myers, with whom she then moved to Pittsburgh. After the death of their child, she began working as a bookkeeper at a drugstore, where she met a physician who encouraged her to become a pharmacist. Stewart was the first African American woman to attend the pharmacy school at the University of Pittsburgh and upon her graduation in 1916, she became the first practicing African American woman pharmacist in the United States. From 1916 to 1919, she managed a drugstore in Bradford, Pennsylvania, and worked also at the Braddock General Hospital, an opportunity made possible by the labor shortage caused by World War I. The strain of two jobs was too much for her health and her marriage. After a divorce, in 1919 she moved back to Pittsburgh and purchased her own drugstore. She became ill, however, and went home to Virginia, leaving her store in the hands of William Stewart, a fellow graduate of the school of pharmacy. In 1920, she and Stewart married and moved to Youngstown, Ohio, where she became the first African American pharmacist—and the first African American employee—at Youngstown City Hospital. In 1922, the Stewarts moved to Toledo and opened the first African American–owned-and-operated drugstore there, serving a community of both African American and white families and becoming active leaders in the Toledo community.

Stewart was also active in the black clubwomen's movement. In 1944, she was president of the Ohio Association of Colored Women. From 1948 to 1952, she was president of the National Association of Colored Women and authorized the writing of the association's history, *Lifting as We Climb*. Stewart also served in many other roles, including as a member of the Women's Advisory Committee of the United States Department of Labor, as a delegate to the International Conference of Women of the World held in Athens, Greece, as vice-president and international vice-president-at-large of the Pan-Pacific and Southeast Asia Women's Association, and on the executive board of the U.S. commission of the United Nations Educational, Social, and Cultural Organization (UNESCO).

After a life of leadership and service, Stewart died on November 27, 1987.

Health Care

Lillian D. WALD

1867–1940

HAMILTON COUNTY

L ILLIAN D. WALD was born on March 10, 1867, in Cincinnati, Ohio. After moving several times with her family, she left Ohio in 1889 to attend the New York Hospital Training School for Nurses, from which she graduated in 1891. In 1893, Wald founded both the Visiting Nurse Service of New York and the Henry Street Settlement in New York City, the first public health nursing agency. In fact, she coined the term "public health nursing."

Wald was instrumental in establishing the United States Children's Bureau to promote the health and welfare of women and children in the United States. She worked with the American Red Cross to establish the first rural nursing services, and with the Metropolitan Life Insurance Company to secure the first third-party payment system for nursing services in the United States. She was also the originator and first president of the National Organization for Public Health Nursing (which later became the National League for Nursing), the first agency responsible for establishing standards for nursing education in the United States. In addition, Wald authored two books, *The House on Henry Street* (1915) and *Windows on Henry Street* (1934; reprinted 1984).

Wald was active in the women's rights movement, devoting four decades to securing the vote and equal rights for women. She has been the subject of several biographies and the recipient of many national and international honors and awards, including being inducted into the American Nurses Association Hall of Fame (1976).

Farah Moavenzadeh WALTERS

1945–

CUYAHOGA COUNTY

ARAH MOAVENZADEH WALTERS was born in 1945 in Teheran, Iran, and in 1964 immigrated to the United States (as did her sister Farah Majidzadeh who also appears in this volume). Walters received a B.S. from the Ohio State University and an M.S. in nutrition from Case Western Reserve University; she also completed the executive MBA program at Case Western. In 1992, Walters was appointed president and chief executive officer of University Hospitals Health System and University Hospitals of Cleveland. She was the first female executive in the United States to head an independent academic medical center. She recognized that the future of health care lay in the development of broad-based networks that would include primary care services, ambulatory centers, community hospitals, home care, and ancillary services. During her tenure with these two organizations, she orchestrated their growth into a regional integrated health care delivery system that offers a full range of health care services with numerous hospital partners, its own health insurance company, and medical services in both centrally located and satellite operations. In June 2002, after ten years of excellence in hospital management and leadership, Walters retired.

Walters's accomplishments in local and national leadership are equally outstanding. She was one of only a handful of hospital CEOs in the United States appointed to serve on Hillary Rodham Clinton's National Health Care Reform Task Force (1993). She has served on numerous local and national boards of corporations, government groups, community organizations, and professional organizations, including the Kerr-McGee Corporation, the Commission to Study the Ohio Economy and Tax Structure, the United Way, Cleveland Tomorrow, the Greater Cleveland Roundtable, the Ohio Business Roundtable, and the Association of American Medical Colleges.

Walters has received numerous awards and honors, among them the Cleveland YWCA Woman of Achievement Award (1988), Distinguished Alumnus of the Year Award from Case Western Reserve University (1993), and the Women Mean Business Award from the Ohio Federation of Business and Professional Women's Clubs (1996). In 2000, she was inducted into the Business Hall of Fame by *Inside Business* magazine, and in 2001 she was a recipient of the Ellis Island Medal of Honor.

99

Health Care

OHIO
WOMEN'S
HALL OF
FAME

Faye WATTLETON

1943–

MONTGOMERY COUNTY

FAYE WATTLETON was born on July 8, 1943, in St. Louis, Missouri. She graduated in 1964 from the Ohio State University with a degree in nursing and in 1967 from Columbia University with an M.A. in maternal and infant care. While interning at a hospital in New York, Wattleton saw the need for birth control and life-saving abortions. She volunteered at Planned Parenthood, and in 1971 became the executive director of the chapter in Dayton, Ohio. In 1977, she became the first woman, the first African American, and the youngest president of the Planned Parenthood Federation of America.

Wattleton has built a distinguished career as an educator, administrator, and leader in the field of women's reproductive rights. During her tenure at Planned Parenthood, she led the nation's oldest voluntary reproductive rights organization through a period of growth and success. She spearheaded innovative initiatives to provide medical and educational services, and she emerged as a powerful voice as a health advocate. Wattleton remained with Planned Parenthood until 1992, playing a major role in national debates and in shaping public policies and programs around the world. In 1995, Wattleton accepted a position as president of the Center for Gender Equality, a not-for-profit research and policy development institute created to advance women's equality and full participation in society. She is continuing to provide insightful leadership and dedication to issues of social reform.

Wattleton's list of honors and awards is long. Among them are the National Mother's Day Committee Outstanding Mother, the Jefferson Award for the Greatest Public Service performed by a Private Citizen, the American Public Health Independent Sector's John Gardner Award, the Women's Honors in Public Service from the American Nurses Association, and the American Humanist Award. In addition, Wattleton has received twelve honorary degrees, and in 1993 she was inducted into the National Women's Hall of Fame.

OHIO
WOMEN'S
HALL OF
FAME

Profiles of Two Hundred Ohio Women

LAW AND

GOVERNMENT

BECAUSE OF THE INTERRELATEDNESS OF LAW AND government, this section treats these two areas as dynamic parts of a whole. The women showcased here have taken on one or both of these centrally important responsibilities in the making, shaping, and maintaining of the legal and political systems at local, state, and national levels. Some have served admirably in government management and administration. Others have served as defenders of justice, making sure that the laws are applied equitably and fairly. Still others have served as judges responsible for interpreting laws through the court system and for monitoring the extent to which we live up to the bedrock principles of truth, justice, equality, and the pursuit of happiness. All of these women have fashioned careers that illustrate invaluable contributions in this male-dominated arena and that help us to document the vital and long-lasting effects of their efforts in the state and in the nation.

FLORENCE ELLINWOOD ALLEN

SANDRA SHANK BECKWITH

PATRICIA ANN BLACKMON

PATRICIA M. BYRNE

JEAN MURRELL CAPERS

MAUDE CHARLES COLLINS

EVA MAE (PARKER) CROSBY

SARA J. HARPER

DOROTHY O. JACKSON

STEPHANIE TUBBS JONES

BLANCHE E. KRUPANSKY

MARGARET DIANE QUINN

ALICE ROBIE RESNICK

MARJORIE M. WHITEMAN

MARY ELLEN WITHROW

MARGARET W. WONG

Florence Ellinwood ALLEN

1884–1966

CUYAHOGA COUNTY

FLORENCE ELLINWOOD ALLEN was the first woman to be elected a judge in the United States. She ran for the judgeship of the Common Pleas Court in Cuyahoga County in 1920 immediately after the ratification of the Nineteenth Amendment to the Constitution, which granted women universal suffrage and set in motion an era of new possibilities for women in law, government, and political leadership. Born on March 23, 1884, in Salt Lake City, Utah, Allen entered the College for Women at Western Reserve University in Cleveland. She was elected to Phi Beta Kappa in her junior year, graduated with honors in music in 1904, and spent two years studying music in Berlin. After an injury prevented a performance career, Allen became a music critic for the *Cleveland Plain Dealer* from 1906 to 1909. In 1908 she received an M.A. in political science from Western Reserve University and after studying law at the University of Chicago, she received a degree in 1913 from New York University School of Law.

In 1914 she was admitted to the Ohio bar, placing her in the small group of women entering the legal profession in the first decades of the twentieth century. After establishing her own law practice, she was appointed assistant prosecutor for Cuyahoga County and elected judge of the Court of Common Pleas in 1920. In 1922, as an independent, she ran for and won a seat on the Supreme Court of Ohio, the first woman to sit on a court of last resort. She was re-elected in 1928 and continued in this position until 1934, when President Franklin D. Roosevelt nominated her to the U.S. Sixth Circuit Court of Appeals. She became the first woman in the United States to sit on the bench of a federal court of general jurisdiction. In 1958 she became the first woman to serve as chief judge of a Circuit Court of Appeals.

Judge Allen also authored five books that speak to the range of her interests and work, including her autobiography, *To Do Justly* (1965). She retired from the Court of Appeals in 1959 and died at home in Waite Hill, Ohio, on September 12, 1966, at the age of 82.

Courtesy of the Ohio Historical Society

Law and Government

Sandra Shank BECKWITH

1943⁻

FRANKLIN COUNTY

SANDRA SHANK BECKWITH was born in Norfolk, Virginia, on December 4, 1943, and moved with her family to Columbus, Ohio, in 1947. She graduated from the University of Cincinnati (1965) and the University of Cincinnati College of Law (1968), where she received the Betty Kuhn Memorial Prize as the top woman graduate. In 1967, Beckwith began her career in private practice with her father, Charles L. Shank, in Harrison, Ohio. From 1977 to 1979, she was judge of the Hamilton County Municipal Court, the first woman and the second-youngest person ever appointed to that court. Thereafter, she was elected to the court (1981), becoming the first woman to be elected.

In 1987, Beckwith became the first woman to be elected to the Court of Common Pleas, Division of Domestic Relations. In 1989, she was the first woman appointed as a member of the Board of County Commissioners of Hamilton County by Governor James A. Rhodes. In 1990, she ran for election to this board and became the first woman to be elected. Subsequently she was elected president by her fellow commissioners, becoming the first woman to hold this office. While serving as county commissioner, Beckwith also practiced law with the firm of Graydon Head & Ritchey, LLP from 1989 to 1992.

In addition, Beckwith has been a member of several professional organizations

104

in her field, and she has served on the boards of numerous organizations, including the United Way of Cincinnati, Great Rivers Girl Scout Council, the National Association of Women Judges, Friends of Women's Studies, and the College of Law Alumni Association at the University of Cincinnati. She has also received several awards and has been recognized multiple times by the Ohio Supreme Court for superior judicial service.

Patricia Ann BLACKMON

1950–

CUYAHOGA COUNTY

Patricia Ann Blackmon, born on August 11, 1950, in Jackson, Mississippi, graduated magna cum laude from Tougaloo College and received a J.D. from Cleveland-Marshall College of Law. In 1976, she was admitted to the Ohio bar and helped organize the first law firm in Ohio made up of African American women—Johnson, Keenon, and Blackmon. This group focused on civil rights and women's issues, and in 1983 succeeded in winning a judgment of fifty thousand dollars on behalf of a battered wife, the first time in Ohio that a battered woman had received such a large damage award. In 1976 Blackmon was admitted to practice before the U.S. District Court and in 1981 before the U.S. Supreme Court. From 1985 to 1986, Blackmon managed the UAW Legal Services Plan; from 1986 to 1989, she served as chief prosecutor for the city of Cleveland; and in 1990, she was appointed a staff attorney for the Ohio Turnpike Commission. In 1991, Blackmon ran for a judgeship and became the first African American woman to be elected to the court of appeals for any district in the state of Ohio.

Currently, Blackmon serves as a judge in the Eighth Judicial District. In 1993, she was appointed director of the National Association of Women Judges for the Seventh District, which covers Ohio, Michigan, and West Virginia. In 1994, she was appointed by the Supreme Court of Ohio to the Board of Commissioners on Grievances and Discipline of lawyers and judges.

In addition to her work on the bench, Blackmon is a member of the Ohio, Cleveland, Cuyahoga, and Norman Bar Associations, Delta Sigma Theta Sorority, and Olive Baptist Church.

Law and Government

Patricia M. BYRNE

1925–

CUYAHOGA COUNTY

PATRICIA M. BYRNE, born in Cleveland, Ohio, in 1925, graduated from Vassar College in 1946 and received an M.A. from the School of Advanced International Studies at Johns Hopkins University in 1947.

Byrne began her career as a foreign service officer in 1949. Her first appointment was as junior foreign service officer in Athens, Greece. After that, she served as political officer in Saigon, Vietnam; officer in charge of Laos affairs in the Department of State in Washington; deputy principal officer in Izmir and political officer in Ankara, Turkey; member of the U.S. delegation to the Geneva Conference on Laos; and political officer in Vientiane, Laos. She then received assignments in the Department of State as chief of dependent area affairs in the Bureau of International Organization Affairs; chief of Far East personnel; and special assistant to the deputy undersecretary for administration.

In 1969, Byrne was sent to Paris as Asian affairs officer and in 1973 to Colombo, Sri Lanka, as deputy chief of mission. In 1976, she was appointed ambassador to the Republic of Mali and in 1980 ambassador to the Union of Burma. In 1985, she was appointed deputy U.S. representative in the United Nations Security Council with the rank of ambassador at the U.S. mission to the United Nations in New York.

Byrne was the first woman to attend the National War College (1968–69), and she is also a graduate of the Department of State's Senior Seminar, which focuses on domestic issues for senior diplomatic officers who will be assigned abroad. In 1984, she was a foreign affairs fellow on detail to the Institute for the Study of Diplomacy at Georgetown University.

Byrne is a member of the American Foreign Service Association, Diplomatic and Consulat Officers, Retired; the American Academy of Diplomacy; and the Washington Institute of Foreign Affairs. She has received several awards, including a Presidential Merit Award in 1983, Senior Performance Pay Awards (1987 and 1990) for excellence in job performance, and Officer of the National Order of the Republic of Mali (1979).

Courtesy of the U.S. Department of State

Jean Murrell CAPERS

1913–

CUYAHOGA COUNTY

JEAN MURRELL CAPERS, born on January 11, 1913, in Georgetown, Kentucky, moved to Cleveland, Ohio, with her family when she was six years old. She received a degree in education from Western Reserve University, ranking at the top of her class, and began teaching in the Cleveland public schools in 1932. She had been teaching only five years when a law was passed requiring single female teachers who married to lose their jobs and their tenure. Caught in this dilemma during the Great Depression, Capers began working at the Phillis Wheatley Association, a social service agency founded by Jane Edna Hunter (also included in this collection). In 1941, while working during the day, Capers enrolled in the Cleveland Law School, a night school. She graduated in 1945 and passed the bar immediately. These early events had a catalytic effect, on her interest in law, government, and public service.

Capers was always an active community volunteer, most notably with the National Association for the Advancement of Colored People (NAACP), where she saw the importance of civic engagement in sustaining justice and equality. Often she worked with elected officials and voter registration initiatives, activities which became an inspiration for her to attend law school and to pursue her own career in public life. In 1945 and in 1947, Capers ran for the City Council of Cleveland, 11th Ward and lost. In 1949, she ran a third time and won, becoming the first African American woman to become a member. After ten years on the council, Capers was defeated, but during her tenure she had pushed tirelessly for "first-class citizenship" for African Americans. Through her ongoing work with the NAACP, Capers continued to be instrumental in campaigns, especially for mayoral offices, which she considered critical to the sustaining of justice and equality. These activities secured her position as a local and national political leader.

In 1977, Governor James A. Rhodes appointed Capers a judge of the Cleveland Municipal Court. She ran that same year to fill the remainder of the unexpired term and again for a subsequent full term. At the end of her second term, Judge Capers retired from the bench at the mandatory age of seventy, but she continues to practice law in Cleveland.

Law and Government

OHIO WOMEN'S HALL OF FAME

Maude Charles COLLINS

1893–1972

VINTON COUNTY

MAUDE CHARLES COLLINS, born in 1893 in Vinton County, made history in 1925 when she became Ohio's first woman sheriff. Earlier that year, her husband, Sheriff Fletcher Collins, had been killed in the line of duty. Maude, as the spouse of a deceased public office holder, was asked to complete the term of office. In such appointments, women were not expected to be active or to provide leadership, only to hold the office until the election, which typically was not far away. Collins, however, broke with these expectations, not only enjoying her work but demonstrating that she was quite good at it. When her appointed term ended, she ran for election to the office on the Democratic ticket, winning the primary and the general election by a landslide. With this victory behind her, Collins came to be known as "Sheriff Maude."

As sheriff, Collins spearheaded the operations and investigations of the county sheriff's department. One of the cases that she investigated and solved—a double homicide—garnered national attention. Collins was a clever detective, as illustrated by another of her cases in which she suspected deception. At the crime scene, she had found incriminating imprints from a pair of boots belonging to a male suspect, but theorized that they had been made by someone other than the owner of the boots. When Collins recreated the footprints wearing the boots herself, she determined that the person who had worn them at the crime scene was someone of her own weight and stature and actually a female. This evidence led to a confession from a woman that Collins suspected.

108

When Collins closed this case, she was at the end of her elected term as sheriff. Instead of returning to private life, however, she ran for clerk of courts and won. Later, she worked as a matron at the Columbus State School until she retired.

Eva Mae (Parker) CROSBY

1911–2002

FRANKLIN COUNTY

Eva Mae (Parker) Crosby was born in Selma, Alabama, in 1911. She moved with her family to Cleveland, Ohio, when she was five years old and then to Oberlin when she entered high school. Crosby graduated from Oberlin College in 1933 and then entered the Ohio State University Law School (now the Moritz College of Law at the Ohio State University), where she became the first African American woman to graduate. After graduation, Crosby returned to Oberlin, started a law practice, and also became a real estate developer. Crosby had a passionate commitment to justice and equality. One of her major projects as a developer was building upscale brick homes and selling them at cost to selected buyers in order to create a racially diverse neighborhood. She succeeded, but not without having to overcome resistance from the neighboring white community. Later, Crosby would serve as the only woman on the Oberlin charter commission, a group that drafted the laws—including a fair housing ordinance—under which the city was required to operate.

Crosby ended her law practice and real estate business after she met and married Normal Crosby, a minister and mortician, and the two began raising a family. Soon, however, she was involved in her children's education, teaching in the schools where they attended. In 1963, when Crosby and her family moved to Columbus, she continued to teach in the public schools. In 1966, however, Crosby's husband died, and she took control of the Crosby Funeral Home and continued to run it for the next thirty-six years. During these years, she also continued to practice law, providing legal services in her home for those who could not otherwise afford them.

Crosby served on several boards and committees, including the board of St. Anthony Hospital and the Mid-Ohio Health Planning Committee. In 1999, Crosby was honored by Black Women of Courage for her work on social issues.

Law and Government

Sara J. HARPER

1926–

CUYAHOGA COUNTY

Sara J. Harper was born in Cleveland, Ohio, on August 10, 1926. She received a B.S. from Western Reserve University and went on to become the first African American woman to graduate from the Western Reserve University Law School. Harper's political life, however, had begun much earlier. At eight years old, she attended political meetings with her parents, distributed literature, and brought election-day lunches to her mother, who was a Republican booth worker. These activities constituted the fertile ground from which her long and illustrious career has grown.

Harper's first adult involvement in public service was on the executive committee of the Mt. Pleasant Community Council, where she chaired the schools committee and participated in the life and welfare of the community. In December 1970, the scope of her participation was broadened when Governor James A. Rhodes appointed her a judge of the Cleveland Municipal Court. She sought election to this position in 1971 and was successful in winning a six-year term and in being re-elected in 1977 for a second term. During this time, Harper also became the first woman to be appointed to the U.S. Marine Corps Reserve Judiciary (1972), a position which required her to spend at least fifteen days a year with the Marines while she continued to serve in the municipal court. She retired from the Marine Corps Reserve in 1986 with the rank of lieutenant colonel.

On November 8, 1990, Harper became one of two African American women judges to serve on the Ohio Court of Appeals, as judge with the 8th District Court. In 1992, she became the first African American woman to be assigned to the Ohio Supreme Court.

Harper has served on many advisory boards, including the Alcohol and Drug Addiction Services Board of Cuyahoga County and the Ohio Judicial College, and she has been the recipient of many awards, including the Superior Judicial Service Award from the Supreme Court of Ohio in 1981, the Public Policy Leadership Award from the Court of Claims of Ohio Victims of Crime Program, and the NAACP's Unsung Heroine Award. In addition, in 1981, Harper was presented with the key to the City of Cleveland.

110

OHIO
WOMEN'S
HALL OF
FAME

Dorothy O. JACKSON

1933–

SUMMIT COUNTY

Dorothy O. Jackson was born in Akron, Ohio, on November 9, 1933. After graduating from East High School, she attended Actual Business College. In 1957, she accepted a position as secretary for Goodwill Industries, where she learned sign language and became an advocate for the disabled. She served as an interpreter for public events and also trained Akron police and fire personnel in sign language. Jackson began a lifelong commitment to the delivery and management of social services for groups of citizens in need. During her twelve years at Goodwill, she excelled at her work and rose through the ranks to become assistant director of public relations. In 1969, Jackson moved to the Akron Metropolitan Housing Authority to become the social and tenant services administrator. In this position, she facilitated the authority's programs, providing educational services, a high level of personalized tenant care, and a sense of community. After sixteen years with the housing authority, in 1984 Jackson became the deputy mayor for the city of Akron, the first African American woman to hold this position.

For two decades, Jackson has provided leadership as deputy mayor and has used her management expertise and her skills in public relations to work together with all levels of government. She spearheads the coordination of Akron's annual town meetings, organizes commissions to address social services and community relations, and convenes meetings for the mayor with governmental and community agencies. She has also lead in developing the city's child abuse program and its camping program for disabled youth.

Jackson is also known as a top volunteer who gives time and energy to many community organizations. In recognition of this work, she has received numerous honors and awards, including the Ohio Black Women's Leadership Caucus Rosa Parks Award, the NAACP Million Dollar Medallion, the United Way Distinguished Service Award, the American Lung Association Crystal Cross Award, and the Jewish National Fund Tree of Life Award. In 1989, the Dorothy O. Jackson Park in Kiryat Ekron, Israel, was dedicated in her honor.

Law and Government

OHIO
WOMEN'S
HALL OF
FAME

Stephanie Tubbs JONES

1949‒

CUYAHOGA COUNTY

STEPHANIE TUBBS JONES, born on September 10, 1949, in Cleveland, graduated from the Flora Stone Mather College of Case Western Reserve University in 1971 with a degree in social work. In 1974, she received a J.D. from the Case Western Reserve University School of Law. Prior to her career in law and government, Jones was a trial attorney for the Equal Employment Opportunity Commission's district office in Cleveland. Jones served also as assistant Cuyahoga County prosecutor and as general counsel and equal employment opportunity administrator for the Northeast Ohio Regional Sewer District. She was also the first African American woman to sit on the common pleas bench in the state of Ohio, and she was a municipal court judge in the city of Cleveland.

In 1999, Jones was the first African American woman elected to serve Ohio's 11th Congressional District. In Congress, she is an advocate for children's rights. She was a sponsor, for example, of the Child Abuse Protection and Enforcement (CAPE) Act of 1999. She is a member of the Committee on Banking and Financial Services and the Committee on Small Business. Jones is a member of the Democratic Caucus, the Congressional Black Caucus, the Women's Caucus, and four other caucuses in which she works to build alliances and get critical jobs done in the interest of her constituencies—to end the practice of predatory lending, support credit unions, protect America's steel industry, and aid small businesses.

Jones is active also on advisory boards and in numerous community organizations, including the National Council of Negro Women, Delta Sigma Theta sorority, the Task Force on Violent Crime, and the Substance Abuse Initiative.

OHIO
WOMEN'S
HALL OF
FAME

Profiles of Two Hundred Ohio Women

Blanche E. KRUPANSKY

1925–

CUYAHOGA COUNTY

BLANCHE E. KRUPANSKY was born in Cleveland on December 10, 1925. When she entered Western Reserve University School of Law in 1946, she was the only female in her class. She completed a four-year undergraduate program and a three-year law program in a total of five years, receiving her law degree at the age of twenty-two. Krupansky was admitted to the Ohio bar in 1949, practiced law, served as an assistant attorney general for the state of Ohio, and was the assistant chief counsel for the Ohio Bureau of Workers' Compensation. In 1959, Krupansky ran for judicial office. To do so, she fought in the courts for the right to appear on the ballot using only her own family name, rather than her married name, and secured this right for the many generations of women to come.

When she was elected to the Cleveland Municipal Court, Krupansky was the third woman to serve in that judicial forum. She is unique, however, in being a woman judge who has served on all four levels of the state court system during her more than thirty years of judicial service. She spent fifteen years on the trial bench, more than fifteen years in the appellate courts, seven years in the Cleveland Municipal Court, eight years in the common pleas court, and four years and eight months as the first woman on the Eighth District Court of Appeals in Cuyahoga County, before she was sworn in as a justice of the Ohio Supreme Court, only the second woman to be appointed. After two years of distinguished service as an Ohio Supreme Court justice, Krupansky returned to the Eighth District Court of Appeals to serve another eleven years before retiring in 1995.

Krupansky is the recipient of many awards, including a Women of Achievement Award from the Women's City Club of Cleveland; the Distinguished Alumna Award from Case Western Reserve University; and the Nettie Cronise Lutes Award from the Ohio State Bar Association's Women in the Profession Section, an award that commemorates the first woman admitted to practice law in Ohio.

113

Law and Government

Margaret Diane QUINN

1951–

MUSKINGUM COUNTY

MARGARET DIANE QUINN was born in 1951 in Zanesville, Ohio. In the early days of her career in law enforcement, she was an oddity—a female police officer. Supervisors suggested to her, for example, that she wear a meter maid hat instead of a police officer's cap in order to appear more feminine on the streets. Quinn, however, was not distracted from her goals by such suggestions even though she certainly could not miss the obvious implication: She had, without a doubt, chosen a male-dominated profession. In the early 1970s, police women were more visible on television than in real life, and Quinn faced the challenge of being very much on her own.

Quinn was the first woman to work patrol for the Zanesville Police Department and the first to serve as patrol sergeant, lieutenant, captain, and chief. As the first female chief of a large municipal department in the state of Ohio, Quinn became the leader of a fifty-six-person police force—the same unit that had earlier encouraged her to try to look more feminine. Quinn was also the first woman to be president of the Ohio Association of Chiefs of Police, an organization of 530 members that at the time of her election included only three women.

In addition to her work in law enforcement, Quinn is active in the Zanesville community in other ways. She is the past president of the Zane chapter of the American Business Women's Association and is recognized in Zanesville as an outstanding woman who is an asset to her community and the state.

Alice Robie RESNICK

1939 –

LUCAS COUNTY

ALICE ROBIE RESNICK was born on August 21, 1939, in Erie, Pennsylvania, but grew up in Toledo, Ohio. She graduated from Siena Heights College in 1961 with a degree in history and from the University of Detroit College of Law in 1964. In that year, Resnick opened a private practice and also was appointed an assistant Lucas County prosecutor. In this latter role, Resnick excelled and began creating a distinctive record of service.

As a Lucas County prosecutor, Resnick tried more than one hundred felony cases, including ten death penalty cases. In 1970, she appeared before the U.S. Supreme Court to argue the constitutionality of Ohio's death penalty statute. In 1975, she was elected judge of the Toledo Municipal Court and was reelected in 1981; in that same year, the other six judges of the court selected her as the presiding administrative judge. By 1982, however, Resnick had moved on, having been elected judge of the Ohio Sixth District Court of Appeals in Toledo. From 1983 to 1987, she sat by assignment on the Supreme Court of Ohio. In 1988, she became presiding judge of the Sixth District Court, but in that same year was elected justice of the Supreme Court of Ohio, the position to which she was reelected in 1994. With these achievements, Resnick became the fourth woman elected to a statewide office in Ohio and the second elected to the Supreme Court.

Throughout her years of leadership in law and government, Resnick has been an advocate for women. She founded and co-chaired the Ohio State Bar Association/ Supreme Court of Ohio Joint Task Force on Gender Fairness, a task force that addressed issues in domestic relations cases. She chaired the Ohio Women's Legal Assistance and Education Coalition, and she initiated the formation of the Ohio Women's Bar Association.

Resnick's contributions have been recognized by many awards and honors, including Woman of Achievement Awards from the Girl Scouts and the YWCA (1994); the Nettie Cronise Lutes Award (1995); a Making a Difference Award from the National Association of Women Judges, District 7 (1996); and the Gertrude W. Donahey Award (1999) from the Ohio Democratic Party. In addition, in 1998, the Ohio Women's Bar Association initiated an award in her honor and named her the first recipient.

Law and Government

Marjorie M. WHITEMAN

1898–1986

HENRY COUNTY

This Digest [Whiteman's Digest of International Law] will fill an important gap in the legal materials available for the United States Government, to the Bar and to the public in this country, and to governments and scholars throughout the world. . . . These volumes will be a documentary record of the complexity and compactness of our world and of the interrelationship of its nations and people.

—Dean Rusk, former Secretary of State

MARJORIE M. WHITEMAN, born in 1898 in Liberty Township, Ohio, graduated magna cum laude and Phi Beta Kappa from Ohio Wesleyan University in 1920. She went on to receive a law degree from Yale University and further training from National University. Whiteman gained fame as a scholar for writing the monumental fifteen-volume *Digest of International Law* (1963–69), which remains today a classic text in the field of international law. It was the fifth such work published by the Department of State since 1877 and the first since the appearance of an eight-volume digest in 1944. For Whiteman, this publication was the result of twenty years of scholarly work.

Whiteman's contributions extend beyond these volumes, however. From 1945 to 1951, Whiteman was legal advisor to Eleanor Roosevelt in her capacity as the U.S. Representative to the United Nations General Assembly. Whiteman was also a part of the U.S. delegation to the Pan-American Conference in Bogotá, Colombia, in 1948, when the Organization of American States was formed. Over the course of her more than forty-year career, Whiteman was legal advisor and counselor on international law to ten secretaries of state.

Whiteman also served as vice-president of the American Society of International Law, from which she received the Manley O. Hudson Medal for preeminent scholarship and achievement in international law and in the promotion of the establishment and maintenance of international relations on the basis of law and justice (1985).

Mary Ellen WITHROW

1930–

MARION COUNTY

Mary Ellen Withrow, born on October 2, 1930, in Marion, Ohio, began her career in government in 1969, when she became the first woman to be elected to the Elgin local school board in Marion County. In 1975, she was appointed deputy auditor of Marion County, and in 1976 she began serving the first of two consecutive terms as Marion County treasurer. In 1982, Withrow became the forty-second treasurer of the state of Ohio and was reelected to this position in 1986 and 1990. In 1994, Withrow made history, when she was sworn in as the fortieth treasurer of the United States and became the first person in history to hold the post of treasurer at all three levels of government—local, state, and national.

During her years as treasurer of Ohio, Withrow initiated a variety of programs designed to improve Ohio's economy and strengthen the state's business climate. She left office having earned the state more than $2 billion in investment income. For such excellence in financial management, she received an award from the Treasury Department's Joint Financial Management Improvement Program, and in 1990 she was named the nation's most valuable state public official by *City and State* newspaper.

As treasurer of the United States under President Clinton, Withrow was responsible for the operations of the U.S. Mint and the Bureau of Engraving and Printing, and she was also the national honorary director of the U.S. Savings Bond program, representing the secretary of the treasury nationwide in promoting the sale of savings bonds. She was part of the "State Quarters" project and the Sacagewea dollar coin project, and she has the distinction of being the treasurer who redesigned the $5, $10, $20, $50, and $100 banknotes. Withrow served as treasurer from March 1, 1994, through January 20, 2001, and her signature appeared on the nation's paper money throughout that period.

Withrow has served on the advisory boards of many organizations, including the United Way, and has received many awards , such as a Women Executives in State Government Fellowship to Harvard University.

117

OHIO
WOMEN'S
HALL OF
FAME

Margaret W. WONG

1950—

CUYAHOGA COUNTY

MARGARET W. WONG, born in the former British Colony of Hong Kong in 1950, immigrated to the United States in the late 1960s on a student visa. She worked as a waitress to pay her way through college and law school and became one of the first noncitizens licensed to practice law.

Wong is now a U.S. citizen and the founder and managing partner of her own nationally and internationally recognized law firm. She focuses on immigration and naturalization law and is one of the best-known immigration attorneys in the country. She has received a top rating from Martindale-Hubbell, the leading attorney rating organization, and she was named one of the ten "best and brightest" female entrepreneurs in Northeast Ohio by the National Association of Business Owners.

Wong has also distinguished herself as a community leader in the Cleveland area and in the state of Ohio. She is former president of the Federal Bar Association, Cleveland chapter. She serves on several advisory boards, including the Greater Cleveland Growth Association, Notre Dame College, the Ohio Commission on Higher Education, the Greater Cleveland Roundtable, the United Way, and the Asian Bar Association. Wong is also a founder and consultant of two of Cleveland's finest restaurants, Pearl of the Orient-East and Pearl of the Orient-West, and she is founder and consultant to the Apothe-Care Pharmacy Group.

For her outstanding achievements and contributions to the United States, Wong has been awarded the Ellis Island Medal of Honor.

118

LITERATURE

OHIO WOMEN'S ACHIEVEMENT IN LITERATURE MIGHT
lead one to conclude that there must indeed be something in Ohio's
soil or water that nurtures creativity and genius. The women profiled
in this section illustrate excellence across literary genres—journalism,
poetry, nonfiction, and fiction, including children's literature, science
fiction, and mysteries. These highly productive women have made Ohio
a beacon of influence in the nation and in the world. These writers inspire, entertain, and teach; they nourish our hearts, minds, and souls
with their words; they fill us with pride and joy as they make their own
places in the world of letters. We embrace them as they are simultaneously embraced by the nation and the world.

MILDRED WIRT BENSON

RITA DOVE

NIKKI GIOVANNI

VIRGINIA ESTHER HAMILTON

TONI MORRISON

ANDRE NORTON

HELEN STEINER RICE

HARRIET BEECHER STOWE

Mildred Wirt BENSON

1905–2002

LUCAS COUNTY

A PIONEERING FICTION WRITER and journalist, Mildred Wirt Benson, born on July 5, 1905, in Ladora, Iowa, devoted her life to writing. She received her first award for creative writing at the age of fourteen for a story published in *St. Nicholas* magazine. She was the first woman to earn an M.A. in journalism from the University of Iowa, where she sold nearly a hundred short stories while still a student. By age twenty-five, using the pen name Carolyn Keene, she published *The Secret of the Old Clock,* the first of the Nancy Drew mysteries, for the Stratemeyer Syndicate. Thus began a series featuring an adventurous young female sleuth that would engage young readers (as well as moviegoers and television watchers) for the next seventy years and counting.

Benson went on to write twenty-three more of the first twenty-seven Nancy Drew books between 1930 and 1953 before the series was taken over by other syndicate authors. In addition to these pacesetting novels, Benson also created other series, including the Ruth Darrow Flying Stories (Benson was a pilot), the Penny Parker Mystery Stories, and the Mildred A. Wirt Mystery Stories, totaling more than 130 published books and 100 magazine stories and articles for young readers.

In 1944, Benson began a career in journalism with the *Toledo Times* and later the *Toledo Blade,* serving first as a city hall and courthouse reporter and later as a writer of "Happy Landings," a column on aviation. Benson received numerous honors and awards for her work as a journalist, including the Amos Ives Root Award for excellence in aviation journalism and awards from the Ohio Newspaper Women's Association (1970, 1973, 1974, and 1975). In 1992, she was inducted into the University of Iowa School of Journalism and Mass Communication's Hall of Fame.

At the time of her death at ninety-six years of age, Benson was still writing a weekly column on active senior citizens, *On the Go with Millie Benson.* Her final column, which she wrote on the day of her death, celebrated her love of books and libraries.

Literature

Rita DOVE

SUMMIT COUNTY

WORLD-RENOWNED POET RITA DOVE, born on August 28, 1952, in Akron, Ohio, graduated from Miami University in Ohio in 1973 and received an M.F.A. in creative writing from the Iowa Writers Workshop at the University of Iowa in 1977. Dove's first volume of poetry, *The Yellow House on the Corner,* was published in 1980 and was followed by *Museum* (1983), *Thomas and Beulah* (1986), *The Other Side of the House* (1988), *Grace Notes* (1989), *Selected Poems* (1993), *Lady Freedom among Us* (1994), and *Mother Love* (1995). Dove has also written two plays, a short story collection, a novel, and an essay collection, and she has participated in musical collaborations with composers Tania León (1996), Alvin Singleton (1996), Bruce Adolphe (1997), and John Williams (1997). Dove has garnered much critical acclaim as a multitalented writer who exhibits interests across a broad range of subject matter.

Dove has been the recipient of numerous prestigious awards, including a Fulbright Fellowship and grants and fellowships from the National Endowment for the Arts, the National Endowment for the Humanities, the Guggenheim Foundation, the Mellon Foundation, the Academy of American Poets, the General Electric Foundation, and many others. Most notably, in 1987 Dove was awarded the Pulitzer Prize for *Thomas and Beulah*, and in 1993 she became the youngest person and the first African American to be honored as Poet Laureate of the United States. Recent achievements include a nomination in 2000 for the National Book Critics Circle Award for *On the Bus with Rosa Parks* and in 2001 the Duke Ellington Lifetime Achievement Award in the Literary Arts from the Ellington Fund.

122

In addition, Dove has held many academic positions at universities across the country, served in various roles in professional organizations in creative writing, and received twenty honorary degrees. Currently, she is Commonwealth Professor of English at the University of Virginia in Charlottesville.

Profiles of Two Hundred Ohio Women

OHIO WOMEN'S HALL OF FAME

Nikki GIOVANNI

1943–

HAMILTON COUNTY

Courtesy of HarperCollins Publishers; Todd
Wright, photographer

Giovanni's gift for verse came to transcend the rhetoric of revolution and to form the essence of . . . love embracing life.

—L. M. Collins, *Tennessean*

NIKKI GIOVANNI, named Yolande Cornelia after her mother, was born in Knoxville, Tennessee. When she was very young, her parents relocated to Wyoming, Ohio, a suburb of Cincinnati, where she attended the public schools. In 1960, she enrolled at Fisk University, where she worked with the Writer's Workshop and edited the literary magazine. After graduating magna cum laude in 1967, she entered graduate school at the University of Pennsylvania, and in the late 1960s, she emerged as one of the New Black Poets. Her poetry established her as a revolutionary voice, deeply committed to the civil rights movement and to social and political equality, as demonstrated by her first published collection of poems, *Black Feeling, Black Talk,* in 1968.

Over the decades since 1968, Giovanni has published more than twenty-five books, including poetry collections and essay collections, and has made several recordings of her poems set to music. While her poetry has consistently exhibited a deliberate political and social consciousness, she has included themes and concerns that have reflected her own evolving experiences, for example, as a single mother and as a woman progressing through the life cycle and overcoming serious illness. Her most recent collections include *Grand Mothers: Poems, Reminiscences, and Short Stories about the Keepers of Our Traditions* (1994); *Racism 101* (1994); *The Sun Is So Quiet: Poems* (1996); and *Love Poems* (1997).

Giovanni's numerous acknowledgments and awards include being named Woman of the Year by *Ebony Magazine* (1970), *Mademoiselle* (1971), and *Ladies' Home Journal* (1972); the NAACP Image Award for Literature (1988 and 1998); and the Langston Hughes Award for Distinguished Contributions to Arts and Letters (1996). Currently, Giovanni holds the title of University Distinguished Professor at Virginia Tech in Blacksburg.

123

Literature

Virginia Esther HAMILTON

1936–2002

GREENE COUNTY

VIRGINIA ESTHER HAMILTON, one of the most influential authors of children's literature in the nation, was born on March 12, 1936, in Yellow Springs, Ohio. Her literary career began in elementary school when she began writing stories for pleasure, many of them about growing up on the farm that had been in her family since her great- great-grandmother guided her son out of slavery and settled in this area. After graduating from Antioch College in 1955 and the Ohio State University in 1958, Hamilton moved to New York and continued studying writing at the New School for Social Research. In New York, Hamilton began a career that ultimately established her as a nationally and internationally recognized literary giant.

In 1967, Hamilton published her first book, *Zeely*, a novel that helped alter the negative images of Africans in children's literature. She followed that with *The House of Dies Drear* (a mystery, 1968), *The Time-Ago Tales of Jadhu* (a folklore collection, 1969), *The Planet of Junior Brown* (a novel, 1971), *W.E.B. Du Bois* (a biography, 1972), and *Time-Ago Lost: More Tales of Jadhu* (a folklore collection, 1973). She is perhaps best known for the folklore collection *The People Could Fly* (1985), but it was her 1974 publication, *M.C. Higgins, the Great*, that became the catapult for her remarkable career. This exceptional novel of a young male's hopes, dreams, and relationships was the first book in history to be awarded both the National Book Award and the Newbery Medal, given by the American Library Association for the most distinguished contribution to literature for children.

124

Drawing from her African American and American Indian heritage, Hamilton wrote more than thirty books in several genres, including fiction, science fiction/fantasy, biographies, and folklore. She received numerous honors and awards, including, in addition to the two cited above, the Regina Medal, the Edgar Allan Poe Award, and the Laura Ingalls Wilder Award. Most notably, Hamilton was also the first children's writer to receive the prestigious MacArthur "genius" grant in 1995. Hamilton died in Yellow Springs, Ohio, on February 19, 2002.

Profiles of Two Hundred Ohio Women

Toni MORRISON

1931–

LORAIN COUNTY

Courtesy of Toni Morrison

Toni Morrison, the eighth woman and first African American woman to receive the Nobel Prize in Literature (1993), was born Chloe Anthony Wofford in Lorain, Ohio, on February 18, 1931. She graduated from Lorain High School in 1949 and received a B.A. in English and classics from Howard University in 1953 and an M.A. from Cornell University in 1955. Morrison began her career as an instructor of English at Texas Southern University in Houston, returning to Howard as a faculty member in 1957. In 1964, she became an associate editor with a textbook subsidiary of Random House in Syracuse, New York. Morrison was soon transferred to the central offices in New York City where she became a senior editor.

During her years at Howard, Morrison began writing fiction and continued to do so as she accepted other teaching positions at colleges and universities and became an editor at Random House. In 1970, she published her first novel, *The Bluest Eye,* to much critical acclaim. Her second novel, *Sula* (1973), was an alternate selection by the Book-of-the-Month Club and was nominated for the 1975 National Book Award in fiction. Her next novel, *Song of Solomon* (1977), won the National Book Critics Circle Award and the American Academy and Institute of Arts and Letters Award. She left Random House in 1983 when she was named the Albert Schweitzer Professor of Humanities at the State University of New York in Albany. In 1987, she published *Beloved,* a bestseller and winner of the Pulitzer Prize for fiction. In 1989, she was named the Robert F. Goheen Professor in the Council of Humanities at Princeton University, where she continues today to teach creative writing and participate in the African American studies, American studies, and women's studies programs. In being named the Goheen Professor, Morrison became the first African American woman writer to hold a named chair at an Ivy League University.

In addition to her seven novels, Morrison has also written a play, *Dreaming Emmett,* which premiered in Albany on January 4, 1986, and several volumes of literary criticism, including *Playing in the Dark: Whiteness and the Literary Imagination* (1990). With such a stellar record of achievements, Morrison clearly holds a secure place in American letters as one of our most celebrated writers.

125

Literature

Andre NORTON

CUYAHOGA COUNTY

Aᴌɪᴄᴇ Mᴀʀʏ Nᴏʀᴛᴏɴ, born in Cleveland, Ohio, on February 17, 1912, officially changed her name to Andre Norton after making the decision to enter the male-dominated world of science fiction/fantasy writing in 1934 with the publication of *The Prince Commands*. Norton graduated from Collinwood High School in Cleveland, where she wrote her first book, *Ralestone Luck* (her second book publication in 1938), and enrolled in Flora Stone Mather College of Western Reserve University with the intention of becoming a history teacher. During the Great Depression, however, she faced difficult financial problems and was never able to complete her degree, although she continued to take night courses in writing and journalism from Western Reserve. For two decades, Norton was a librarian with the Cleveland Public Library, working ultimately in all but two of the forty-seven branches of the library across the city. Before she left this position to become a reader for the Gnome Press, she had published eight more novels and two short stories, establishing herself as a prolific writer with a growing readership and now one of the most celebrated female science fiction/fantasy writers of our times.

Norton has written more than 130 science fiction and fantasy books, with perhaps the best known being the Witch World series, begun in 1963, which was nominated for the Hugo Award, and the Solar Queen series, begun in 1955, which includes *Sargasso of Space* (1955), *Plague Ship* (1956), and *Voodoo Planet* (1959), all written as Andrew North.

126

Over her long career, Norton has received many awards. Among these honors, she was the first woman to receive the Gandalf Grand Master of Fantasy Award and the Nebula Grand Master Award, and she was the first woman to receive the Invisible Little Man Award for Life Achievements. She founded and directs the High Hallack Genre Writers' Research and Reference Library in Murfreesboro, Tennessee.

OHIO
WOMEN'S
HALL OF
FAME

Profiles of Two Hundred Ohio Women

Helen Steiner RICE

1900–1981

LORAIN COUNTY

HELEN STEINER RICE, known as the "Poet Laureate of Greeting Card Verse," was a woman ahead of her time. Born in Lorain, her plans for college and a career in law were interrupted by the untimely death of her father. Steiner began working at the Lorain Electric Light and Power Company and was soon promoted from demonstrating the art of creating silk lampshades to advertising and then public relations, where she had the opportunity to develop a talent for public speaking. She eventually opened her own lecture service.

In 1924, Steiner was named manager of advertising for the Ohio Public Service Company in Lorain and served also as Ohio State Chairman of the Women's Public Information Committee of the National Electric Light Association. She contributed several articles to the *Electric Light and Power* magazine and won a *Forbes Magazine* prize for "How Sound Public Relations Can Best Be Developed and Maintained." Speaking before many business and civic organizations nationwide, Steiner promoted the importance of women as partners in the workplace and argued eloquently for the hiring and promoting of women workers.

In 1929, Steiner married Franklin Rice, a Dayton bank vice-president who committed suicide after the 1932 stock market crash, leaving his family financially ruined. Steiner moved to Cincinnati to work for Gibson Greeting Cards as editor of their card lines and wrote poetry for greeting cards for the next five decades. Although greeting card verses during this era used only humorous messages, Rice wrote inspirational verses for her personal correspondence and her friends. In 1963, her poem "The Priceless Gift of Christmas" was featured on the nationally televised *Lawrence Welk Show*. After that exposure, Helen Steiner Rice cards, books, and other merchandise, which reflected the author's deep concern for others and her abiding love of God, were in great demand. In 1967, she published *Just for You: A Special Collection of Inspirational Verses,* the first of seventy-four books of poetry, which marked the beginning of a billion-dollar industry for inspirational writers. Shortly before her death, she established the Helen Steiner Rice Foundation, which continues to be an invaluable community resource, awarding grants to charitable programs that assist the needy and the elderly.

127

Literature

Harriet Beecher STOWE

1811–1896

HAMILTON COUNTY

The little lady who made the big war.
—attributed to President Abraham Lincoln

Harriet Beecher Stowe was born in Litchfield, Connecticut, into a family made famous by her father, Lyman, a nationally known clergyman; her brothers, Henry Ward and Edward, who were also famous preachers; and her sister, Catherine, a respected educator. When her father became president of Lane Theological Seminary in Cincinnati, Ohio, in 1832, she moved to Cincinnati with him and in 1836 married Calvin Ellis Stowe, a professor at Lane. The Stowe family soon grew to include seven children.

In the 1830s and 1840s, Stowe began publishing magazine stories that earned her money that helped to support the family. During these years of living across the Ohio River from slaveholding territory, Stowe heard stories from fugitive slaves and visited slave plantations, seeing slavery firsthand and considering it an outrage against humanity. In 1850, Stowe moved to Brunswick, Maine, where her husband became a professor at Bowdoin College.

In 1851, Stowe was inspired to write a novel, *Uncle Tom's Cabin: Or, Life Among the Lowly,* published serially in 1851 and 1852 in the *National Era,* a newspaper that promoted antislavery principles. In 1852, the novel was published in book form, selling more than three million copies before the Civil War. While the story did not question some of the patriarchal and kindly stereotypes of slavery, it did offer vivid descriptions of suffering and oppression that inflamed Northern sentiments and inspired many to take a moral stand. In its own day, *Uncle Tom's Cabin* experienced unprecedented success, and over the generations since 1851, it has been translated into forty languages and presented often on stage and in movie productions. It has recently experienced a resurgence, not just in terms of its own ongoing popularity, but also by inspiring a rethinking of stereotypes and alternate renderings of a powerful human tale.

Stowe's other works include *The Mayflower* (1843); *Dred: A Tale of the Great Dismal Swamp* (1856); another antislavery novel, *The Minister's Wooing* (1859); and *Lady Byron Vindicated* (1870). Stowe died in Hartford, Connecticut.

MILITARY

SERVICE

OVER THE CENTURIES, WOMEN HAVE BEEN PRAISED
for patriotically serving the nation by waiting at home while fathers,
husbands, brothers, and sons took to the land, air, and sea in defense of
home and country. The women in this section, however, did not "wait."
They stepped up and out to serve, willingly placing their lives on the
line and sometimes making the ultimate sacrifice. These are women
who have served valiantly and well in the line of duty and beyond.

In the past, gender stereotypes confined women in the military to
maintenance and support roles, which meant that their work might be
acknowledged in a basic way as valuable but not vital to the nation's
causes. For example, women were expected to transport and care for
the wounded, deliver mail and supplies, or organize operations for personnel and their families. They were not expected to be combat ready.
They were, however, always professional, and they served with the
honor and excellence expected of anyone in the armed forces. These
pioneers blazed the trails, and new generations of women are now
following those paths in ways heretofore unprescribed and even
unimagined.

MARY ANN BALL BICKERDYKE

CHRISTINE M. COOK

SARAH M. DEAL

CHARITY EDNA ADAMS EARLEY

KATHLEEN V. HARRISON

SHARON LANE

MARIE BARRETT MARSH

HELEN GRACE McCLELLAND

BETTY ZANE

Mary Ann Ball BICKERDYKE

1817–1901

KNOX COUNTY

MARY ANN BALL BICKERDYKE was born in Knox County, Ohio, on July 19, 1817. She married Robert Bickerdyke, a Cincinnati widower with two sons, in 1847 and moved to Galesburg, Illinois. Robert died three years later. In Galesburg, Bickerdyke became known for her leadership and especially for her understanding of herbal medicines. At the start of the Civil War, she was chosen by her community to take charge of medical supplies being sent to soldiers in the camp hospital near Cairo, Illinois. Bickerdyke left her stepsons in the hands of her fellow church members and began a military service that was distinctive and unparalleled for her day.

Without military sanction, Bickerdyke entered the camp hospital and was incensed by the devastating conditions in which soldiers were suffering and dying. She cleaned up the hospital, taught the men to cook, obtained a broader variety of foods for them to eat (rather than just uncooked beans, salt pork, hardtack, and coffee), and ministered to their wounds and spirits. After the battle of Fort Donelson, without any authority to do so, she boarded the river steamer *City of Memphis* and took charge of the wounded. That night, she walked the battlefield alone with a lantern looking for anyone alive who might have been missed, a service that she rendered frequently.

Bickerdyke's reputation for excellence was recognized by both the American Sanitary Commission, which ultimately sanctioned her work, and General William T. Sherman, who asked her to serve with his soldiers as they marched through Georgia. Bickerdyke resigned her commission as a sanitary agent on March 21, 1866, the day that the very last Illinois volunteer received his discharge at Camp Butler in Springfield, Illinois. After the war, her activism continued in support of other causes, for example, responding to the devastation in Kansas by hordes of grasshoppers and working with immigrants in the slums of New York.

In Kansas, the state legislature passed a resolution of gratitude to her and placed her portrait in the State Capitol. Galesburg, Illinois, erected a monument to her on the courthouse lawn. In 1943, a victory freighter was named the *Mary A. Bickerdyke.*

Military Service

Christine M. COOK

1956–

ERIE COUNTY

CHRISTINE M. COOK was born in Marshfield, Wisconsin, on August 15, 1956. Her military career began in 1974, when she enlisted as a private in the U.S. Army. She served four years on active duty as a linguist, translator, and interpreter. Upon completion of this duty, she enlisted in the Maryland Army National Guard and completed training at the Maryland Military Academy Officer Candidate School; she was commissioned in 1980 as an officer in the Army National Guard. In the Guard, she served twelve months as an ambulance platoon leader in Company B of the 58th Support Battalion. During this time, she also managed to complete a B.S. in business administration at the University of Maryland.

In July 1981, Cook transferred into the 137th Supply and Service Battalion of the Ohio Army National Guard, where she filled various roles over the next six years, including becoming the first female battalion training officer and battalion administrative officer in the state of Ohio. In November 1989, she was selected as the plans and actions branch chief for the Ohio Adjutant General's Department, where she supervised the operations of enlisted and officer personnel sections, family assistance office, health services, education services, and selective retention incentive programs. During this time, Cook developed the Family Assistance Program which provided statewide support to twenty-one thousand servicemember families during both Operation Desert Shield and Operation Desert Storm. In March 1997, Cook was appointed director of the Ohio Veterans Home (OVH) in Sandusky, the first woman to be appointed to this post since the home was established in 1888.

Cook is a highly accomplished member of the military who has worked diligently to achieve the rank of colonel. Her leadership has established her as the first woman in the over two-hundred-year history of the Ohio National Guard to assume command of two separate battalions and, later, a regiment. She is also the recipient of many honors and awards including the Meritorious Service Medal with two oak clusters, and the Army Commendation Medal.

OHIO
WOMEN'S
HALL OF
FAME

Profiles of Two Hundred Ohio Women

Sarah M. DEAL

1969-

WOOD COUNTY

S ARAH M. DEAL, who was born in Bowling Green, Ohio, on September 14, 1969, graduated from Kent State University's aeronautics program in 1992. She was commissioned a second lieutenant in the U.S. Marine Corps on May 17, 1992. Although she had obtained a private pilot's license in January 1989, she had no expectation to serve as a pilot in the Marines, in part because there was a ban on women in combat positions. Deal went instead to Quantico, Virginia, for basic training and then to air traffic control school. With the encouragement of her recruiting officer, however, she took the aptitude test for the Marine Flight School in anticipation that the ban might one day be lifted. In 1993, Deal became the first woman to be selected to attend the Marine Flight School in Pensacola, Florida.

Deal earned her wings as a naval aviator in April 1995, becoming the first female Marine pilot in the 220-year history of the Marine Corps. On October 1, 1996, she was promoted to the rank of captain and became the adjutant for the commanding officer of Marine Aircraft Group 16 at Marine Corps Air Station Miramar in San Diego. She began flying the CH-53 Super Stallion helicopter, the second-largest helicopter in the world and the largest used by the U.S. military, used to support and supply ground troops. Deal has also become an active member of the Women Military Aviators and the Ninety-Nines, an international organization of licensed women pilots. Through these groups she is an advocate for the efforts of other women in the field of aviation.

In 1996, Deal was awarded the Young Alumni Special Achievement Award by Kent State University. In 1996 she was also honored by *Working Woman* magazine as one of the "350 Women Who Changed the World, 1976–1996," and in 1998 she received the Kent State University School of Technology Distinguished Alumnus Award and a certificate of commendation for representing the United States of America, an award given for exceptional performance not normally required of a Marine.

133

Military Service

Courtesy of Stanley Earley, Jr., M.D.

Charity Edna Adams EARLEY

1918–2002

MONTGOMERY COUNTY

CHARITY EDNA ADAMS EARLEY was born on December 5, 1918, in Kittrell, North Carolina. She moved to Ohio to attend Wilberforce University and after graduating from there in 1938 began teaching mathematics and science in Columbia, South Carolina. At the beginning of World War II, she was selected as one of the first officer candidates of the Women's Army Auxiliary Corps, and on August 29, 1942, became the first African American woman to be commissioned. Earley was appointed commanding officer of the 6888th Central Postal Directory Battalion, the only organization of African American women to serve overseas (in England and France) during World War II. After the Battle of the Bulge, Earley and her unit faced the daunting task of sorting and delivering a backlog of mail that filled three airplane hangars. In spite of the race and gender discrimination that she and the other women in her battalion faced, they broke all records for redirecting military mail at the height of war.

After leaving the army in 1946, Early completed an M.A. in vocational psychology at the Ohio State University and held positions at the Veterans Administration in Cleveland, Tennessee A&I University, and Georgia State College (now Savannah State College). In 1949, after her marriage to Stanley A. Earley Jr., a medical student at the University of Zurich, she moved to Switzerland. Upon gaining proficiency in German, she took courses at the University of Zurich and the C. J. Jungian Institut Zürich.

After leaving Switzerland and settling in Dayton, Earley turned her attention to community service, participating on many committees, task forces, and corporate boards related to education, business, and community leadership. This included serving on the boards of Sinclair Community College, the Dayton Metropolitan Housing Authority, the Dayton Power and Light Company, and on the American Red Cross National Board of Governors.

Earley received numerous awards for both military and community service, including induction into the Ohio Veterans Hall of Fame in 1993; recognition in a special program in her honor, by the National Postal Museum in 1996, and the awarding of honorary degrees from Wilberforce University and the University of Dayton. In 1989, she published her autobiography, *One Woman's Army: A Black Officer Remembers the WAC.* Earley died in Dayton on January 13, 2002.

OHIO
WOMEN'S
HALL OF
FAME

Kathleen V. HARRISON

1959–

FRANKLIN COUNTY

KATHLEEN V. HARRISON, one of the most decorated women in the Marine Corps, was born in Reynoldsburg, Ohio, on February 13, 1959. She received a B.A. in Spanish from Miami University of Ohio in 1981. In 1994, she completed the postgraduate intelligence program at the Joint Military Intelligence College in Washington, D.C., where later she earned an M.S. in strategic intelligence in 1999.

Harrison joined the U.S. Marine Corps in 1981 and has served in a variety of tactical and operational intelligence positions in the fleet Marine forces, unified combatant commands, and the joint staff. As the intelligence officer for Marine Aircraft Group (MAG) 70, she was the first woman to serve in an operational aviation unit eligible for combat deployment. In 1986, she was selected as the administrative assistant to the director of intelligence, headquarters Marine Corps. Fluent in both Spanish and German, she served concurrently as a Marine Corps foreign liaison officer. She participated in, and was the first female marine to receive a combat fitness report for, Operation Just Cause, the invasion of Panama in 1989. She has been deployed as the National Intelligence Support Team (NIST) detachment commander for Operation Provide Comfort, the Kurdish humanitarian relief operations in Iraq and Turkey, as deputy intelligence officer for Operation Provide Promise, and the NIST detachment commander in Italy, Croatia, and Macedonia. She served as the senior intelligence officer for the Guantanamo Bay Naval Base, the ground defense security force and Operation Sea Signal, the Cuban migration. She was also the branch head for command and command support for the Doctrine Division at Quantico, Virginia.

Harrison has received countless decorations and awards for the excellence of her military service, and in 1996 she was an Olympic torchbearer in the 15,000 mile Olympic relay from Los Angeles to Atlanta.

135

Sharon LANE

1943–1969

STARK COUNTY

Courtesy of Richard L. McElroy, Psalm 139

Sharon Lane, born in Zanesville, Ohio, on July 7, 1943, moved with her family to Canton, Ohio, and graduated from Canton South High School in 1961. She then enrolled in the Aultman Hospital School of Nursing from which she graduated in April 1965. After working three years as a nurse, Lane joined the U.S. Army Nurse Corps, where she received six weeks officer training at Fort Sam Houston, Texas, and was commissioned as a first lieutenant. She was stationed first at Fitzsimmons General Hospital in Denver, Colorado, where she could have easily remained, but volunteered instead for service in Vietnam. On April 24, 1969, she arrived in South Vietnam to serve at the 312th Evacuation Hospital at Chu Lai.

At Chu Lai, Lane cared for wounded and dying soldiers and civilians, taking great satisfaction in her work, despite the danger and suffering that surrounded her. She worked long, grueling hours but still found time to befriend Vietnamese children. Those around her, including the Vietnamese people, appreciated her dedication, tenderness, and concern. They considered her a devoted and courageous person who was steadfast in ministering to others in times of war.

On June 8, 1969, at 5:55 A.M., an enemy rocket killed Lane while she was on duty in the hospital. A child was also killed, and twenty-five other Vietnamese and Americans were wounded. Of the more than fifty-eight thousand Americans killed in Vietnam, only eight were women, and Lane was the only U.S. Army nurse to be killed by enemy fire. Posthumously, Lane was awarded the Bronze Star, the Purple Heart, and the Vietnamese Gallantry Cross, all for valor and bravery under fire.

Lane was buried with full military honors in Canton, Ohio. In 1973, a statue was dedicated to her memory at the Aultman Health Foundation. In 1986, the Stark County Vietnam Veterans of America Chapter 199 renamed the chapter the Sharon A. Lane Memorial Chapter 199 in honor of her sacrifice and is dedicated to performing community service on her behalf. Several hospitals throughout the country have named buildings or sections of hospitals for her, and in March 2001, the Sharon Ann Lane Clinic was dedicated in Chu Lai, Vietnam. Lane was inducted in the Ohio Veterans Hall of Fame in 1995.

Marie Barrett Marsh

1919–1997

TRUMBULL COUNTY

Marie Barrett Marsh was born on December 3, 1919, in Youngstown, Ohio. Marsh entered Youngstown College in 1937, where she was named the first homecoming queen. In 1940, she also began taking flying lessons through the civilian pilot training program that was offered on campus, becoming one of only six women in the nation to complete the advanced training program. After graduation in 1941, Marsh taught school for one year in Mecca, Ohio, and was secretary to the superintendent of schools at Youngstown for one year. In 1943, however, she was accepted in the Army Air Force Pilot Training Program and became one of only 1,074 women—out of an original 25,000 applicants—who completed the program. Marsh was assigned as a Women Airforce Service Pilot (WASP) to the headquarters of the Weather Wing in Asheville, North Carolina. She flew all sorts of planes and served as a Pentagon liaison for her base, flying personnel of the Weather Wing to bases located across the United States. Women pilots, like Marsh, who flew military planes on routine missions, helped to make it possible for male pilots to be more freely assigned in combat zones, an area that was not open to women.

After the war, Marsh returned to Warren, Ohio, married her college sweetheart, John Marsh, and concentrated on her family. She was a role model for her own eight children and for others, and continued to offer plane rides to local people. In 1962, she became a night school teacher, teaching shorthand and typing at Warren G. Harding High School and on the Warren campus of Kent State University. For the next twenty-one years, she helped women and men who were returning to school to better their opportunities and improve their job status.

In 1999, Youngstown State University named an alumni award in her honor, the Marie B. Barrett Marsh Half Century Club Award. It is presented annually to an alum who graduated more than fifty years before and who has consistently demonstrated support of the University through leadership and public service. Marsh died on April 29, 1997.

Military Service

Helen Grace McCLELLAND
1887–1984

KNOX COUNTY

HELEN GRACE McCLELLAND was born in Austinburg, Ohio, in 1887, and moved with her family to a Knox County farm, near Fredericktown, in 1897. McClelland had early ambitions to be a doctor, but was dissuaded from pursuing what was perceived to be a male profession. In 1908, she entered the Pennsylvania Hospital School of Nursing, graduating in 1912. After graduation, she accepted a position as head nurse in Weiser, Idaho, on the Snake River. In 1913, she moved to the Norfolk Protestant Hospital in Virginia before volunteering with the American Ambulance Service in 1915 to serve in France. She returned home in 1916 to work in the hospitals of Norfolk before joining the Army Nurse Corps and returning in 1917 to serve for two years during World War I as a member of an American surgical team to British Casualty Clearing Station 61 near the Convent of St. Sixte in Belgium.

Close to the front line in France, McClelland experienced bombings first hand. Teams were sent forward to the front for forty-eight hours at a time, but there were occasions when two days were stretched to several. The work was long and hard. While on an extended tour, McClelland's base was bombed. Her tentmate, Beatrice Mary MacDonald, was wounded, making her the first nurse to be wounded in WWI; the camp suffered heavy casualties. McClelland rendered aid to the wounded and dying amid enemy fire. For this bravery, she was awarded the Distinguished Service Cross, the nation's second-highest combat award, becoming one of only three women ever to receive it. She was also cited by British field marshal Sir Douglas Haig for "gallant and distinguished service in the field." She also received from England the Royal Red Cross, First Class for meritorious service.

After the war, McClelland returned eventually to the Pennsylvania Hospital as a staff nurse, where she was named director of the nursing department in 1933, a position she held until her retirement in 1956. McClelland shepherded many innovations during her tenure, including the implementation of shorter work days, ongoing professional development for faculty and nurses, and changes in the curriculum. Under her leadership the program received national accreditation.

In 1995, McClelland was inducted posthumously into the Ohio Veterans Hall of Fame.

138

OHIO
WOMEN'S
HALL OF
FAME

Betty ZANE

C. 1759–C. 1828

BELMONT COUNTY

Elizabeth "Betty" Zane, born in Moorefield, Virginia, circa 1759, was the granddaughter of Robert Zane, a prominent member of the first wave of immigrants from Dublin, Ireland. She was raised by her Uncle Isaac in Philadelphia, where she attended school. At the age of thirteen, Zane demonstrated the highly independent and fearless spirit that would make her a heroine twice over during the transformation of the American colonies into a powerful nation.

During the Revolutionary War, Zane was awakened in her uncle's home by the sound of horses ridden by British soldiers. While the men were being fed by her uncle and his wife Sarah, Betty quietly stole all forty horses and trotted them to General George Washington who was camped nearby. After this incident, the Zane family was closely watched. Fearing for Betty's safety, her aunt and uncle sent her to live with her brothers Ebenezer, Jonathan, and Silas, all prominent leaders at Fort Henry, located within the city limits of present-day Wheeling, West Virginia.

Her second opportunity for military heroism came in 1782, when Fort Henry was attacked by a combination of British soldiers and Indians, in what is now considered the last battle of the American Revolution. When the ammunition of the fort was exhausted, the athletic and fearless Zane convinced her brother Silas, the commander of the fort, to permit her to run the forty yards to her brother Ebenezer's house for a new supply of powder. Amid gun fire, Zane ran the distance and returned carrying

a keg of powder that had been dumped into a tablecloth and tied around her waist.

In her lifetime, Zane received no medals or awards for her courage. She went on with her life, married twice, and raised a large family. She lived on the Ohio side of Wheeling during her first marriage and later on a farm near Martins Ferry, Ohio, where she died around 1828. Her story was immortalized by the great-grandson of Ebenezer Zane, Zane Grey, in his book *Betty Zane*. A statue memorializing her heroic run was dedicated at her gravesite on May 30, 1928.

Military Service

MUSIC

WOMEN IN OHIO HAVE BEEN AMONG THE MOST noteworthy contributors to the world of music. They have demonstrated excellence in performance and creativity across many areas of music, including classical, jazz, folk, and popular. These women have lifted our spirits and inspired us on many levels. We celebrate them locally, but they are admired for their talents across the nation and indeed around the world. Adding to such stellar accomplishments in this field have been women who have been staunch patrons, making sure that music can be a daily part of community life, and others who have helped to document and preserve the richness of what humans can do through sound. We applaud the collective contributions of these talented and dedicated women.

KATHLEEN BATTLE

TRACY CHAPMAN

GEORGIA GRIFFITH

ADELLA PRENTISS HUGHES

EUSEBIA SIMPSON HUNKINS

NANCY WILSON

Kathleen BATTLE

1948−

SCIOTO COUNTY

Courtesy of the Columbus Dispatch

KATHLEEN BATTLE, born in Portsmouth, Ohio, on August 13, 1948, studied music education at the University of Cincinnati, earning a B.A. and an M.A. from the College Conservatory of Music. She began her professional career as a music teacher, but her extraordinary lyric soprano voice and her unique artistry destined her for much wider national and international acclaim. Battle made her professional debut at the 1972 Spoleto Festival in Brahms's *Ein deutsches Requiem* under the baton of Thomas Schippers. Five years later, she debuted at the Metropolitan Opera in Wagner's *Tannhäuser*. Since then, she has been awarded several honorary doctoral degrees, including one from her alma mater. In 1999, she was inducted into the Image Hall of Fame of the NAACP.

Battle has captivated audiences around the world, appearing on the stages of leading opera houses, including the Royal Opera House and Covent Garden, as well as the opera houses of Vienna, Paris, San Francisco, Chicago, and New York. She has performed with the world's greatest orchestras, including the New York Philharmonic, Chicago Symphony Orchestra, Boston Symphony Orchestra, Philadelphia Orchestra, Los Angeles Philharmonic, Berlin Philharmonic, Vienna Philharmonic, and Orchestre de Paris. She has appeared at the most prestigious festivals: Salzburg, Ravinia, Tanglewood, Blossom, the Hollywood Bowl, the Mann Music Centre, and Caramoor. Her repertoire ranges from jazz and spirituals to an uncommonly wide spectrum of classical music. She has enjoyed collaborations with Grover Washington Jr., Cyrus Chestnut, Christian McBride, James Carter, and Wynton Marsalis; Jessye Norman, Luciano Pavarotti, Plácido Domingo, Itzhak Perlman, Jean-Pierre Rampal, Christopher Parkening, James Levine, and André Previn. She has made many recordings and television appearances, and she has shared her voice and artistry with millions around the world.

In addition to many other accolades, Battle received in 1991 an Emmy Award for Outstanding Individual Achievement in a Classical Program on Television in the USA, and she has also received five Grammy Awards, three as Best Classical Vocal Soloist. Her memorable concerts, prolific recordings, and frequent tours that demonstrate her lasting audience appeal are evidence that Battle is one of the most acclaimed vocalists of our times.

143

Music

Tracy CHAPMAN

1964–

CUYAHOGA COUNTY

TRACY CHAPMAN was born in Cleveland, Ohio, on March 30, 1964. In 1986, she received a B.A. in anthropology and African studies from Tufts University. Always interested in music, Chapman started playing the guitar and writing poetry, prose, and songs as an adolescent. While in college she began playing with an African drum ensemble and also performing her own songs in Boston clubs and coffeehouses. In 1986, she made her first recording, "For My Lover," for *Fast Folk Musical Magazine,* a Boston folk magazine that was distributed with a record. In April 1988, her debut album was released by Elektra Records. Within three months, her song "Fast Car" topped the charts in both the United Kingdom and the United States, and Chapman became a household name in popular music.

With songs that have reached platinum and triple platinum levels in sales (the Recording Industry Association of America certified 3 million sales for *New Beginnings*), Chapman has been consistently praised for both lyrics and music. Noted particularly for her feminist insights and political consciousness, she demonstrates an understanding of the social and political conditions that surround contemporary problems and issues, and she demonstrates a personal commitment to such issues by participating frequently in concerts in support of social and political causes such as Amnesty International and AIDS.

Chapman received her first major accolade as a performing artist in 1989 when she was named Favorite New Artist in the Pop/Rock category at the American Music Awards. Chapman went on to receive numerous other prestigious awards, including Best International Newcomer at the BRIT Awards (1989); four Grammy Awards; and four Bay Area Music Awards (1997). Chapman has appeared often on television programs and has performed around the world as a solo artist and with other famous musicians, including B. B. King, Bruce Springsteen, and Luciano Pavarotti. She performed at the White House in 1998. The high school essay contest Crossroads in Black History, which she established in 1990, is evidence of Chapman's compassion for others.

144

OHIO
WOMEN'S
HALL OF
FAME

Profiles of Two Hundred Ohio Women

Georgia GRIFFITH

1931–

FAIRFIELD COUNTY

GEORGIA GRIFFITH, born on November 12, 1931, in Lancaster, Ohio, was the first blind person to attend Capital University, graduating with highest honors in music education in 1954. She began her career teaching private music lessons to sighted students and managing a resource room for students with disabilities at a local school, where she continued for sixteen years until hearing loss and a simultaneous loss of balance (which affected her ability to walk) made teaching music impossible. In 1970, therefore, Griffith shifted her attention to earning a Braille Literacy Proofreading Certificate in music from the Library of Congress, which she received the following year. With this certification, she proofread more than two thousand pages of Braille-notated music each year until cutbacks in federal funding curtailed the volume of Braille work being done by the Library of Congress. This work made Griffith the preeminent authority in the United States on Braille music, and in 1974 Capital University presented Griffith with the Distinguished Alumni Award and Chair.

In order to help a sighted and hearing friend do research, Griffith taught herself nine foreign languages so that she could participate fully in the project. Acquiring her own computer in 1981, she began using a VersaBraille System, which translates computer text into Braille, to volunteer with the National Braille Association as a proofreader for all of Beethoven's symphonies. When she had finished, the symphonies covered four thousand Braille pages of painstaking work. In 1987, when friends in Lancaster and Columbus celebrated this feat by giving Griffith a printer that would make such work easier, President Ronald Reagan added his message of congratulations for the event.

145

With enhanced technological capacity, Griffith began accessing the world through CompuServe and soon became the systems operator of the National Issues Forum and the Handicapped Users Database on CompuServe. She was hired as the Information Specialist for the Center for Special Education Technology to monitor electronic networks for information about new technologies for individuals with disabilities and provide information and support for families about appropriate uses of the technology. Today, Griffith manages five information services on the CompuServe network as a home business.

OHIO WOMEN'S HALL OF FAME

Adella Prentiss HUGHES

1869–1950

CUYAHOGA COUNTY

Adella Prentiss Hughes combines the artistic perceptiveness of a musician with the efficiency of a locomotive.

—*Fortune Magazine*, 1931

BORN IN CLEVELAND, OHIO, on November 29, 1869, Adella Prentiss Hughes attended Miss Fisher's School for Girls (later Hathaway Brown) and Vassar College, where she both performed in and arranged tours for the college glee club and banjo group. After graduating Phi Beta Kappa in 1890, touring Europe, and studying piano in Berlin, Hughes returned to Cleveland. She began performing as an accompanist, and she also began organizing concerts. Working first through the Fortnightly Musical Club and then on her own, she established the Symphony Orchestra Concerts series in 1901 and brought to Cleveland's Grays Armory many notable ensembles and conductors. She also organized smaller concerts, recitals, and lectures in several other venues around the city and began demonstrating her expertise in arts management, a career in which she would excel over the next four decades.

The success of Hughes's concerts was based on a financing schema in which she secured investors for an event and reimbursed them from the proceeds of the concert. With this model of fundraising, Hughes founded the Musical Arts Association in 1915 (which still exists today as the Cleveland Orchestra's parent organization). Three years later, in 1918, she was instrumental in founding the Cleveland Orchestra and became its first general manager. Under her leadership, the orchestra grew to national prominence, made its first recordings, embarked on its first tours, made its first radio broadcasts, became a pioneer in educational work, and built its own concert hall (Severance Hall). At the second anniversary of the orchestra, Hughes was greeted as the "Mother of the Cleveland Orchestra," a title she retained throughout her career.

Hughes is recognized for the tremendous impact she had on the cultural life of the city. Her honors include being one of only four women whose portrait hangs in Cleveland City Hall's Hall of Fame; being named during Cleveland's Bicentennial in 1996 as one of the city's ten greatest leaders; and being honored by the Fortnightly Musical Club by a scholarship given in her name.

146

Eusebia Simpson HUNKINS

ATHENS COUNTY

Eusebia Simpson Hunkins was born in Troy, Ohio, on June 20, 1902. She studied piano and music theory in Dayton until she received a fellowship to the Juilliard School in New York. During her studies at Juilliard, she traveled as a Juilliard Foundation representative to Cornell College in Mount Vernon, Iowa, where she taught piano and composition. Later, she also studied composition at the Aspen Music Festival, at Tanglewood, and in Salzburg, Austria.

In 1931, she married Maurel Hunkins, who had been the assistant conductor of the Chautauqua Symphony and Opera when she performed with the orchestra as a piano soloist. The couple lived in New York City, where Hunkins composed and taught music and conducted choral groups, while her husband served as director of student activities at New York University. In 1946, they moved to Athens, Ohio, when Maurel Hunkins was appointed Dean of Students of Ohio University. There, Hunkins began conducting research on Appalachian folk music, which inspired her to compose folk and children's operas, including *Spirit Owl, The End of the Rainbow,* her major operatic work *What Have You Done to My Mountain?,* and *Smoky Mountain,* which has been published and performed more than four thousand times.

Hunkins's other works include compositions for violin, cello, flute, string quartet, orchestra, band, liturgical drama, and ballet. She was active in the National Opera Association, cofounder of the Opera for Youth Project, founder and past president of the Hocking Valley Arts Council, and member of the National Federation of Music. In 1976, Hunkins directed the Federation's participation in the celebration of the United States Bicentennial in Washington, D.C. She died on September 9, 1980.

Courtesy of Nancy J. Hunkins

147

Music

Nancy Wilson

1937⁻

ROSS COUNTY

NANCY WILSON was born on February 20, 1937, in Chillicothe, Ohio, but grew up in Columbus, where she attended West High School. At the age of fifteen, while a student at West, she was chosen to represent the school in a talent contest sponsored by local television station WTVN. She won. The prize was an appearance on a twice-a-week television show, *Skyline Melodies,* which she ended up hosting. She also performed regularly with Rusty Bryant's Carolyn Club band and sat in whenever possible with other touring artists, including jazz saxophonist Julian "Cannonball" Adderley. Graduating in 1954, Wilson attended Central State University but continued to perform. In 1956, she left college to tour the Midwest and Canada for two years with the Rusty Bryant band. In 1959, she left the band to pursue a career as a jazz vocalist in New York. After a short time, she signed with Cannonball Adderley's manager, John Levy, who secured for her a contract with Capitol Records, thus setting the stage for the rest of her remarkable career as an internationally renowned song stylist.

Wilson recorded her first hit, "Save Your Love for Me," with Adderley in 1962; was named the top female vocalist by *Downbeat* and *Playboy* magazines in 1963; and won her first Grammy in 1964 for "How Glad I Am." Wilson has appeared on television countless times, including hosting *The Nancy Wilson Show,* a variety show on the NBC network during the 1967–68 season, for which she won an Emmy Award. She has appeared periodically on other television shows, such as *I Spy, Room 222, Hawaii Five-O, Police Story, The Cosby Show, New York Undercover,* and, most recently, *Moesha* and *The Parkers.* In addition, she has hosted the National Public Radio program *Jazz Profiles* since its debut in 1996.

Over her career, Wilson has made more than sixty albums, more than half of which have appeared on the Billboard charts, leaving a legacy of high-quality listening pleasure for generations to come. In 1991, she was presented with her own star on the Hollywood Walk of Fame.

Courtesy of the Columbus Dispatch

Profiles of Two Hundred Ohio Women

PUBLIC SERVICE

DISTINCTIVE AMONG THE WOMEN WHO ARE
chronicled in this volume are those who have held elective office and
been responsible for the oversight of government at all levels. It is quite
remarkable that, despite discrimination and male dominance in public
service, women have filled such a surprising array of roles. On the local
levels, they have won positions on school boards, city councils, and
county commissions. On the state level, they have been active as members and leaders of the state legislature. On the national level, they
have served in the United States Congress. In order to excel in this male-
dominated world, they have had to be tenacious, but they have also
had to be highly competent, professional, and responsive to their constituencies. The evidence of their success is in both the quality of their
achievements and the length of their service as documented, for example, in the profiles that follow.

FRANCES PAYNE (BINGHAM) BOLTON

MARY O. BOYLE

ELLEN WALKER CRAIG-JONES

JO ANN DAVIDSON

GERTRUDE W. DONAHEY

NANCY P. HOLLISTER

BETTY D. MONTGOMERY

HELEN RANKIN

MARIAN REGELIA ALEXANDER SPENCER

ETHEL G. SWANBECK

CLARA E. WEISENBORN

Frances Payne
(Bingham) BOLTON

1885–1977

CUYAHOGA COUNTY

Courtesy of the Payne Fund

Frances Payne (Bingham) Bolton was born in Cleveland, Ohio, on March 29, 1885, to a wealthy family. She was educated in private schools in Cleveland, New York, and France. In 1907, she married Charles C. Bolton and began a life of active philanthropy in a socially prominent family. On February 27, 1940, she was elected as a Republican to the Seventy-sixth Congress by special election to fill the vacancy caused by the death of her husband. She thus became one of four members of her family to serve in Congress, including her husband, her grandfather (Senator Henry B. Payne), and her son (Congressman Oliver Bolton), with whom she served simultaneously at one point. More striking for her day, however, Bolton became the first woman from Ohio to fill this role. Serving from 1940 to January 3, 1969, she was reelected fourteen times, becoming one of the longest-serving women in this male-dominated legislative body.

In Congress, Bolton proposed sixty-one bills, dealing mainly with social services, public health, education, and industrial issues, many of which were related to women and children. For example, in 1943, she authored the Bolton Act, which established the U.S. Cadet Nursing Corps, an indication of her long-standing interest in the field of nursing. In addition, she was the first woman to head a congressional mission abroad (1947), the first appointed as congressional delegate to the United Nations General Assembly (1953), and the first to attend a meeting of congressional leaders at the White House (with President Eisenhower).

After leaving Congress, Bolton continued her philanthropic and volunteer work with many organizations. She was appointed to the Board of Governors of the Middle East Institute and served as a trustee of Lakeside Hospital, the School of Advanced International Studies, Lake Erie College, Tuskegee Institute, the U.S. Capitol Historical Society, and Central School of Practical Nursing in Cleveland. She received several honorary degrees and awards, including the Human Relations Award from the National Coalition of Christians and Jews (1976). Among her other honors, she was named Churchwoman of the Year by the Religious Newswriters Association (1954), and the school of nursing at Case Western Reserve University was named for her.

151

Public Service

Mary O. BOYLE

1941–

CUYAHOGA COUNTY

M ARY O. BOYLE, a lifelong resident of Cleveland, Ohio, was born on December 23, 1941. In 1962, she received a B.S. from St. Mary's College, Notre Dame, and in 1995 completed the Harvard University program for senior executives in state and local government at the John F. Kennedy School of Government. In 1978, Boyle was the first woman to be elected to the Ohio House of Representatives to represent Cleveland Heights. She was named "Rookie of the Year" in her first term and majority whip in her third. In 1984, Boyle was elected Cuyahoga County's first woman county commissioner (representing 1.4 million people in a county larger than ten states with a budget exceeding that of fifteen states); she served three terms as the commission's president. In 1994, Boyle sought the Democratic nomination for the United States Senate and in 1998 became the first woman in Ohio history to be nominated to seek this office. Although both campaigns were unsuccessful, Boyle clearly established herself as a highly respected political leader.

In the Ohio legislature, Boyle authored many initiatives, including Ohio's first Conservation Easement Law, permanent homes for abused and neglected children, and the Joint Custody Law. On the Cuyahoga County Board of County Commissioners, she initiated a strong new community planning process; upgraded financial capacity; reorganized and reformed the county's human services operations; and established, coordinated, and expanded services for seniors and children. As president of the county commissioners, she formed a partnership between the County Department of Human Services and Cleveland State University and established the Push to Achievement Program to assist students in earning a degree while sustaining their families. In addition, in 1995 and 2000, Boyle accompanied President Clinton on his historic peace missions to Northern Ireland, and she has served as a member of the boards of Hard Hatted Women, Starting Point, Children's Support Rights, and the Jewish Family Services' advisory group on divorce mediation.

Boyle's honors and awards are many. To mention only three, she was named Public Servant of the Year by the Greater Cleveland and Ohio Nurses Association and Public Official of the Year by the local and state chapters of the National Association of Social Workers, and she received Cleveland State University's Distinguished Public Service Award.

OHIO
WOMEN'S
HALL OF
FAME

Ellen Walker CRAIG-JONES

1906–2000

FRANKLIN COUNTY

Ms. Craig is a treasure. She personifies what it means to be at peace with one's self. Her quality of life is from within, but it is reinforced by serving others. Her effervescent spirit is truly contagious.

—Grayce Williams, 1994

ELLEN WALKER CRAIG-JONES was born in Franklin County on June 5, 1906. She spent her life as a social activist deeply involved in community development and pursuing ways to provide opportunities for children and youth, as illustrated by her work with Buckeye Boys Ranch. In 1972, at the age of sixty-six, she was elected mayor of Urbancrest, Ohio, and became the first African American woman to be elected to such a position in Ohio. She served as mayor until 1975, overseeing the modernization of various village programs and the annexation of sixty acres of land. Prior to her tenure as mayor, she had served twelve years (1960–72) on the Urbancrest Village Council, including ten years as chairman of the Service Finance Committee. Throughout these years of service, Craig-Jones was a passionate advocate for her community, leading, for example, a community-wide effort to establish a child-care facility and securing services for senior citizens, whom she called "seasoned citizens."

Craig-Jones was the cofounder of the Urbancrest Volunteer Civic Improvement Association, the Urbancrest Chapter of the Blue Star Mothers of America, and the Urbancrest Community Recreation Club, serving as its first president. She was on the advisory board of the Urbancrest Youth Council and a member of the board of trustees of the Mid-Ohio Regional Planning Commission. She held memberships in several community organizations, including the Union Baptist Church, to which she devoted fifty years of active service.

153

Craig-Jones received more than eighty honors and awards, including proclamations from the City of Columbus and keys to the cities of Cleveland, Cincinnati, and Springfield.

Public Service

OHIO
WOMEN'S
HALL OF
FAME

Jo Ann DAVIDSON

1927-

FRANKLIN COUNTY

Jo Ann Davidson was born on September 28, 1927, in Findlay, Ohio, but moved to Reynoldsburg as an adult and raised her family there. Always active in community organizations, such as the PTA, the Girl Scouts, and her church, she also had an interest in politics. In 1965, after an unsuccessful bid for city council, she was instrumental in forming the Reynoldsburg Republican Women's Club. Her involvement with the Republican Party went well beyond Reynoldsburg, however, to both the Franklin County Republican Central Committee, which she chaired for several years, and the national arena, in which she served as a delegate to several Republican national conventions and as a member of the 1976 platform committee.

In 1967, Davidson ran again for Reynoldsburg City Council and won. In 1978, after ten years of service in this position, she was elected clerk of Truro Township. In 1980, she was elected to the Ohio House of Representatives, where she served the maximum ten terms and provided leadership for many important legislative initiatives, including welfare reform, electric deregulation, and criminal justice reform, and in 1995 she became the first woman Speaker of the Ohio House, a position she held until January 2001. Amid the responsibilities of elected office, Davidson also continued to be active in community organizations, serving as Vice-President of Special Programs for the Ohio Chamber of Commerce and volunteering with the March of Dimes, American Heart Association, Reynoldsburg PTA, and Girl Scouts of America.

Davidson also serves on the boards of the University of Findlay, Franklin University, and the Ohio State University. She holds honorary degrees from each of these institutions, and she has received several other honors and awards, including the National Republican Legislators Association's Legislator of the Year award (1991); YWCA Woman of Achievement Award (1992); and *Governing* magazine's Public Official of the Year Award (1999).

154

Gertrude W. DONAHEY

1908-

FRANKLIN COUNTY

Courtesy of Gertrude W. Donahey

GERTRUDE W. DONAHEY was born on August 4, 1908, in Tuscarawas County. Graduating from Mann's Business College in Columbus, she worked in the Business and Finance Division of the Office of Ohio Adjutant General. During these years, Donahey also served as the Democratic National Committee operation support chairman for Ohio (1963–69); a delegate to two national conventions (1964 and 1968); Ohio representative on the national platform and resolution committee; and state central committeewoman from her congressional district. From 1964 until 1970, she was executive assistant in Ohio for U.S. Senator Stephen M. Young. In 1970, with the support of the Federated Democratic Women of Ohio, Donahey was elected treasurer of the state of Ohio, which made her the first woman in Ohio to be elected to a statewide administrative office.

Donahey served as state treasurer from 1971 to 1983, demonstrating that she was one of the leading vote-getting Democrats for over a decade in a state dominated by Republicans. As treasurer, she was chairman of the State Board of Deposit, treasurer of the Commissioners of the Sinking Fund, and treasurer of the Public Facilities Commission. In 1981, she was elected president of the National Association of State Auditors, Comptrollers, and Treasurers. Throughout her service in these public roles, Donahey built a distinctive reputation for her administrative expertise and management skills.

Donahey has received many honors and awards, including an honorary degree from Rio Grande College in Rio Grande, Ohio, and an award was created in her honor by the Ohio Democratic Party. She was named one of Ohio's five outstanding women in 1976 by the Ohio Extension Homemakers, inducted into the Ohio Senior Citizens Hall of Fame (1979), and awarded the Zeisberger Heckewelder Medallion by the Tuscarawas County Historical Society (1984).

155

Public Service

Nancy P. HOLLISTER

1949–

WASHINGTON COUNTY

N ANCY P. HOLLISTER, born on May 22, 1949, in Marietta, Ohio, made history in Ohio when she became the first woman elected lieutenant governor of the state in 1994. In 1998, she made history again when, with the resignation of George Voinovich from office on December 28, 1998, to prepare for his new role as senator, she served as acting governor for eleven days and became the first woman to lead the state.

Having attended Kent State University, Hollister settled into family life in her hometown of Marietta, became active in community life, and was soon elected to public office as a member of the Marietta City Council (1980–84). In 1984, she was elected mayor, serving until 1991. As mayor, she strengthened ties between community leaders and business and industry, encouraged tourism, expanded city services, and was instrumental in creating a joint Ohio/West Virginia labor-management council that secured funding for a new multimillion-dollar Ohio River bridge. In 1991, she was appointed director of the Governor's Office of Appalachia, where she managed economic development, funding, and policy issues for twenty-nine southeastern rural counties. In 1994, she was elected lieutenant governor. In this position, Hollister chaired the State and Local Government Commission and the Governor's Workforce Development Board, cochaired the Ohio Farmland Preservation Task Force, and served as the governor's director of the cabinet. She oversaw the Ohio Bureau of Employment Services, the Ohio Department of Agriculture, the Governor's Office of Appalachia, the Ohio Coal Development Office, the Office of Housing and Community Partnership, and the Ohio School-to-Work Initiative. She was also the chief architect of Jobs Bill III, an economic stimulus package for both urban and rural communities that was the first of its kind in Ohio history. In 2002, Hollister was elected to her third term in the Ohio House of Representatives, where she has served on the Public Utilities and the Retirement and Aging Committees, and is the chair of the Energy and Environment Committee.

Hollister has received several awards for her achievements, including the 1995 Bernard P. McDonough Award for Excellence in Leadership, the 1996 Ohio Federation of Business and Professional Women's Award for Government, the 1997 Ohio Proud Award for Outstanding Service, and the 1997 Ohio Rural Development Partnership Distinguished Public Service Award.

OHIO
WOMEN'S
HALL OF
FAME

Betty D. MONTGOMERY

1948–

WOOD COUNTY

Betty D. Montgomery, born on April 3, 1948, in Fremont, Ohio, received a B.A. in English and Art from Bowling Green State University (1970) and a J.D. from the University of Toledo College of Law (1976). She began her career in law and public service as a criminal clerk for the Lucas County Common Pleas Court. In 1976, she became the assistant prosecuting attorney in Wood County; in 1978, the prosecuting attorney in the City of Perrysburg; in 1981, prosecuting attorney of Wood County; and in 1988, she was elected to the Ohio State Senate, where she served as chair of the Senate Criminal Justice Subcommittee, the Correctional Institution Inspection Committee, and the Lucasville Legislative Committee, and as vice-chair of the Senate Judiciary Committee and the Ohio Criminal Sentencing Commission. In the senate, she sponsored legislation that created the Lake Erie license plate, which has raised more than $1.5 million for the Lake Erie Protection Fund; drafted legislation that now serves as model environmental legislation for the country; and drafted Ohio's first living will law and Victim's Rights Law. These achievements established Montgomery as a public servant who is dedicated to developing crime-fighting resources and protecting the citizens of Ohio.

In 1990, Montgomery became the first woman to be elected attorney general of Ohio. She reorganized the Bureau of Criminal Identification and Investigation and increased state support for local law enforcement in order to upgrade crime-fighting resources. She also drafted a series of crime bills that include tougher penalties, actual time sentencing, and the establishment of a DNA laboratory and database, and her national award-winning Consumer Protection section processes a record number of complaints on behalf of consumers and prosecutes consumer fraud cases with record success. In 2002, Montgomery was elected auditor of the state.

Montgomery has received many honors and awards, including Best Brief Award six consecutive years for briefs filed with the U.S. Supreme Court by the National Association for Attorney General; the Ohio State Bar Association's Distinguished Service Award; and the United Conservatives of Ohio's Watchdog of the Treasury Award.

157

Public Service

Helen RANKIN

1936–

HAMILTON COUNTY

HELEN RANKIN, born on September 12, 1936, in Cincinnati, Ohio, was appointed to the Ohio House of Representatives in 1978 to serve in place of her late husband, James W. Rankin. That year, she sought election to the seat and won, subsequently serving eight elected terms, from 1978 to 1994, and becoming the first and longest-serving African American woman in the Ohio General Assembly.

During her tenure in the General Assembly, Rankin dedicated herself to ensuring support for humanitarian initiatives. She was on several committees, including Aging and Housing, Education, Colleges and Universities, Finance and Appropriations, Human Resources, Elections, Highways and Highway Safety, Transportation and Urban Affairs, Children and Youth, and Reference, and she was an advocate for funding education; health care issues, including mental health; mental retardation and disability issues; and support for first-time homebuyers. One example of her advocacy was her introduction of a bill to provide benefits for mammography and cytologic screenings for women over forty.

Rankin has also been active in the Hamilton County Women's Democratic Club, the National Council of State Legislators on the Committee on Human Resources, the Board of the Planned Parenthood Association of Cincinnati, the Community Action Agency, and the Ohio Job Training Coordinating Council. For both her community and political work, Rankin has received many honors, most notably the Recognition Award from the Ohio Primary Care Association, Legislator of the Year from the National Association of Social Workers, the Outstanding Achievement Award from the Black Student Community of Capital University, and Outstanding Woman of the Year from the Harriet Tubman Black Women's Democratic Club. She also received a tribute from Alpha Phi Alpha Fraternity and was named an Honorary Buckeye Colonel.

Courtesy of The Ohioana Library Association

158

Profiles of Two Hundred Ohio Women

Marian Regelia Alexander
SPENCER

1920–

GALLIA COUNTY

Courtesy of Marian Alexander Spencer

MARIAN REGELIA ALEXANDER SPENCER and her twin sister Mildred Luvinia were born in Gallipolis, Ohio, on June 28, 1920, and graduated as co-valedictorians of Gallia Academy High School in 1938. Spencer enrolled at the University of Cincinnati and graduated in 1942, despite the barriers she faced as an African American who was not permitted to live on campus, attend certain social events, or be accepted in certain college programs such as medicine or music. These experiences, however, only enhanced her commitment to justice, equality, and civil rights, as did an incident at Coney Island on July 4, 1952. Spencer, with the help of the local and national NAACP, organized a group of African American and white citizens to present themselves at the park entrance. The whites were admitted; the African Americans were refused. The subsequent charges against Coney Island management challenged the policies and succeeded in desegregating the park.

Spencer served as president of Links, Women's City Club, Fellowship House, the Cincinnati Chapter of the NAACP, and the West End Branch of the YWCA and as vice-president of the Metropolitan Branch. She was the chairperson of the U.S. Civil Rights Commission Ohio Advisory Committee in 1980. She has served on the board of directors of the University of Cincinnati, the Opportunity Industrialization Center, the Mayor's Friendly Relations Committee, Hoxworth Blood Center, Alpha Kappa Alpha Sorority, Housing Opportunities Made Equal, Planned Parenthood, Caracole House (an AIDS hospice), Mt. Zion United Methodist Church, and many others.

In 1973, Spencer ran for, but did not win, a seat on the Cincinnati Board of Education on the Citizens School Committee ticket. In 1983, she was the first African American woman elected to Cincinnati City Council. She has been a delegate to two Democratic National Conventions, and in 1988, she cochaired the fair ballot campaign to return proportional representation to city council.

For service both in politics and in the community, Spencer has received numerous awards, including the PUSH Black Excellence Award (1972); the NAACP President's Award for Outstanding Leadership (1980); the YMCA Black Achievers award (1982); the National Association of Social Workers Citizen of the Year (1986); the Urban League's Glorifying the Lions Award (1984); and the Great Living Cincinnatian Award from the Greater Cincinnati Chamber of Commerce (1998).

Public Service

159

OHIO
WOMEN'S
HALL OF
FAME

Ethel G. SWANBECK

1893–1989

HURON COUNTY

Ethel G. Swanbeck, born in 1893, graduated from Case Western Reserve University. She taught in the public schools of Cleveland, Ohio, and at the college level for twenty-seven years. Swanbeck, however, was interested in having a more public role and ran successfully in 1954 for a seat in the Ohio House of Representatives. She served eleven terms, retiring after twenty-two years in 1976 as dean of the Ohio House Republican delegation.

During her time in office, she served as secretary of both the Legislative Service Committee and the Blue Ribbon Committee on Education. She sponsored legislation reforming state commercial fishing laws, fought against lakeshore erosion as a member of the Great Lakes Commission, sought welfare reform as a member of the House Finance Committee's welfare section, and consistently championed educational causes. During these years, Swanbeck also wrote a weekly column for a local newspaper and taped a radio show in Sandusky. Near the end of her service, she took the unusual step of starting flying lessons with the goal, as she stated in 1974, of graduating to "flying grandmother."

Swanbeck was also active in local and state community organizations, including the Ohio State Medical Association, which awarded her its Community Service Award

(1967), and the Ohio Mental Health Association, which named her Woman of the Year in Mental Health (1967). Her other honors include a Civic Service Award from the Fraternal Order of Eagles (1949), a Distinguished Citizen Award from the Huron Chamber of Commerce (1959), the Outstanding Community Service Award from the United States Junior Chamber of Commerce (1965), an honorary degree from Bowling Green State University (1972), and a Distinguished Alumna Award from Case Western Reserve University (1973).

Courtesy of the Ohio Historical Society

160

OHIO
WOMEN'S
HALL OF
FAME

Profiles of Two Hundred Ohio Women

Clara E. WEISENBORN

1907–1985

MONTGOMERY COUNTY

Clara was an achiever of the highest order, one who overcame all of life's obstacles to serve society at all levels. Her exemplary life shines as a model for each of us.

—Ruth Ann Peek, Dayton, Ohio

Courtesy of the Ohio Historical Society

CLARA E. WEISENBORN, born on February 9, 1907, spent her life in Dayton, Ohio. When she was thirteen years old, she had to leave school behind to take care of twelve younger siblings. She went on, however, to overcome challenges and craft a remarkable career as a journalist, political leader, and champion of her community. In later years, Weisenborn became a highly accomplished gardener, writing a column, "Home and Garden," for the *Dayton Journal Herald* for forty-two years. She was a devoted member of her church, teaching Sunday school for fifty-three years. She was a 4-H leader for ten years, and a member of the Vandalia Historical Society.

In 1952, Weisenborn was elected to the Ohio House of Representatives, where she served until 1966. In 1966, she was elected to the Ohio Senate, where she remained until 1974. During her service in the state legislature, Weisenborn was the first woman to chair the Senate Education and Health Committee and the first woman on the Legislative Service Commission. Among the legislation she introduced were initiatives to establish the School of Medicine at Wright State University; control drugs; make wearing eye safety shields mandatory for workers in various shops and chemical laboratories; require licensing for fitting hearing aids; license practical nurses; and preserve historical landmarks in Dayton. Across her years of service, Weisenborn built a reputation as a political leader who understood the importance of working cooperatively with others to address critical community needs.

In addition, Weisenborn was active in many organizations. She served as president of the National Order of Women Legislators. She was active in the Altrusa Club (a business and professional women's group) and served as president of Altrusa International. She served on the board of directors of many organizations, including Barney Children's Medical Center and the Ohio Society for the Prevention of Blindness. In 1970, Hubert Heights named a middle school after her. In 1979, Wright State awarded her an honorary degree and named the Wright State campus gardens in her honor.

161

Public Service

OHIO WOMEN'S HALL OF FAME

RELIGION

WOMEN ARE NOTED FOR THE DEPTHS OF THEIR spiritual commitment. Across the state of Ohio, women from various religious traditions have demonstrated that they are dedicated and steadfast in following the practices embraced by their communities. What is most striking about the women showcased in this section, however, is that they served their communities and their faiths in ways that were not prescribed for women by society in general. Through their religious organizations, these women have founded and run schools, worked as missionaries in dangerous territories, and taken on leadership positions, despite expectations that women should not be so adventurous or so much in the vanguard of social action. Thanks to them, we have not simply a record of special service but models of courage and fine work in the interest of others.

DOROTHY L. KAZEL, O.S.U.

ELIZABETH McMICHAEL POWELL

BENVIN SANSBURY, O.P.

Dorothy L. KAZEL, O.S.U.

1939–1980

CUYAHOGA COUNTY

SISTER DOROTHY L. KAZEL was born on June 30, 1939, in Cleveland, Ohio. In 1960, she entered the Ursuline Sisters of Cleveland, where she worked with marginalized groups, teaching at the beginning of her career business and religion courses at Ursuline Sacred Heart Academy in East Cleveland; catechism to deaf children at St. Philomena Parish; and volunteering at the Martin De Porres Center in Cleveland's Glenville area. In the summer of 1969, Kazel worked with Papago Indian children in Topawa, Arizona, and from 1972 to 1974, she served as a counselor at the Beaumont School for Girls in Cleveland Heights. Her life would be irrevocably changed, however, in 1974, when she became a member of Cleveland's diocesan mission team to El Salvador, where she worked from 1974 to 1980.

In El Salvador, Kazel worked in several parishes, including Chirilagua, La Union, La Libertad, and Zaragoza. She participated in the communities, worked to empower leaders within their own villages, and connected with international programs to help bring much-needed resources to support families. Ultimately, she became entangled in the Salvadoran Civil War. On February 20, 1980, she signed a letter with other missionaries to President Jimmy Carter, stating, "[B]ecause of our own love of liberty and justice for all and the belief in the right of self-determination of nations, springing from our religious and national roots, . . . we make known to you our full support of Archbishop Romero's request [to prohibit the giving of military aid to the Salvadoran government]." By this time, Kazel was working with her mentee, lay worker Jean Donavan, and two Maryknoll Sisters, Maura Clarke and Ita Ford. In December of the same year, all four were abducted, interrogated, physically and sexually abused, and shot by five Salvadoran national guardsmen. They were found the next day. Their tortured bodies became a symbol for dramatic appeals for peace and justice and for the heroism of women who laid down their lives for a noble cause.

The story was chronicled in a 1982 television movie, *Choices of the Heart,* about Jean Donovan; Kazel's story was chronicled by her sister-in-law Dorothy Chapon Kazel in her book *Alleluia Woman* and by Cynthia Clavac, O.S.U., in her biography of Kazel, *In the Fullness of Life: A Biography of Dorothy Kazel, O.S.U.* (1996).

165

Religion

Elizabeth McMichael POWELL

1902–

MAHONING COUNTY

ELIZABETH McMICHAEL POWELL was born in Buena Vista, Georgia, on June 8, 1902, but moved to Youngstown, Ohio, in 1925. She attended the Bible Theological Institute of Youngstown and the Youngstown Baptist Ministers Institute. Throughout her life, she has demonstrated boundless energy and a relentless passion to minister to the needs of others as she has worked tirelessly for the residents of Youngstown and others.

During World War II, Rev. Powell served the war effort, as many American women did, by working at the Ravenna Arsenal. In 1945 she helped organize the South Side Prayer Band to stabilize fragile families. An ardent defender of civil and human rights, she was active in unionizing to improve working conditions for others, served on the Youngstown Human Relations Commission and in the Youngstown chapter of the National Association for the Advancement of Colored People (NAACP), and was a staunch supporter of the modern Civil Rights movement. Prominent among her activist causes, however, was her advocacy of women in the ministry.

Rev. Powell was called to the ministry during a time when the Baptist church frowned on women in the pulpit. In the 1950s, she successfully challenged this patriarchy and was ordained as a Baptist minister in 1956. She became the first female Baptist minister in the Mahoning Valley, and was named pastor of the Elizabeth Baptist Church, where she remained until December 1962, when she founded her own church, the World Fellowship Interdenominational Church where she still serves as pastor at 101 years old.

Rev. Powell has been honored by many groups, including the local and national NAACP, the Youngstown chapter of the National Association of Negro Business and Professional Women's Clubs, Buckeye Elks Lodge No. 73, her church, city mayors, and city council members.

Benvin SANSBURY, O.P.

1797–1873

FRANKLIN COUNTY

Courtesy of the Dominican Sisters of St. Mary of the Springs.

Benvin Sansbury (Elizabeth Sansbury) was born in 1797 in Prince George's County, Maryland, and became a Dominican Sister in 1823 at Cartwright Creek, Kentucky. At the request of Bishop Edward Fenwick of the fledgling Catholic diocese of Cincinnati, Sansbury, along with three other Dominican sisters (Mother Elder, Sister Agnes Harbin, and Sister Mudd), came to Somerset, Ohio, on February 5, 1830, to found St. Mary's Academy, one of the first Catholic schools in Ohio. The academy offered educational opportunities to the children of both the Catholic and non-Catholic pioneer families in the area, educating some of the most prominent settlers of this era, including Angela Gillespie, the first Mother General of the Holy Cross Sisters in America and Ellen Ewing, the daughter of Senator Thomas Ewing and wife of General William Tecumseh Sherman.

In establishing the academy, the founding sisters were critical to the growing community of sisters in Somerset. They farmed and fed themselves, as well as their students. In 1866, a devastating fire destroyed the academy, leaving the sisters without a permanent home. In 1868, Theodore Leonard, a Columbus businessman who had five daughters to educate, offered the sisters land on his old brickyard on which to build an academy in Columbus. They did, traveling to Columbus to open a motherhouse, St. Mary of the Springs, and a new academy, St. Mary's Academy, which operated in Columbus until 1966.

The "O.P." after Sister Sansbury's name indicates that she was a member of the Order of Preachers founded by Saint Dominic in the thirteenth century. Sansbury, therefore, was part of a vibrant and long-standing community of women who were dedicated to changing the world through prayer and service. Today, more than three hundred sisters in the Congregation of St. Mary of the Springs carry forth these traditions. Sister Sansbury died in Columbus in 1873. She and the original founders of St. Mary's Academy are buried on the grounds of St. Mary of the Springs.

167

Religion

SCIENCE

AND

TECHNOLOGY

EVEN TODAY, SCIENCE AND TECHNOLOGY ARE professions dominated, often overwhelmingly, by men. Over the generations, however, there have been determined women who have had the desire to be in these fields and have had the courage and tenacity to act on those desires. The Ohio women highlighted in this section are prominent among them. They cover a range of scientific and technological interests and an equally impressive range of achievements. They have carried out their work in academic institutions, community organizations, business, and industry. Their fascination with the natural world inspired them to make insightful, often groundbreaking discoveries with long-lasting benefits for many areas of our lives. In fields where women have been few and often far between, these scientists, engineers, and conservationists have defied the gravity of social expectations and soared.

MARGARET J. ANDREW

EMMA LUCY BRAUN

JEANETTE GECSY GRASSELLI BROWN

BUNNY COWAN CLARK

NANETTE DAVIS FERRALL

SUSAN F. GUTERMUTH GRAY

HARRIET HYMAN PARKER

FARIDA ANNA WILEY

Margaret J. ANDREW

1908–2000

MONTGOMERY COUNTY

M ARGARET J. ANDREW, a pioneer in science and technology, was the first woman to earn a B.S. in banking and finance from the Ohio State University. Graduating in 1931, her career path took her first to the State of Ohio Liquidation Division and then in 1934 to the Frigidaire Division of the General Motors Corporation in Dayton. She began at Frigidaire with customer research, was promoted to technical specialist, and in 1953 she was appointed experimental engineer, a post at which she blossomed.

As an experimental engineer, Andrew became an inventor and received four patents between 1959 and 1968 for technological innovations—among them a dish rack for domestic appliances, an apparatus capable of cleaning woolens without causing shrinkage, and an apparatus that improved agitation control in automatic washers —that enhanced our lives in ways we now often take for granted. Andrew retired in 1971, after four decades of distinguished service, but her contributions did not end there. She continued her research in the area of food and nutrition, publishing *Home Food Care* in 1982. In this publication she reported on the successful development of a method for cooking, sealing, and freezing food at home. Such techniques were noted for accommodating the changing lifestyles of Americans, especially women, who during this era were broadening the horizons of their work life and sought time-saving ways to handle ongoing responsibilities at home.

In addition to her accomplishments at Frigidaire and afterward, Andrew was active in professional and community organizations. She was the first woman president of the Ohio Valley section of the Institute of Food Technologists, vice-president of the Dayton branch of the American Association of University Women, an elder at Westminister Church, and a member of the Advisory Committee of the Travel and Adventure Series Organization for more than fifty years. In addition, she was a member of the Miami Valley Management Association, the Dayton Council on World Affairs, the YWCA, the YMCA, the Dayton Music Club, the Dayton Federation of Women's Clubs, the OSU Alumni Association, the Dayton Art Institute, and the Ohioana Library Association.

171

Science and Technology

Emma Lucy BRAUN

1889–1971

HAMILTON COUNTY

EMMA LUCY BRAUN was born in Cincinnati, Ohio, on April 19, 1889. In 1910, she graduated from the University of Cincinnati and remained there for an M.S. in geology (1912). During the summer of 1912, Braun studied with the eminent plant ecologist Henry C. Cowles at the University of Chicago, then returned to the University of Cincinnati for a Ph.D. in botany, which she earned in 1914. This achievement alone established her in her own day as one of only a few women professionals in science. This select group included her sister Annette (1884–1978), an entomologist, who was the first woman to obtain a Ph.D. from the University of Cincinnati and internationally known as an authority on Microlepidoptera (moths). Braun and her sister worked and lived together throughout their careers, with Braun building a remarkable career as a distinguished botanist.

Upon completion of her Ph.D., Emma Braun was appointed to the University of Cincinnati faculty, where she remained until her retirement in 1948. During these years and afterward, Braun named and described new species of plants and contributed to the understanding of their distribution, as well as to theories related to the origins of the prairie. She published more than 180 articles in twenty scientific and popular journals and three books, including *Deciduous Forests of Eastern North America* (1950), based on twenty-five years of field study and more than sixty-five thousand miles of travel. It was reprinted several times and remains her most striking scholarly achievement.

172

Braun's stature in the scientific community is illustrated by her election as the first woman president of both the Ohio Academy of Science (1933–34) and the Ecological Society of America (1950). Among her many honors, Braun received the Eloise Payne Luquer Medal from the Garden Clubs of America (1966), a Merit Award from the Botanical Society of America (1956), and an honorary doctor of science degree from the University of Cincinnati in 1964. Braun died on March 5, 1971, in Cincinnati.

Courtesy of The Ohioana Library Association

Profiles of Two Hundred Ohio Women

Jeanette Gecsy Grasselli BROWN

1928–

CUYAHOGA COUNTY

JEANETTE GECSY GRASSELLI BROWN, born on August 4, 1928, in Cleveland, Ohio, received a B.S. in chemistry from Ohio University (she was the only woman chemist in her class), graduating summa cum laude and Phi Beta Kappa, and an M.S. from Western Reserve University. In 1950, she was hired by Standard Oil of Ohio (now BP Amoco) in Cleveland and given the task of finding industrial applications for the infrared spectrometer, used during World War II in military research. She did so and established for herself a remarkable trajectory of excellence in science.

Brown spent thirty-eight years in industrial research. The first woman to be named director of corporate research for BP America, she was upon her retirement in 1989 the highest-ranked woman in this multi-billion-dollar company. Brown has one patent, eighty publications, including nine books in the field of vibrational spectroscopy to her credit. She has lectured at more than a hundred universities in the United States and abroad and at industrial laboratories, on topics related to molecular spectroscopy and analytical problem solving. Her interests in science go well beyond her own laboratory to include not only science education generally, but encouraging women and minorities to consider careers in science and informing the public about the importance of science and technology in the world.

In addition to her professional service, Brown has been active with many community organizations in the Cleveland area, including the Musical Arts Association of the Cleveland Orchestra, the Holden Arboretum, the Great Lakes Science Center, and the Hathaway Brown School. Moreover, she has served on the board of trustees at Ohio University and has been a member of the Ohio Board of Regents, of which she is the immediate past chair, since 1995.

Brown's many honors and awards include receiving twelve honorary doctoral degrees and being the first woman elected to the Ohio Science and Technology Hall of Fame (1991), the first woman to win the prestigious ACS Fisher Award in Analytical Chemistry (1993), the first woman to receive the Theophilus Redwood Lectureship of the Royal Society of Chemistry, United Kingdom (1994), and the first woman inducted into the Hungarian and Austrian Chemical Societies.

173

Science and Technology

Bunny Cowan CLARK

1935–

FRANKLIN COUNTY

Bunny Cowan Clark, born in El Paso, Texas, on September 8, 1935, received a B.S. in physics and math (1958) and an M.S. in physics (1963) from Kansas State University and a Ph.D. in theoretical physics (1973) from Wayne State University. In 1981, she became the first woman to be appointed to the physics faculty at the Ohio State University and has proceeded, despite the difficulties of this male-dominated area, to build a distinctive career, opening a new area of research in nuclear physics, relativistic Dirac phenomenology, serving as an advocate for innovative teaching, especially at the undergraduate level, and dedicating herself tirelessly to the effort to attract women to science by countering the forces and barriers that hinder women from succeeding in certain areas.

Clark has published more than ninety scholarly articles and presented more than 150 talks on her work. She coedited *Relativistic Nuclear-Many Body Physics* (1989), and her research has been funded continuously since 1981 by the National Science Foundation. Clark has also been active in professional organizations, most notably the American Physical Society (APS), where she has filled many leadership roles, including chair of the Committee on the Status of Women in Physics (1991–94), and currently designated as a Friend of the Committee; member of the Executive Committee of the Division of Nuclear Physics, and chair of that division (1997–98).

In addition to her leadership in professional organizations, Clark has also served on the Ohio State University Affirmative Action Council, Council on Academic Excellence for Women, and currently the President's Council on Women's Issues. She has used every mechanism at her disposal to nurture under-represented groups in science careers and was recognized for this work with a University Distinguished Affirmative Action Award (1989) and a University Distinguished Service Award (2000).

In 1987, Clark was named the General Motors Corporation Distinguished University Professor, a position which she currently holds, and she has received many other prestigious awards, including the Ohio State University Distinguished Research Award (1983), Fellow of the American Physical Society (1984), Outstanding Woman Scientist of the Year (1986), YWCA Woman of Achievement (1993), Fellow of the American Association for the Advancement of Science (1996), and the William Fowler Award for Distinguished Research in Physics, Ohio Section, American Physical Society (1999).

Nanette Davis FERRALL

1960-

AUGLAIZE COUNTY

Nanette Davis Ferrall was born on April 15, 1960, in St. Marys, Ohio. She attended St. Marys Memorial High School, excelling in both academics and athletics. She received varsity letters in basketball, gymnastics, and track. She was a member of the choir, the Girls Athletic Association, the M-Club (a local school-based club), Thespians, and Y-Teens, and she was active with the school newspaper, the *Blue Print*. On the evening of graduation day, June 4, 1978, on her way home from a graduation party, Ferrall was involved in a tragic automobile accident in which she suffered a spinal-cord injury that left her paralyzed from the waist down. She was not expected to walk again. Her life turned, but it did not end.

With the support of family and friends and with six months of recovery and rehabilitation behind her, Ferrall enrolled at Wright State University, graduating in 1983. While at Wright State, she met Dr. Jerrold Petrofsky, a professor of biomedical engineering and physiology who had developed a computerized electronic system that stimulated muscles with small jolts of electricity in order to enhance muscle tone and increase circulation to a paralyzed limb. Working with Dr. Petrofsky, Ferrall made history. On November 11, 1982, four years after her accident, she took five dramatic steps and became the first paraplegic ever to walk. In 1986, Ferrall launched an aerobic fitness program for paraplegics and quadriplegics, called Moving Again, at Middletown Regional Hospital, located between Cincinnati and Dayton, where she served for two years as administrative director. This program was designed to put Dr. Petrofsky's technological research into a clinical setting and to demonstrate that people with spinal-cord injuries can do more and live healthier lives than ever before.

Currently, Ferrall teaches elementary school in her hometown, manages her own driving school, gives inspirational speeches on health care and the importance of safe driving, works out several times a week on her computerized stationary bicycle, and plays golf occasionally with the aid of a walker. Ferrall's story was dramatized in a 1985 CBS movie, *First Steps*. The scientific breakthrough that permitted her achievement is on display at the EPCOT Science and Technology Exhibition Center in Orlando, Florida.

175

Science and Technology

Susan F. Gutermuth GRAY

1934⁻

DARKE COUNTY

Susan F. Gutermuth Gray, born on March 4, 1934, is a passionate environmentalist. She lives on a 104-acre farm just west of Greenville, Ohio, where she and her husband, Bob, have preserved a 160-year-old log house. On the farm, they engage in conservation farming, which includes practices to reduce erosion and minimize the use of agricultural chemicals. They are also active in preserving the natural features of the farm, including restoring a natural lowland area, returning eight acres to native prairie grasses, and restoring a ten-acre wetland area. In addition, each year Gray conducts outdoor education classes for adults and for more than five hundred Darke County students on the farm, and conducts courses in natural resources management for fourteen-year-olds and for college students at her lodge in Ontario, Canada. While these achievements alone are noteworthy, they only scratch the surface of a lifelong commitment to the preservation of our ecostructure and the preservation of the historic and cultural significance of the land for future generations.

Gray has been a volunteer with the Brukner Nature Center in Troy, Ohio, since 1975. Through this center, she initiated the Greenville Scenic Rivers Program, a river monitoring program using 4-H children—the Fur, Fish & Game 4-H Club—to examine river life for signs of pollution. She helped develop the Biotic Index, a test of water quality for inland waterways that has become a standard measurement used by the Ohio Department of Natural Resources and adopted by states across the nation and internationally. Further, for three decades, Gray has been a commissioner with the Darke County Park District, speaking at schools, businesses, and community organizations about everything from garbage and recycling to clean air and water to preserving the historic heritage of Ohio. Without compensation or funding for the commission, Gray has been a leader in preserving more than two hundred acres in Darke County.

Gray has received many awards, including the Nature Conservancy Award (1984), the U.S. Wildlife Resource Award (1989) by the Southwest Region U.S. Department of the Interior, U.S. Fish and Wildlife Department, the Chevron Conservation Award (1993), and the Ohio Department of Natural Resources' Cardinal Award (2000).

176

OHIO
WOMEN'S
HALL OF
FAME

Profiles of Two Hundred Ohio Women

Harriet Hyman PARKER

1910−2001

FRANKLIN COUNTY

Harriet Hyman Parker, born in 1910, was a pioneering researcher in the field of human genetics. In 1936, she received a Ph.D. from the Ohio State University, where she was the first Ph.D. student of Dr. Laurence H. Snyder, who is considered the father of human genetics and was author of the first human genetics textbook, *The Principles of Heredity.* As Snyder's graduate assistant, Parker proofed and helped to edit the book. She also studied with Dr. Karl Landsteiner, who won the Nobel Prize in medicine for his discovery of the blood groups, and with Dr. Alexander Weiner and Dr. Philip Levine, who later discovered the Rh factor. With excellent training and research opportunities, Parker went on to make her own mark in genetics.

Parker's research proved for the first time that the heredity of the blood groups was established as early as three months after conception and that blood types (A, B, O, M, and N) are present at birth. These discoveries had many ramifications. Her work made possible the typing of blood in jaundiced newborns, which enabled them to receive transfusions safely, an achievement that gained Parker worldwide praise. Her work was also instrumental for determining paternity, allowing hospitals a scientific way to sort out mix-ups of parentage, as well as for determining nonpaternity. While the use of blood typing as evidence in nonpaternity court cases became quite commonplace, during this era it was revolutionary, changing both medical and legal practices.

For the remainder of her career, Parker taught and advised students at the Ohio State University, where she established the Milton M. and Harriet H. Parker Fund for Psychiatry and Human Genetics to support research, teaching, and treatment in psychiatry and human genetics. The fund is housed in the department of psychiatry in the College of Medicine and Public Health. In addition, she was a devoted volunteer with many community organizations, including the Greater Columbus Arts Council, the Hillel Foundation, and the Columbus Jewish Federation, among many others. In recognition of her accomplishments, Parker received many awards, including being named Woman of the Year by B'nai B'rith Women and Columbus Woman of the Year by the American Association of University Women and receiving an OSU Alumni Citizenship Award.

177

Science and Technology

OHIO
WOMEN'S
HALL OF
FAME

Farida Anna WILEY

1889–1988

SHELBY COUNTY

The most precious things of life are near at hand, without money and without price.

—Farida Wiley

FARIDA ANNA WILEY, born in 1889 on her parents' Percheron horse farm in Orange Township, quickly developed a fascination with birds. Even as a young girl she made regular reports on bird sightings to the United States Biological Survey. After both her parents died tragically when she was young, she moved to New York City to live with her older sister, Bessie. In 1919, Bessie helped her get a job teaching blind children at the prestigious American Museum of Natural History. Wiley continued with the museum for the next sixty-four years, inspiring children and adults and creating a career as a world-class ornithologist.

Completely self-taught in the natural sciences, Wiley authored and edited several books, including *Theodore Roosevelt's America* and *Ferns of Northeastern United States;* was a frequent contributor to *Natural History* and *Audubon* magazines; and compiled and edited the works of John Burroughs, a preeminent naturalist whose research focused on the effects of natural surroundings on the development of children. Wiley was also a staff member of the Audubon Camp on Hog Island in Maine from 1946 to

Courtesy of the Shelby County Historical Society

1967, where she taught Audubon Society members the birding techniques that she had developed. She was an instructor in ornithology and the natural sciences at Columbia University, the Pennsylvania State University, and New York University, and she worked with children in the New York public schools.

Wiley died peacefully in New York at the age of ninety-nine, after having led daily nature walks at 7 A.M. in Central Park, her haven, for nearly half a century.

SOCIAL

ACTIVISM

ACTIVISM IS A COMMITMENT TO THE PRACTICE AND emphasis of vigorous action. Social activism is an application of such a commitment to social responsibility and change. Women in Ohio have a long history of social activism, vigorous engagement in keeping social responsibility as a central issue in society, and vibrant leadership in social change. The causes they have supported have been multiple, from abolitionism to woman suffrage; from civil rights to women's rights; from social justice to education to health and well-being. The list is endless. The women showcased in this section have set a dazzling pace in seeing the needs around them and responding with energy, dedication, and laudable goals. They provide lessons for us all about what passion and commitment to changing the world can do in the hands of individuals and groups.

FRANCES JENNINGS CASEMENT

BETSY MIX COWLES

FRANCES DANA GAGE

CAROLE GARRISON

JEWEL FREEMAN GRAHAM

ELIZABETH J. HAUSER

DONNA L. HAWK

JANE EDNA HARRIS HUNTER

JANET KALVEN

BETTYE RUTH BRYAN KAY

MAGGIE (MARGARET) ELIZA KUHN

FANNIE M. SCOTT LEWIS

HELEN HOFF PETERSON

YVONNE POINTER (TRIPLETT)

HENRIETTA BUCKLER SEIBERLING

ELEANOR CUTRI SMEAL

HARRIET TAYLOR UPTON

Frances Jennings CASEMENT

1840–1928

LAKE COUNTY

Frances Jennings Casement was born in Painesville, Ohio, on April 23, 1840. She graduated from the Painesville Academy in 1852 and from Willoughby Female Seminary in 1856. Her social consciousness was influenced by both the politically active men and some equally active women in her life. The men were her abolitionist father, Charles C. Jennings, who served in the Ohio House of Representatives from 1854 to 1856, and her abolitionist husband, John (Jack) S. Casement, who served in the Union Army as a brigadier general under General William Tecumseh Sherman, who was in charge of laying the Union Pacific Railroad in 1869 and who was elected the nonvoting representative to the U. S. Congress from the Wyoming Territory in 1868. The women were Susan B. Anthony and Elizabeth Cady Stanton, whom Casement met when they worked closely with her husband in his lobbying efforts for Wyoming statehood and women's suffrage.

All of these influences came together for Casement in 1883, when she organized the Equal Rights Association (ERA) in Painesville. In the early meetings of the ERA, Casement began with social conversation, lectures, and discussions, and then she would read articles from *Woman's Journal* to the group and shift the discussion toward equal voting rights, equal rights for women in the work world, rights for women during divorce, and so on. Soon, however, Casement was able to focus the meetings, which included both men and women, on just the political issues. By 1884, the ERA had grown in size and reputation, and the group was invited to attend the first Annual Convention of the Ohio Woman Suffrage Association. Eventually, Casement became president of this organization, and she was also instrumental in resolving the competition that had developed between the National Woman Suffrage Association, led by Elizabeth Cady Stanton and Susan B. Anthony, and the American Woman Suffrage Association, led by Lucy Stone, Henry Blackwell, and Julia Ward Howe. In 1890, the National American Woman Suffrage Association (NAWSA) formed, and the combined group fought for another thirty years before the Nineteenth Amendment to the U.S. Constitution would be ratified in 1920, granting women equal voting rights. In that same year, NAWSA honored Casement as a pioneer in the movement. Casement died on August 24, 1928, at age eighty-nine.

Social Activism

OHIO WOMEN'S HALL OF FAME

Betsy Mix COWLES

1810–1876

ASHTABULA COUNTY

I N 1811 AT AGE ONE, Betsy Mix Cowles moved with her family to Austinburg, Ohio, where as a very young woman she began a teaching career, teaching in several eastern Ohio communities in the 1820s. Cowles later enrolled at Oberlin College in the Ladies Course, graduating in 1840, and then continued to teach and hold several administrative positions as well. She set up "infant schools" near her home and later became preceptress at the Grand River Academy at Austinburg. She is credited for starting the public schools of Canton and Massillon and the normal schools at Hopedale, Ohio, and Bloomington, Illinois. She was named superintendent of the Painesville Township Schools, a position that was not usually held by women during this era, and she lived through the Civil War at her last teaching post in Delhi, New York. As a teacher and administrator, Cowles earned the respect of those around her and served as a pioneering role model, especially for the young women whose lives she touched.

In addition to her career in teaching, Cowles was an active supporter of the antislavery and women's rights movements. In 1837, she founded the Ashtabula County Female Anti-Slavery Society, wrote articles for the *Anti-Slavery Bugle*, and attended antislavery conventions. Early in her career, she demonstrated her support of the rights of African Americans by holding Sunday school classes for both African American and white children, despite the complaints of white parents, and by participating actively in the Underground Railroad. In 1850, Cowles was elected president of Ohio's first Women's Rights Convention held in Salem, Ohio, on April 19–20, 1850. At the next year's convention in Akron (where Sojourner Truth made her famous

"Ain't I a Woman" speech), Cowles presented a carefully documented report comparing the inequality between the wages of men and women. In 1852, she founded the Ohio Women's Rights Association, which sought "the extension of human freedoms, for the elevation of the [human] race, without respect to sex, color, or other conditions."

Cowles committed herself passionately to struggles for freedom and justice throughout her life, continuing in her social reform activities until her death in 1876.

182

OHIO
WOMEN'S
HALL OF
FAME

Profiles of Two Hundred Ohio Women

Frances Dana GAGE

1808–1884

WASHINGTON COUNTY

F RANCES DANA GAGE, born on October 12, 1808, in Union Township, grew up with a limited formal education but well instructed by her reform-minded family about the social issues of her day. In 1829 she married James L. Gage, a lawyer from McConnelsville, Ohio, and started what would become a very large family. Despite these responsibilities, however, she remained passionately committed to abolition, temperance, and women's rights, interests that led her to write a consistent stream of letters to the periodical press. By 1850, she was a frequent contributor to the *Ladies' Repository* of Cincinnati and a contributor also to the *Ohio Cultivator,* a bimonthly farm paper in which her letters, written under the pen name "Aunt Fanny," appeared in the Ladies' Department, providing practical advice about the daily lives of farm women, and also presenting her views on social issues. By the time a call went out for the first Ohio Women's Rights Convention to be held in Salem, Ohio, in April 1850, Gage was recognized as an author and public speaker.

Gage was unable to attend the first convention but sent a letter of support and drew up a petition to the state legislature asking that the words "white" and "male" be left out of the new state constitution. A year later she was elected to preside at the second convention held in Akron in 1851 (the site of Sojourner Truth's "Ain't I a Woman" speech, which Gage later made famous when she rendered it in one of her articles), and in 1853 she presided over a national convention held in Cleveland. During these years Gage worked with Susan B. Anthony, Elizabeth Cady Stanton, and other prominent members of the women's movement. She also contributed poems and articles to *Lily* and *Saturday Visiter,* building a well-deserved reputation as a radical reformer.

During the Civil War, in addition to working with recently freed slaves on Parris Island in the Sea Islands off South Carolina, Gage also traveled up and down the Mississippi River delivering care packages, caring for the sick and wounded, and raising funds for Union soldiers and freed slaves. In 1867, Gage suffered a stroke but continued to write, publishing articles, children's stories, poems, and five novels. She died in 1884.

183

Social Activism

Carole GARRISON

1942–

SUMMIT COUNTY

CAROLE GARRISON was born on October 18, 1942, in Chicago, Illinois. She earned a Ph.D. in public administration with a concentration in criminal justice from the Ohio State University and is currently chair of the Department of Criminal Justice and Police Studies at Eastern Kentucky University. Garrison could very well be celebrated for the interesting and remarkable career that she has had as an academic. She was visiting scholar at the Center of Alcohol Studies at Rutgers University, cofounder of the Akron Women's History Project, the founding director of women's studies at the University of Akron, and the codirector and founder of the Kent State/University of Akron Institute for the Study of Gender and Education. She has served as coordinator of the North Central Women's Studies Association, chaired the Ohio Council of Criminal Justice Educators, chaired the American Society of Criminology's Division of Women and Crime, and served on the National Council for Research on Women. These and other contributions establish her as a noteworthy educational leader.

Garrison's contributions, however, have gone well beyond the boundaries of academe. For well over twenty years, she has operated as an agent of change in the interest of others. While a professor at the University of Akron, for example, she was a member of the first Ohio Women's Policy and Research Commission, serving as co-vice-chair under Governors Celeste and Voinovich; she helped to stimulate training opportunities for Ohio female police officers; and she started Women in Criminal Justice in 1982, an organization committed to fostering communication and cooperation among women working in the criminal justice system in Summit County. On a national level, Garrison has served on the board of the U.S. Department of Defense's Advisory Commission on the Status of Women in the Military. On an international level, she has served as executive director of the Cooperation Committee for Cambodia, a network of all the humanitarian organizations in Cambodia, and volunteered as a district electoral supervisor in Cambodia as part of the United Nations peacekeeping mission.

Garrison has received many awards, including a Distinguished Service Medal (1976) by the Atlanta Bureau of Police Services for her work as a police officer in Atlanta, Georgia, and a Professional Woman of the Year Award (1985) from Akron Area Women's History Project.

184

OHIO
WOMEN'S
HALL OF
FAME

Profiles of Two Hundred Ohio Women

Jewel Freeman GRAHAM

1925−

GREENE COUNTY

J EWEL FREEMAN GRAHAM, born in Springfield, Ohio, in 1925, graduated magna cum laude from Fisk University in 1946 with a degree in sociology, from Case Western Reserve University with an M.A. in social service administration, and from the University of Dayton with a law degree in 1979. In 1964, she was appointed professor of social welfare at Antioch College, where she was a dedicated teacher, advisor, director of the Social Work Program of the anthropology/sociology department, director of the Program for Interracial Education, and interim associate dean of the college. In 1972, she was named one of the Outstanding Educators of America, and in 1975 she was named Social Worker of the Year by the Miami Valley Chapter of the National Association of Social Workers. In addition to such noteworthy accomplishments, Graham has made indelible marks through a variety of local, national, and international leadership roles with the Young Women's Christian Association (YWCA).

At age fourteen, Graham joined the racially segregated Clark Street branch of the YWCA Girl Reserves (the precursor of Y-Teens). She delighted in the programs and, along with forty to fifty other girls, participated in service projects; staged plays, talent shows, and dances; and arranged programs with speakers. Her first professional position was with the YWCA, when, after their adoption of an interracial charter, she was appointed a program director of the YWCA of Grand Rapids, Michigan, and worked with white teenagers. Later, she worked for three and a half years for the YWCA of Detroit. In 1970, she was elected to the national board of the YWCA of the United States of America, where she chaired the Racial Justice Task Force and the advisory committee to the YWCA's self-study team to determine future YWCA directions. In 1973, she was elected national vice-president; in 1975, member of the World YWCA Executive Committee; in 1979, president of YWCA of the U.S.A.; and in 1987, president of World YWCA, a post she held until 1991.

In addition to her honors and awards as an educator, Graham has been frequently recognized for her organizational leadership. Among these honors, she is listed in Who's Who in the United States and in 1987 she was selected by the *Dayton Daily News* as one of the Top Ten Women in the Miami Valley.

Social Activism

Courtesy of the Ohioana Library

Elizabeth J. HAUSER

1873–1958

TRUMBULL COUNTY

ELIZABETH J. HAUSER, born on March 15, 1873, in Girard, Ohio, became a suffragist at age sixteen, when she attended a state suffrage meeting in Salem, Ohio, with Harriet Taylor Upton (also profiled in this section). In 1892, at age nineteen, she began a career as a journalist, working as editor of the weekly newspaper *Girard Grit,* but by 1895 she had resigned this position to become personal secretary to Upton, who at that point was treasurer of the National American Woman's Suffrage Association (NAWSA).

In 1903, with Hauser serving as the point person, Upton moved NAWSA's headquarters from New York City to Warren, Ohio. After the move, Hauser served as headquarters secretary and worked closely with all of the prominent suffragists of the era, including Susan B. Anthony, Carrie Chapman Catt, and Anna Howard Shaw. She was also active in the Ohio Woman Suffrage Association, functioning as corresponding secretary, press chairman, and editor of the official bulletin of the organization, and she served as chair of the Cleveland Woman Suffrage Party.

When NAWSA headquarters returned to New York in 1909, Hauser became national press committee vice-chair, attending national and international meetings, publicizing the suffrage campaign, and handling communications for the suffrage, Democratic, and Republican conventions. A striking example of her leadership was her work in helping to organize the Parade in the Rain at the 1916 Republican convention in which ten thousand activists marched through Chicago during a rainstorm that forced the cancellation of other events.

After the ratification of the nineteenth amendment in 1920, Hauser directed her efforts toward voter education, helping Carrie Chapman Catt to organize the League of Women Voters and becoming a member of that organization's first official board as a regional director. Hauser continued to be active in the League throughout her lifetime, serving in various capacities including national director and national secretary.

In 1927, Hauser returned to journalism. She became a reporter and editor for the *Warren Tribune Chronicle,* for which she wrote many articles on local and state history and had a regular column, "The Tribune Trailer."

OHIO
WOMEN'S
HALL OF
FAME

Donna L. HAWK

1943‒

COLUMBIANA COUNTY

DONNA L. HAWK, born on March 12, 1943, in Wellsville, Ohio, joined the Sisters of St. Joseph in 1957, graduating from Nazareth Academy in Cleveland in 1960. She graduated from St. John's College in 1967 and received an M.A. from John Carroll University in 1973. She began her career as a teacher, ultimately becoming principal of the St. Patrick's Elementary School from 1970 to 1972. Hawk's impact in her community, however, did not stop at the school doors. She is a national leader in the development of support systems for the homeless and programs designed to inspire and help women to attain stability and economic independence.

Hawk volunteered with the West Side Catholic Shelter from 1978 to 1980 and was employed there from 1980 to 1983. Hawk developed a special compassion for the women in the shelter, many of whom had become homeless to free themselves from domestic violence. Joining hands with Sister Loretta Schulte in 1983 to address these problems more directly, Hawk opened Transitional Housing, Inc. (THI) in 1986, a comprehensive housing program. Hawk and Schulte put together an innovative financing package to purchase and renovate a motel on Cleveland's West Side and began implementing programs that would change homeless women's lives.

Since 1986, THI has provided residents with on-site counseling with an emphasis on building self-esteem and recovering from chemical dependencies. Residents are required to enter an educational or job-training program to prepare themselves for the world of work with the goal of overcoming their dependence on public assistance and abusive relationships. They also benefit from employment counseling and parenting classes, and they are encouraged to volunteer to help others. This combination of services, along with safe, decent, affordable housing, can be instrumental in helping women reinvent themselves and start more positive lives.

Hawk has also been actively involved in supporting the homeless at state and national levels. She is a founding member of the Emergency Shelter Coalition in Cleveland, which became the Northeast Ohio Coalition for the Homeless (NEOCH). She was the first board president of NEOCH. In 1989, she led the Cleveland delegation to the Housing Now! march in Washington, D.C. Hawk has received several honors and awards, including the Liberty Bell Award from the Cleveland Bar Association and induction into the hall of fame of Nazareth Academy.

Social Activism

Courtesy of the Phillis Wheatley YWCA

Jane Edna Harris HUNTER

1882–1971

CUYAHOGA COUNTY

JANE EDNA HARRIS HUNTER was born on December 13, 1882, on the Woodburn plantation near Pendleton, South Carolina, and graduated from Ferguson Academy. After a failed marriage, she enrolled in the Cannon Street Hospital and Training School for nurses in Charleston and completed advanced nurse training in 1904 at the Hampton Training School for Nurses in Virginia. In 1905, Hunter moved to Cleveland, where she found no opportunities for African American nurses and encountered the more problematic challenge of locating decent housing and social opportunities for single African American women. She sought assistance from the YWCA but was denied because of her race, an incident which inspired her to dedicate her life to social reform.

Hunter broke the color barrier as a nurse in Cleveland when she received her first professional assignment from Dr. L. E. Siegelstein, coroner for Cuyahoga County, and from Dr. Christian LaTrobe Mottley, an African American physician. Despite her own struggles, she did not forget her desire to help other African American women who were migrating into the city. After several years, she approached the YWCA again, this time soliciting their support in setting up a separate branch and separate housing for blacks. In September 1911, Hunter founded the Working Girls Association, which became the Phillis Wheatley Association the next year. Hunter became the first president and executive secretary of the Wheatley Association and manager of a twenty-three-room home that ultimately provided a full range of services.

Hunter also continued her education. She took courses in social work at Western Reserve University, received a law degree from John Marshall College of Law in Cleveland, and passed the Ohio Bar in 1926. Throughout these years, Hunter was a national leader in the black clubwomen's movement; a founding member of the Women's Civic League of Cleveland in 1943, affiliated with the National Urban League; a member of the Progressive Business Alliance; an officer with national prominence in the Republican Party's Colored Women's Committee; and active with several other local, national, and international organizations.

Hunter received honorary degrees from Fisk, Allen, Central State, and Tuskegee Universities and a nomination for the prestigious Spingarn Award from the NAACP (1937). In 1940, she wrote her autobiography, *A Nickel and a Prayer.*

OHIO
WOMEN'S
HALL OF
FAME

Janet KALVEN

1913–

HAMILTON COUNTY

JANET KALVEN was born on May 21, 1913, in Chicago, Illinois. She graduated Phi Beta Kappa from the University of Chicago in 1934 with a B.A. in mathematics and philosophy and from Boston University in 1971 with an M.A. in adult education and human relations. In 1942, Kalven joined the Grail, an international women's organization founded in Holland in 1921 that came to the United States in 1940. Over the decades, the organization has blossomed into an international ecumenical movement that embraces several religious traditions, including Judeo-Christian, Native American, and Zen, and is committed to transforming the world into a global community of justice, peace, and love.

As a passionate member of the Grail, in 1944 Kalven cofounded Grailville Education and Conference Center on a three-hundred-acre organic farm in Loveland, Ohio. The center is a nonprofit adult education and retreat center and an international women's religious community. During the almost six decades of its operation, Kalven has coordinated and developed a wide range of educational opportunities so that women of all ages and backgrounds have an environment in which to learn to trust themselves and work cooperatively as part of an interracial and often international team. Among these opportunities is a series of residential programs that include a semester at Grailville for college women and a seminary quarter at Grailville for women in graduate theological study. These alternative programs offer women a lively experiential education that integrates a feminist spirituality with concerns for social justice, ecology, and the arts.

In addition to her work at Grailville, from 1972 to 1986 Kalven served as associate director of the Self-directed Learning Program at the University of Dayton, and she has coauthored and coedited several books, including *Your Daughters Shall Prophesy: Feminist Alternatives in Theological Education* (1980), *With Both Eyes Open: Seeing Beyond Gender* (1988), and most recently *Women Breaking Boundaries: A Grail Journey, 1940–1995* (1999).

189

Social Activism

OHIO WOMEN'S HALL OF FAME

Bettye Ruth Bryan KAY

1929–1996

LUCAS COUNTY

Bettye Ruth Bryan Kay was born on March 7, 1929, in Birmingham, Alabama. She attended Carson-Newman College in Jefferson City, Tennessee, but graduated from the University of Minnesota in 1950. Kay built a career as an educator in the public schools, spending many years teaching in the Toledo Public Schools across all grade levels but mainly at Libbey High School. In 1976, she received an M.A. in special education from the University of Delaware. Her special focus was on learning-disabled students. In 1973, she taught in the first program for autistic children in a U.S. public school, and in 1977 she received the National Society for Autistic Children's Teacher of the Year award. With this experience and expertise, Kay went in a different but complementary direction in 1983, when she seized the opportunity to provide a remarkable service to autistic adults.

In that year, Kay left the Toledo school system to become director of Bittersweet Farms in Whitehouse, Ohio, where she helped to establish the first specialized center for autistic adults in the United States. Bittersweet Farms, a name taken from a vine found on the property and meant to represent the bittersweet lives of its residents, is an intermediate care facility designed to meet the educational, vocational, developmental, and social needs of individuals with autism within a holistic and integrated program. With remarkable passion and enthusiasm, Kay became a highly visible advocate, ultimately establishing a premier model for a farmstead community. She organized Bittersweet Farms around the notion of increasing the autonomy and self-reliance of autistic adults in order to enable choices, maximize dignity, and encourage community interaction, and she dedicated her life to creating an environment that respected their needs, their abilities, and their possibilities.

Through this work both in the public schools and on Bittersweet Farms, Ruth was recognized for her expertise and her dedication. She became a national leader, giving lectures and workshops and offering innovative educational solutions for people with special needs. She died on December 25, 1996, leaving behind a legacy of high-quality holistic care for both children and adults.

190

Maggie (Margaret) Eliza KUHN
1905–1995

CUYAHOGA COUNTY

MAGGIE (MARGARET) ELIZA KUHN, born on August 31, 1905, in Buffalo, New York, graduated at age sixteen from West High School in Cleveland, and earned a B.A. in 1926 from the Flora Stone Mather College for Women at Western Reserve University. In 1930, she became head of the Professional Department of Business Girls at the Young Women's Christian Association (YWCA) in the Germantown section of Philadelphia. During World War II, she was a program coordinator with the YWCA's USO division. By 1948, when she became program coordinator for the General Alliance of Unitarian and Other Liberal Christian Women in Boston, Kuhn was well on her way in the area of community organization and development.

Over the next three decades, Kuhn continued to achieve. In 1950, she was appointed assistant secretary of the Department of Social Education and Action, Board of Christian Education, at the United Presbyterian Church in the USA at the national headquarters in Philadelphia, where she helped encourage churchgoers to take progressive stands on important social issues of the day. In 1969, as a program executive for the Presbyterian Church's Council on Church and Race, Kuhn also served on a subcommittee on the problems of the elderly. These activities were fortuitous, since in 1970, when she reached sixty-five, retirement age, she did not want to stop working.

After her retirement as program executive, Kuhn and a group of five friends met to address the problems of retirees. They formed a group called the Consultation of Older and Younger Adults for Social Change. The organization grew, and in 1972 was renamed the Gray Panthers, with Kuhn clearly identified as a charismatic leader. By 1973, there were eleven chapters of the organization, and in 1975 the group held its first national convention in Chicago. By 1990, the Gray Panthers had opened a public policy office in Washington, D.C., and was operating as a nationally recognized activist group that addressed age discrimination, pension rights, nursing home reform, and other issues affecting the elderly.

By the time of her death in 1995, Kuhn had had a remarkable impact, raising national awareness about aging and creating a means for strategic action. She chronicled her views and experiences in several books, including her autobiography, *No Stone Unturned: The Life and Times of Maggie Kuhn*, with Christina Long and Laura Quinn.

Social Activism

Fannie M. Scott LEWIS

1926–

CUYAHOGA COUNTY

F ANNIE M. SCOTT LEWIS was born on June 6, 1926, in Memphis, Tennessee. As a young woman, she moved to Cleveland in search of a better life, but found that her new home, the Hough community, held the typical challenge of a poor urban inner city neighborhood. Instead of being overwhelmed, however, Lewis found spiritual strength and, with the encouragement of Lugenia Dixon, became actively involved in the grass-roots politics of the area.

Lewis has worked with Community Action for Youth, the Hough Community Council, the League Park Center, the Ward Club (a club in the Seventh Ward), and other community-based groups. Through a broad range of activities, she became knowledgeable about work at the precinct level and developed a clearer understanding of people's everyday lives and needs. She worked with more than a hundred youth through the Neighborhood Youth Corps. In 1968, she became citizen participation director for the Cleveland Model Cities Program, overseeing an increased investment in the Hough community, and in 1980 she was elected Hough (Ward 7) representative to the Cleveland City Council. In this position she was an advocate for community change, her success measured by a number of developments, including five housing programs, revitalization of the neighborhood's only shopping center, home weatherization and rehabilitation programs, the establishment of a merchants' association, the creation of several parks, and the creation of new commercial development and employment opportunities.

In addition, while raising her own five children, Lewis opened her home as an office for the community, naming it the "Office of Community Resources and Human Problems." Through this mechanism she has been able to help countless individuals and groups who found themselves in need, ministering to them without compensation, helping them to develop job skills, and helping them to create networks that support success. With a commitment to working hard and helping others, Lewis has made a real difference in the lives of those around her.

192

OHIO
WOMEN'S
HALL OF
FAME

Profiles of Two Hundred Ohio Women

Helen Hoff PETERSON

1902–1998

FRANKLIN COUNTY

HELEN HOFF PETERSON was born on June 3, 1902, in Center-burg, New Jersey. A 1923 graduate of Brown University, she moved to Columbus in 1928. She had already been a volunteer with the Young Women's Christian Association (YWCA), and she continued that involvement in Columbus.

Peterson began her Columbus YWCA work as a member and then chair of the Industrial Women's and Girls' Committee (IWGC). The Depression was beginning, and unemployment was high. In response, the YWCA established the School of Leisure Time Activities, organized by Peterson, to offer free classes to provide valuable information during difficult times. Also under Peterson's leadership, the IWGC established Household Training Centers in response to the exploitation of women and girls who were so desperate for jobs that they were willing to be overworked just for room and board. Through the centers, they were trained in cooking and household skills and received certificates which enabled them to demand reasonable living and work conditions and a living wage. Even after the success of this program, Peterson's concerns with eliminating such inequities and injustices continued. She became an advocate for a state minimum wage law for women and minors in the 1930s, championing legislation, and ultimately serving as a public member on one of Ohio's first wage boards.

As suggested by these activities, civil rights became an ongoing part of Peterson's action agenda. In 1946 she was elected to the YWCA's National Board, on which she served until 1955. She was active in the effort to integrate the organization at all levels locally and nationally. In Columbus, she was a member of the monitoring team that ensured the safety of participants when the YWCA swimming pool was integrated, and she served as chair of the committee that established the first interracial neighborhood nursery school in 1945 at the First Congregational Church. Further, prior to World War II, when by presidential order all racial discrimination in defense industries was banned, Peterson was the only woman to serve on the Ohio Fair Employment Commission to hear discrimination cases. Over the next decade, she traveled extensively to present workshops on issues related to social justice and peace.

For more than fifty years, Peterson encouraged women to work actively for change, and through her own activism helped to ensure that the city of Columbus would be a better place, with social justice and opportunities for all.

Social Activism

OHIO
WOMEN'S
HALL OF
FAME

Yvonne POINTER (Triplett)

1952–

CUYAHOGA COUNTY

Yvonne Pointer (Triplett), born in Cleveland, Ohio, on December 28, 1952, fell victim to tragedy on December 6, 1984, when her oldest daughter, Gloria Pointer, was abducted, raped, and murdered. The crime was not solved. Instead of succumbing to the inevitable frustrations of the failure to apprehend the murderer, however, Pointer found the resolve to commit herself to bringing about the changes that would make communities safer.

Convinced that drugs, violence, and gangs would not go away by themselves, Pointer began a campaign to make a difference. When she learned of the Midnight Basketball program, a successful effort in Chicago to offer youth positive outlets for their energy, she lobbied successfully to bring the program to Cleveland. In addition, she founded the Positive Plus Support Group (for women) and Parents against Child Killing (PACK); she is an active member of Parents of Murdered Children, Inc. (POMC); she is a mentor for students in the Cleveland Municipal School District; she has established the Gloria Pointer Scholarship Fund to award an annual five-hundred-dollar athletic scholarship to an inner-city student; and she has written a book, *Behind the Death of a Child*. Pointer is also on the executive board of the Cleveland NAACP, and she has served as a regional liaison with the Office of Attorney General of Ohio. In other words, Pointer has succeeded in turning personal tragedy into social action, much to the benefit of her local community and the state.

Pointer's activism in the face of crime and violence has garnered her many hon-

194

ors and awards. Among them are the FBI's Director's Community Leadership Award (1993), the National Council of Negro Women's Tribute to Black Women Community Leaders Award (1994), and having her name permanently placed, along with those of fifteen other Clevelanders, in the rotunda of Cleveland City Hall for volunteering their time to the city.

Henrietta Buckler SEIBERLING

1888–1979

SUMMIT COUNTY

Henrietta Buckler Seiberling was born on March 18, 1888, in Lawrenceburg, Kentucky, but spent her childhood in El Paso, Texas, where her father was a judge in the Court of Common Pleas. She graduated from Vassar College with a degree in music and psychology. In 1917, she married John Frederick Seiberling and moved to Akron. After experiencing family and financial problems, Seiberling and her husband decided to live separately. By 1930, Seiberling was drawn to the Oxford Group, a religious revival group founded by Dr. Frank N. D. Buchman in the 1920s. This evangelical fellowship stressed prayer and charitable work as a way of life, and Seiberling began volunteering her time to various causes.

Through the Oxford Group, Seiberling met Anne Smith and her husband Bob, who admitted to Seiberling that he had a problem with alcoholism. He asked for her support. Shortly afterward, her involvements with the Oxford Group also connected her with Bill Wilson, a New York stockbroker who discussed with her the role that the Oxford Group had played in helping him to stop drinking. Seiberling introduced the two men on May 12, 1935, an encounter that ultimately led to the formation of Alcoholics Anonymous (AA). Anne and Bob Smith, Bill Wilson, and Henrietta Seiberling worked together to develop and refine the principles that would become the foundation of AA. They began holding sessions with alcoholics at Oxford Group meetings in June, 1935, which proved so popular that they began holding separate meetings at the King School in Akron, the first site of official AA meetings, first as part of the more general Oxford Group and ultimately as the official Alcoholics Anonymous group. By 1938, AA had spread to several other cities, and eventually it evolved into an organization that has now helped millions of people worldwide fight alcoholism and regain control of their lives.

While Seiberling received no awards for her dedication to this effort during her lifetime, there are two clear tributes to the difference that she made. One is the evidence of millions of rebuilt lives. The other is recorded in *Alcoholics Anonymous Comes of Age* (1957), in which Bill Wilson credits her with creating the connections that made AA possible.

195

Social Activism

Eleanor Cutri SMEAL

1939‒

ASHTABULA COUNTY

Eleanor Cutri Smeal, born on July 30, 1939, in Ashtabula, Ohio, graduated Phi Beta Kappa from Duke University and holds an M.A. in political science from the University of Florida. For more than twenty-five years, Smeal has played a pivotal role in defining and shaping the national and international action agendas for the contemporary women's movement, has promoted the involvement of women in feminist action, and has served as a frontline lobbyist, organizer, and political strategist.

Between 1977 and 1987, Smeal served three terms as president of the National Organization for Women (NOW). In this role, her involvement in women's causes escalated. Over the course of three decades of service, her activisim included causes as varied as the integration of girls into Little League and lobbying for national legislation related to women's interests, for example, the Equal Credit Opportunity Act (1976), the Pregnancy Discrimination Act (1978), the Civil Rights Act of 1991, the Violence against Women Act (1994), and the Freedom of Access to Clinic Entrances Act, (1994). She campaigned to make Social Security and pensions more equitable for women and to achieve pay equity for women who are segregated in low-paying jobs. In 1984, she published *How and Why Women Will Elect the Next President,* which brought attention to the voting clout of women and to gender differences in the way women and men vote, information that was subsequently used in election and polling analyses. In addition, Smeal also led the drive to ratify the Equal Rights Amendment and she led the first national March for Women's Lives (1986), which drew more than one hundred thousand participants to Washington, D.C.

On August 26, 1995, Smeal pioneered the use of the Internet as a feminist organizing and research tool. She cofounded The Feminist Majority Foundation and launched it on-line as one of the first nonprofit and first women's organization sites on the World Wide Web. As president of this organization, Smeal continues to broaden and intensify actions related to women's issues locally, nationally, and internationally.

Smeal has received numerous awards and honors. Recent among them is the 2002 NOW Woman of Vision Award in recognition of her career and her international campaign to stop gender apartheid in Afghanistan and to counter the Taliban's brutal abuse of women.

Harriet Taylor UPTON

1854-1945

PORTAGE COUNTY

Harriet Taylor Upton was born on December 17, 1854, in Ravenna, Ohio, and moved with her family to Warren in 1862. In 1880, she went to Washington, D.C., to serve as hostess and companion to her widowed father, Congressman Ezra B. Taylor. There she was a favorite in society, appreciated especially for her literary abilities. In 1890, she wrote a children's book entitled *Our Early Presidents, Their Wives and Children*. She also wrote articles for magazines and newspapers and later in life authored two additional books, on the Western Reserve and Trumbull County.

While in Washington, she met and married George Upton. She also met and began a lifelong friendship with Susan B. Anthony. The immediate result of the friendship was that in 1890 Upton joined the National American Woman's Suffrage Association (NAWSA). She worked closely with Anthony and other suffragist leaders to fight for passage of the suffrage amendment. In the NAWSA leadership, she became press secretary, auditor, and treasurer, holding the latter position for fifteen years. In 1903, she was responsible for bringing NAWSA national headquarters to Warren, where it remained until 1909. Upton was also active on the state level, serving as president of the Ohio Woman's Suffrage Association for eighteen years.

After the passage of the Nineteenth Amendment in 1920, Upton became the first woman vice-chair of the Republican National Executive Committee, a position which she held for four years. She was appointed manager of women's work in Senator Warren Harding's presidential campaign. In 1928, she was appointed by Governor Cooper as special representative to the Welfare Department, the first woman to be assigned such a duty. Through this position she was instrumental in several social changes, including child labor laws, and prison reform. She held this position until 1931.

On a local level, Upton was also active. For example, she was the first woman to serve on the Warren Board of Education, holding this post for fifteen years, four as president. She was a founder of the Warren Red Cross and elected temporary chairman of the new chapter. She was also a charter member of the Mary Chesney Chapter of the Daughters of the American Revolution, founded in Warren in 1916, and she founded the League of Women Voters.

In 1931, Upton lost her home in a sheriff's sale and moved to Pasadena, California, where she died in 1945.

Social Activism

SPORTS

AND

ATHLETICS

THE DISCIPLINE THAT IS REQUIRED FOR EXCELLENCE in sports and athletics can be intimidating, but the women in this section were not intimidated. They were inspired—inspired to engage in world-class sports, to choose advocacy of athletics for women as a career path, to use athletics to rebuild their lives, to believe in themselves as capable women. All of these choices require focus, creativity, and dedication, and those highlighted here exhibit each trait with style. They are admired across the state, the nation, and even, in some cases, globally as symbols of strength, resilience, and high performance.

TINA (MARIE) BISCHOFF

MARY L. BOWERMASTER

IVY S. GUNTER

CAROL HEISS (JENKINS)

STEPHANIE HIGHTOWER

DOROTHY KAMENSHEK

CINDY NOBLE (HAUSERMAN)

ANNIE OAKLEY

PAIGE PALMER-ASHBAUGH

EMMA PHALER

RENEE POWELL

MARGARET UNNEWEHR SCHOTT

MARIA SEXTON

Tina (Marie) BISCHOFF

1958–

FRANKLIN COUNTY

Courtesy of Tina M. Bischoff

Tina (Marie) Bischoff, born in 1958 in Columbus, Ohio, is a world-champion long-distance swimmer and top competitor in world-class endurance events around the world. At the age of twelve, Bischoff became an All-American long-distance swimmer, and by fourteen she was a National Long Distance Champion. This early success was just the beginning of a long list of remarkable athletic feats.

In 1976, at age of eighteen, Bischoff swam the English Channel in nine hours and three minutes, thirty minutes better than the previous mark. That same year, she won the Amateur Long Distance Swimming Race sponsored by the Amateur Swimming Association; the Syrian Women's Long Distance Swimming Championship, a seventeen-mile swim between Jablah and Latakia, Syria, in the Mediterranean, becoming the contest's first champion. She won the South American International Women's Amateur Swimming Championship by swimming a fifty-mile distance in nine hours, one minute, and she won the International Long Distance Swim in the Nile. In 1980, Bischoff won the Naples to Capri Swim in Italy and the Nile swim again. In 1983, she was inducted into the International Marathon Swimming Hall of Fame.

Since these championships, Bischoff has sought ever more demanding challenges, competing in events that are sometimes labeled "athletic odysseys" because of their torturous requirements. For example, in 1989 she won the women's competition in the Ultraman World Championships and finished eighth overall. This three-day event, held in Hawaii, is composed of four demanding competitions—a swim, two bike rides, and an ultramarathon—covering 320 miles. In 1994, she set world-record times in the Double Ironman Triathlon.

201

Mary L. BOWERMASTER

1919⁻

BUTLER COUNTY

Mary L. Bowermaster was born on July 26, 1919, in Franklin, Ohio. Before 1981, her life was fairly typical of a wife and mother. However, in that year, at age of sixty-two, she was diagnosed with breast cancer and given a poor prognosis for recovery. Bowermaster did undergo a mastectomy and received extensive radiation treatments, both of which created for her a deep physical and mental challenge. As a method of rehabilitation, she began entering senior track-and-field competitions, even though before her surgery, she indicates that she had done nothing more competitive than chase her two athletic sons when they were late for dinner in the 1950s.

In the beginning, she competed at the local level, but after she proved successful, she began entering state and national competitions. With each venture, she set state, national, and world records in her age group in the 100- and 200-yard dash, the high jump, and the long jump. In 1983, she began competing in world championship events, in places such as San Juan, Puerto Rico, Rome, Melbourne, and Portland, Oregon. In the year 2000, at age eighty-one, she set four world records.

During these years of competition, Bowermaster also became a spokesperson for cancer recovery and senior fitness, speaking before women's groups, civic groups, and cancer support groups throughout Ohio and the United States. She has appeared on national television, including ESPN, *48 Hours,* and *CBS Sunday Morning.*

Bowermaster's messages of life after cancer and life as a senior have been inspirational for untold numbers of people, especially women and cancer survivors, and she has received numerous honors and awards for her invaluable services, including being inducted into the Ohio Senior Citizens Hall of Fame (2000) and the U.S. Masters Track and Field Hall of Fame (2000); being named U.S. Masters Track and Field Athlete of the Year (1987, 1989, 1990, 1991, and 2000); and being named Ambassador of Goodwill, Sanford Golden Age Games (1986).

Profiles of Two Hundred Ohio Women

Ivy S. GUNTER

1950–

SANDUSKY COUNTY

Gunter is a 22-year survivor. The disease cost her a leg and her hair, but not her motivation, as she encouraged fellow survivors to reach out to each other for support and to treasure life.
—Meg Pirnie, *Columbus (Georgia) Ledger-Enquirer,* 2002

Ivy S. Gunter, born on June 22, 1950, in Bellevue, Ohio, began modeling professionally at fifteen while still in high school. Throughout her college years and in the first years of her marriage, she continued to maintain an active professional schedule in top venues in Atlanta, Chicago, and ultimately New York. Having signed with New York's prestigious Wilhelmina Agency, she was photographed for layouts in such magazines as *GQ* and *Cosmopolitan* and for designers such as Calvin Klein and Yves St. Laurent. She was living a dream life, with great expectations for ongoing success. In 1980, however, she was diagnosed with bone cancer. She had a tumor in her right leg that necessitated amputation at the knee and chemotherapy, which caused her hair to fall out. Through her religious beliefs and with the support of family and friends, Gunter found the determination and resilience to continue to excel despite this dramatic shift in her life and career.

One might predict that Gunter continued to model. As she says, "I'm pretty stubborn. Even though I was bald-headed and one-legged, I took a bag of wigs and started modeling again." First with lacquered black crutches decorated with sequins and then with a perfectly designed prosthesis, she was modeling again in six months, evidencing only a slightly stiff gait on the runway. What is not so predictable, however, is Gunter's commitment to athletics and to sports competition. In 1982 she learned to snow ski and to water ski, which she had never attempted before. Since then, she has garnered several bronze and gold medals in the National Handicapped Sports and Recreation Association's competitions, and she spends much of her time speaking before groups and helping to broaden the horizons of both cancer survivors and disabled persons, encouraging them, by illustration of her own life, to experience new and different challenges. Gunter also appears frequently on national television shows and in documentaries, and her book *On the Ragged Edge . . . of Drop Dead Gorgeous* (1993), written with Paul Kartsonis, profiles her courage, survival, and humor.

Sports and Athletics

Carol HEISS (Jenkins)

1940–

SUMMIT COUNTY

CAROL HEISS (JENKINS), born on January 20, 1940, grew up in Queens, New York. She began ice skating at age six, and within five years she was the U.S. Novice Ladies Champion in figure skating. From that point Heiss went on to create a phenomenal record of accomplishments: Junior Ladies Champion (1952); fourth place, world championships (1953); silver medals, U.S. championships (1953–56); silver medal, world championships (1955); gold medals, U.S. championships (1957–60); gold medals, North American championships (1957 and 1959); silver medal, 1956 Olympics; gold medal, 1960 Olympics. Beyond these accomplishments, Heiss was the youngest competitor (at eleven) to win the Novice Championship and Junior Championship back to back and the first woman to land a double axel in competition (1953).

Heiss retired from competition in 1960, and, after a short stint as a professional skater and one movie role, she moved with her husband, fellow Olympian Hayes Alan Jenkins, to Akron, Ohio. Since retirement, she has continued in sports as a skating instructor and a sports commentator for NBC, spending much of her time as a dedicated wife and mother of three and as an active member of boards and community groups in Akron. Heiss has also served on the U.S. Olympic Committee and the United States Figure Skating Association Board of Directors. In recognition of her accomplishments, Heiss has been recognized by the Women's Sports Foundation and inducted into several halls of fame, including the World Figure Skating Hall of Fame.

Throughout her competitive career, Heiss set an incredibly high watermark for sports competition, paving the way for other women Olympians in winter sports who would follow, as evidenced in 2002 by Leann Parsley from Granville, Ohio, who won a silver medal in the first Olympic women's skeleton competition and is setting the pace for yet another generation of women in sports.

Courtesy of Carol Heiss Jenkins

OHIO
WOMEN'S
HALL OF
FAME

Profiles of Two Hundred Ohio Women

Stephanie HIGHTOWER

1961–

FRANKLIN COUNTY

Courtesy of Stephanie Hightower

STEPHANIE HIGHTOWER, born in 1961, grew up in a military family that placed great emphasis on the value of having a good education and being goal-oriented. She was encouraged to do well in school, but the highlight for her was running track and working toward her desire to be in the Olympics. Hightower achieved all three goals (a good education, running track, and being in the Olympics) and more.

Hightower graduated from the Ohio State University with a degree in communications. While there, in addition to her academic accomplishments, she flourished as a world-class athlete. In track and field, Hightower was a four-time All-American and a fifteen-time Big Ten champion. Her event was hurdles, and she was undefeated in four years of Big Ten competition. She holds eleven Big Ten and Ohio State records and set a new world record in the sixty-yard hurdles. In 1993, she was inducted into the Ohio State Women's Varsity "O" Hall of Fame.

In 1980, Hightower was selected for the United States Olympic Team. Ultimately, the United States boycotted the summer games, and athletes were unable to compete. However, Hightower again made the team in 1984 as an alternate. In addition, she has served on the U.S. Olympic Committee and has been selected as a staff member for the 2004 Olympic Team in track and field. Further, as a professional athlete, Hightower competed many times in the Millrose Games, becoming a five-time champion in the hurdles (1980, 1982–85). In 2001, she was inducted into the Millrose Games Hall of Fame.

Hightower's career in public service began during her years of professional competition when she became communications director for the Columbus Urban League as part of the Olympic Job Opportunity Program. When she retired from track and field in 1988, she became communications director with the Ohio Department of Mental Health and was also involved with the Columbus Area Sports Corporation. When Gregory Lashutka decided to campaign for mayor of the city of Columbus, she agreed to manage his speaker's bureau and, following his election, became his press secretary. In 1999, with passionate interests in education, Hightower decided to run for a position on the Columbus Board of Education. She was successful and is currently serving her first term as president.

205

Sports and Athletics

Dorothy KAMENSHEK

1925–

HAMILTON COUNTY

DOROTHY KAMENSHEK was born on December 21, 1925, in Cincinnati, Ohio, where she lived until 1943, when she was drafted by the All-American Girls Professional Baseball League (AGPL) as one of the original players. The league was started by Phillip K. Wrigley (business magnate and owner of the Chicago Cubs) to keep baseball alive during World War II, when many of the male players were at war. Kamenshek was chosen to play in Rockford, Illinois, as a member of the Rockford Peaches. She started in the outfield but was soon switched to first base, where she remained until her retirement.

Kamenshek's lifetime fielding average was an astounding .950. In 1946 and 1947, she won the league's hitting titles with averages of .316 and .306, respectively. She finished second in two other years. Her lifetime average was .292, the highest of all long-term players in the league. In 3,736 at bats, she struck out only eighty-one times. From 1945 to 1953, when she retired, she was selected every year to the league's All Star Team. This stellar record has earned Kamenshek many awards, including being selected by *Sports Illustrated* as one of the top one hundred women athletes of the twentieth century and being honored in a standing exhibit at the Major League Baseball Hall of Fame in Cooperstown, where her performance in baseball was one of only four records from among the AGPL singled out for attention.

The pioneering spirit that Kamenshek brought to baseball was the same spirit that she brought to her work after baseball. In the off-seasons, Kamenshek studied physical education and health education at the University of Cincinnati, graduating, however, in 1958 from Marquette University in Milwaukee. She returned to Ohio to serve as a physical therapist in Hamilton County and after several other positions moved to Los Angeles, where she was a physical therapist for the Los Angeles County Crippled Children's Services. In 1964, she was promoted to supervisor of physical and occupational therapy for Los Angeles County Children's Services, and later to chief of therapy services, the position she held when she retired in 1980.

After her retirement, Kamenshek was honored by Los Angeles County with the Outstanding Management Award (1980).

Cindy NOBLE (Hauserman)

1958–

ROSS COUNTY

CINDY NOBLE (HAUSERMAN) was born on November 14, 1958, in Clarksburg, Ohio. At Adena High School in Frankfort, Ohio, she was an outstanding athlete, including being a player on state champion volleyball, track, and basketball teams. Her achievements continued in college at the University of Tennessee, where she played basketball and participated in three NCAA Division I Final Fours. In 1980, she was chosen to represent the United States on the Olympic women's basketball team. Ultimately, the United States boycotted these games, and athletes were unable to compete. However, she was selected for the team for the 1984 games in Los Angeles. She and her teammates won the gold medal.

Noble has also represented the United States on seven international teams, including being a member of the U.S. Pan American gold medal team in 1984 and the winning U.S. World University Championship team. Noble was also a pioneer in women's professional basketball, playing in the Italian and Japanese women's basketball leagues for three years.

From 1985 to 1989, Noble served as assistant coach at the University of Kentucky before being named head coach for Centre College in Danville, Kentucky. Currently, she has returned to Ohio and is a teacher and coach at Westfall High School in Williamsport. In 1984, Noble's alma mater, Adena High School, honored her by renaming the gymnasium after her. In addition, in 2002, Noble was inducted into the Women's Basketball Hall of Fame and into the University of Tennessee's Lady Vol Hall of Fame.

207

Annie OAKLEY

1860–1926

DARKE COUNTY

Courtesy of the Garst Museum

ANNIE OAKLEY was born Phoebe Ann Mosey in Woodland, Ohio (now known as Willowdell), on August 13, 1860. Growing up in a very poor family, Mosey learned to trap and shoot small game, which she would sell to hotels and restaurants to help support her family. By age fifteen, she had earned a reputation across Ohio for accuracy and skill as a marksman. Her business was so successful that she was able to pay off the mortgage of her family's farm.

At age twenty-one, Oakley, a name she chose as a stage name, was invited by one of her customers to compete as a woman sharpshooter against well-known marksman Frank E. Butler. Oakley defeated Butler, but the relationship that began in that competition resulted in their marriage on June 22, 1882. They toured together with the Sells Brothers Circus, headquartered in Dublin, Ohio. On March 19, 1884, in St. Paul, Minnesota, Oakley met Sioux Chief Sitting Bull, who was so impressed by her skills that he adopted her as his daughter and gave her a Sioux name that translates as "Little Sure Shot."

In 1885, Oakley and Butler joined Buffalo Bill's Wild West, with Oakley receiving top billing and Butler serving as her manager and assistant. On European tours, Oakley was presented in the press as a lady of the Wild Wild West, rather than a person who had honed her skills in the woods of Darke County. Capitalizing on this image, Oakley remained with the Wild West until 1901. In that year, a train accident left her severely injured, but she continued to perform almost until the end of her life.

208

Oakley, immortalized in books, television shows, movies, stage plays, and commercial memorabilia, is now an American icon. A lesser-known fact about her pioneering spirit, however, is that she made two offers during times of war (the Spanish American War and World War I) to assemble a regiment of women sharpshooters to defend the country. Her offers were declined, but in World War I she traveled along the Eastern Seaboard, demonstrating gun safety to servicemen and raising funds for the American Red Cross. Oakley died in 1926 in Greenville, Ohio. In 2000, a stretch of State Route 127 in Darke County was renamed "Annie Oakley Memorial Pike" in her honor.

Paige PALMER-ASHBAUGH

1916−

SUMMIT COUNTY

Courtesy of Paige Palmer-Ashbaugh

P AIGE PALMER-ASHBAUGH, popularly known as Ohio's First Lady of Physical Fitness, was born and raised in Akron, Ohio. She graduated from the University of Akron with a B.A. in physical education and home economics and earned an M.A. in physical education from the University of California at Berkeley. Palmer-Ashbaugh began her career in New York as a model, winning a contest sponsored by Richard Hudnut for "The Perfect Girl Figure." In 1947, she opened the Paige Palmer School of Charm and Fashion Modeling. In 1948, she created the nation's first television exercise show at WEWS in Cleveland, a program that combined beauty, fashion, travel, household concerns, and an impressive parade of celebrity guests. She promoted daily exercise for women and better eating habits long before they were recommended by the medical profession, and she was the first television personality to encourage women to get pap smear tests as a preventive measure for cancer. Palmer-Ashbaugh's program aired for twenty-five years and established her as a pioneer in the field of health and fitness.

In addition to her television program, Palmer-Ashbaugh achieved many other significant markers of success. She was the first person to invent and design exercise equipment strictly for women, "The Complete Home Gym," and to have a line of fitness apparel. Through her salesmanship and persistence, she successfully placed her equipment in every major sporting-goods store in the country, despite their having catered previously only to men. In addition, she turned her experiences as a world traveler into twenty award-winning travel books and wrote countless articles for magazines and newspapers. In recognition of these remarkable achievements, Palmer-Ashbaugh was honored by the United States Congress for improving the quality of life for American women.

Palmer-Ashbaugh is also an art collector and philanthropist. She has served on many boards, including those of the American Cancer Society, the Bath Historical Society, the Crawford Auto-Aviation Museum, and others. Among her many honors and awards, in January 2000, Kent State University dedicated the Paige Palmer Gallery in its university museum in honor of her gift of a 130-piece collection of Ohio art pottery to the museum's permanent collection of decorative arts.

Sports and Athletics

Emma PHALER

1882–1982

FRANKLIN COUNTY

EMMA PHALER was born in Columbus, Ohio, in 1882. After serving one year as secretary of the Columbus Women's Bowling Association, in 1927 Phaler became the executive secretary of the Women's International Bowling Congress (WIBC), a position she held until her retirement in 1965. When she assumed leadership, working with Jeanette Knepprath (from Milwaukee), who served as president (1924–60), the membership of the WIBC stood at 5,357 in twenty-eight cities. When Phaler retired, the membership totaled 2.7 million, bowling in more than 115,000 sanctioned leagues in more than 2,800 cities in the United States, Canada, and many foreign countries.

Phaler is credited with playing many prominent support roles for the WIBC. Her organizing efforts during the formative years are recognized as critical. She facilitated getting the WIBC Annual Convention and Championship Tournament awarded to Columbus in 1927 and 1948, to Cincinnati in 1938, and to Dayton in 1957. She promoted the steady increase in membership and spearheaded the championship tournament's growth to a record 5,071 teams in Minneapolis in 1964. She and Knepprath planned and supervised the WIBC's move to new offices in Columbus, dedicated in 1958. She initiated the Star of Yesteryear category of the WIBC Hall of Fame in 1953. She worked on many committees, devoting time and study to revitalizing the American Junior Bowling Congress and senior programs.

In 1949, Phaler's contributions to bowling were recognized by the Jo Ettien Lieber Award for distinguished service; in 1965 with induction into the WIBC Hall of Fame for meritorious service; and in 1978 by the Flowers for the Living Award.

Profiles of Two Hundred Ohio Women

Renee POWELL

1946–

STARK COUNTY

Courtesy of Renee Powell

RENEE POWELL, born on May 4, 1946, in Canton, Ohio, began playing golf at Clearview Golf Club, the only public course in the world designed, built, and operated by an African American, her father William J. Powell. He modified her first set of clubs for her when she was three. Powell attended Ohio University for two years and was named captain of the women's golf team but transferred to Ohio State in 1967 after her coach decided that she should not compete in a tournament in Jacksonville, Florida, because of racial tensions. During these years, Powell was recognized as the top female amateur golfer in Ohio. She turned professional in 1967 and became the second African American woman to play on the Ladies Professional Golf Association (LPGA) tour and the only African American woman to become a member of of both the LPGA and the PGA of America.

During her thirteen years on the LPGA tour, Powell participated in 250 tournaments, competing in the United States and around the world. She won the Kelly Springfield Open in Brisbane, Australia. She was chosen to represent the United States in the United States versus Japan team matches on four separate occasions, with her team winning all four matches. She made history in the golfing world in 1979 when she became the first woman to be named head professional at a golf course in the United Kingdom, at Silvermere, near London. While in England, Powell designed and promoted golf, tennis, and jogging clothes for McCarthy Sports of London, and she wrote articles for *Par Golf Magazine*.

Leaving the LPGA Tour in 1980, Powell began conducting golf clinics and lecturing nationwide. In 1985, she hosted the first of what would become an annual event, The Renee Powell/Anheuser Busch Golf Tournament to benefit the United Negro College Fund. This event marked an escalation in her commitment to community service, as evidenced by her participation on several advisory boards, as well as by her teaching of golf to women and children. Powell's career has been chronicled in several magazines, including *Golf Digest* and *Ebony,* and she has received many honors and awards, including the 1999 LPGA Service Award for significant contributions to junior golf and being named by *Golf Digest* as one of the top ten teachers in Ohio, the only woman on the Ohio list. In 2003, she was inducted into the North Ohio Section of the PGA Hall of Fame and chosen as the First Lady of Golf in 2003 by the PGA of America.

Sports and Athletics

Margaret Unnewehr SCHOTT

1928–

HAMILTON COUNTY

MARGARET UNNEWEHR SCHOTT was born on August 18, 1928, in Cincinnati. Married to businessman Charles J. Schott, she led the normal life of a corporate spouse until his death in 1968. She assumed leadership of her husband's business empire, including Schottco Corporation, Schott Buick, Inc., Schott Leasing, Southern Ohio Insurance Company, and Alton Brick Company, all in Ohio, and the St. Louis County Landfill Company and Concrete Products, based in St. Louis, Missouri. Schott wasted no time in demonstrating that she was an astute businesswoman, not only capable of running her husband's operations, one of the forty largest business networks in the United States, but of adding to it holdings on her own. Schott became the first woman in the nation to obtain a General Motors dealership, the first woman trustee of the Cincinnati Chamber of Commerce (1972), and perhaps most striking of all, the first woman in the United States to purchase a major-league sports team, when in 1981 she became the principal owner of the Cincinnati Reds baseball club.

Amid some controversy, Schott has provided the leadership and financial support needed to build the Cincinnati Reds into a financially successful winning team. Her dream of quality entertainment for Reds fans came true in 1990 when the Reds became National League Western Division Champions, captured the National League pennant, and won the World Series in a stunning sweep. Schott was jubilant, leading the victory parade in downtown Cincinnati and heading the contingent from the baseball club that was honored by President George Bush in the White House. In 1987, she was inducted into the Communiplex Women's Hall of Fame for women in sports.

Schott remains active with community organizations as well. She has been a board member, for example, of the Ohio Arts Council, the Boy Scouts of America, Maryville College in St. Louis, Rio Grande Community College in Rio Grande, Ohio, Xavier University in Cincinnati, and the Cincinnati Zoo. She has also received many honors and awards, including an honorary degree from Maryville College (now Maryville University) in 1991, being named an honoree in 1989 at the Women in Business luncheon at the White House, being saluted by *Savvy Magazine,* and being named Woman of the Year by the American Legion Auxiliary in 1986.

Maria SEXTON

1918–

WAYNE COUNTY

Maria Sexton, born on December 17, 1918, received a degree in physical education from Western Michigan University (1942), an M.A. from Ball State (1951), and an Ed.D. from Columbia University (1953). In 1953, she was appointed to the faculty at the College of Wooster in Ohio, where she served as chair of the Women's Physical Education Department for over ten years before the men's and women's programs were merged in 1964. Despite her disappointment in not being selected chair of the new department, Sexton remained steadfast in her vision for women in sports, continuing to serve as a professor, coach, and passionate advocate for women's athletics. Over the next twenty years, she laid the groundwork for several women's varsity programs: field hockey (1965), basketball and volleyball (1966), tennis (1971), lacrosse and swimming (1973), softball (1978), track (1980), cross country (1981), and soccer (1985).

Sexton's impact went beyond the College of Wooster, however. She served multiple roles in bridging the gap between the American Athletic Union (AAU) and women physical educators. In addition, among these other national roles, she served as a national basketball, volleyball, and track and field official; a member of the U.S. Olympic committee for track and field (1964–72); chair of the U.S. Olympic committee for basketball (1972–76); manager of the U.S. women's track and field team at three international meets and at the 1967 Pan American Games; and on the Track and Field Committee of the United States Collegiate Sports Council (1967–71). From 1971 to 1972, she was a charter commissioner of the Midwest Association of Intercollegiate Athletics for Women and active in developing, with the Ohio High School Athletic Association, rules for girls in sports. In addition to these activities, Sexton was a premier breeder of Saint Bernard dogs. Her Squaw Valley Kennel, from which she retired in 1999, produced both American and Canadian national champion Saint Bernards.

Sexton's honors and awards are manifold. In 1969 the College of Wooster established the Maria Sexton Award, in 1982 she received an Association of Intercollegiate Athletics for Women Presidential Service Award, and in 1999 she received the National Association of College Women Athletic Administrators' Lifetime Achievement Award.

Sports and Athletics

STAGE AND SCREEN

PERFORMANCE

AMONG THE MOST VISIBLE ARENAS FOR WOMEN'S achievements are the theater, television, and the cinema. Performers in these media are larger than life for those of us who watch and are fascinated from a distance. They speak and act our thoughts and dreams, and they take us on imaginative ventures into geographical territories and internal landscapes that, before their intervention, are sometimes unacknowledged but often completely unknown. They make us laugh. They make us cry. They make us think. Because of their visibility, their names are often on many tongues, but because they are filled with talent and beauty, they are also easily taken into our hearts and homes with joy and admiration. Ohio is remarkable for being the homeplace for so many of these women, as illustrated in the following pages. We can count Ohioans among the pioneers across all categories. Indeed, they are among the very best in this field. We love them as the world does and salute them for the magnificence of their talents and their gifts to us all.

HALLE BERRY

AMELIA SWILLEY BINGHAM

ROSEMARY CLOONEY

DORIS DAY

RUBY DEE

PHYLLIS DILLER

SUZANNE FARRELL

LILLIAN GISH

ELSIE JANIS (BIERBOWER)

MAIDIE NORMAN

JOSEPHINE LINDEMAN SCHWARZ

Halle BERRY

1966–

CUYAHOGA COUNTY

Courtesy Karen Samfilippo; Fadil Berisha, photographer

HALLE MARIA BERRY was born on August 14, 1966, in Cleveland, Ohio, where she attended suburban schools. Despite experiencing discrimination in a predominantly white community, Berry's resilient spirit prevailed. In high school, she was active in school organizations, a leader in student government, and a member of the honor society. At seventeen, Berry won the Miss Teen Ohio beauty pageant, the first of several high-profile competitions in which she competed, winning Miss Teen All American, capturing first runner-up in Miss USA, and representing the United States in Miss World.

After high school graduation, Berry attended Cuyahoga Community College but soon left to pursue a career in modeling and to study acting in Chicago. Leaving Chicago for New York, she was successful in securing her first television role in the short-lived situation comedy *Living Dolls.* Her first big break came in 1989, when Spike Lee cast her as a crack-addicted woman in *Jungle Fever,* playing opposite Samuel L. Jackson. She received much acclaim for this performance and went on to other television and movie roles, including a recurring role on the popular nighttime soap opera *Knots Landing* in 1991.

With movie roles as her goal, however, Berry was soon in other big-screen productions, including *The Last Boy Scout, Boomerang, The Flintstones, Losing Isaiah, Executive Decision, Bulworth, X-Men,* and *Swordfish.* She also received television movie and miniseries roles, including *Queen, The Wedding,* and *Introducing Dorothy Dandridge,* for which she won the 2000 Golden Globe Award and an Emmy for Best Actress in a miniseries or television movie.

With the film *Monster's Ball,* Berry reached her highest critical acclaim to date. For her portrayal of a death row convict's wife, she received the 2002 Screen Actors Guild Award and made history as the first African American to receive the Academy Award for Best Actress. Berry followed the critical acclaim of *Monster's Ball* with more action films: *Die Another Day,* a James Bond film, and *X-Men 2.* In addition, she has continued her modeling career as a spokesperson for Revlon, Inc., and has taken on a new role as a volunteer for the Juvenile Diabetes Association, having been recently diagnosed with this disease.

217

Stage and Screen Performance

Amelia Swilley BINGHAM

1869–1927

DEFIANCE COUNTY

A MELIA SWILLEY BINGHAM was a major player in the world of Broadway theater, both onstage and off, but her stage career began in Hicksville, Ohio, where she was born on March 20, 1869. Her father owned the Swilley House, a hotel that stood at the site of the present-day Hicksville Bank. She attended college at Ohio Wesleyan, and during vacations waited tables in the hotel dining room.

Across the street from the hotel was the acoustically perfect Huber Theater, used to try out Chicago and New York stage productions. Lloyd Bingham, actor/manager of the theater, and Amelia were married in 1890. Bingham spent the next three years apprenticing in theaters around the country and debuted on Broadway on December 18, 1893, at the old Bijou Theater. Noted for sparkling performances in both melodramas and comedies, Bingham gained renown. In 1900, Bingham's success made it possible for her to acquire the Bijou. Within a year, she organized the Amelia Bingham Stock Company and leased the theater, becoming the first American woman to succeed as a Broadway actress, producer, and manager. In addition, she became the first president of the Professional Women's League, an advocate for theatrical roles for mature women, and an active charitable worker with the Actors' Fund of America. Despite Bingham's active life in New York, neither she nor her husband ever forgot Hicksville. She was a regular visitor to the Defiance County Fair; gave motivational speeches to young people; championed the Hicksville Hart's Boys Band and Hart's All-Girl Band; and attended Armistice Day gatherings.

218

Bingham died of pneumonia in 1927 at her home in New York. The *New York Herald Tribune* and the *Times* both noted that there were more than two thousand mourners. Her memorabilia are in the Museum of the City of New York, but the Hicksville Historical Society has many copies of photographs and theater bills. Her books, part of a $200,000 estate that was quite large for her day, were left to the Hicksville Schools.

Courtesy of Mary Smith

OHIO
WOMEN'S
HALL OF
FAME

Rosemary CLOONEY

1928-2002

HAMILTON COUNTY

Courtesy of Concord Records; Fergus Greer, photographer

Rosemary Clooney was born on May 23, 1928, in Maysville, Kentucky, but moved with her family to Cincinnati, Ohio, when she was thirteen years of age. In 1945, she and her sister Betty successfully auditioned to perform on Cincinnati's WLW radio station. They were featured on live shows for two years, singing with a wide range of performers including both jazz sextets and country and western groups. By 1947, they had been invited to tour with Tony Pastor's big band. After three years, Betty Clooney decided to stop performing, but Rosemary continued, having signed with Columbia Records in New York. In 1950, she recorded "Beautiful Brown Eyes," which sold more than half a million copies; in 1951, "Come on-a My House," which sold more than a million copies; and over the next two years, six more hits, including "Hey There," which sold more than three million copies. By this point, Clooney was well on her way to becoming a legendary vocalist most noted for her jazz sensibilities, and a star of both movies and television.

With such remarkable success as a "girl singer," "Rosie" became a household name. In 1953, she appeared on the cover of *Time* magazine, and her career shifted to Hollywood musicals. Most notable among several other films, *White Christmas* (1954), in which she costarred with Bing Crosby and Danny Kaye, was the top-grossing film of the year. By 1956, she was married with five children and also starring in her own television variety show, *The Rosemary Clooney Show* (1956–57), for which she received an Emmy Award nomination. During the next decade, she struggled on a personal level and her career waned, setbacks she addressed in her autobiography, *This for Remembrance* (1977). By 1977, Clooney had reestablished her career and began performing and recording again. In 1994, she returned to television to appear with her nephew, George Clooney, in a recurring role on *ER,* a performance for which she received a second Emmy Award nomination. Clooney's many other honors and awards include the most prestigious Lifetime Achievement Award, which she received during the 2002 Grammy Awards Ceremony. Clooney died on June 29, 2002.

Doris DAY

HAMILTON COUNTY

DORIS DAY, the quintessential "all-American girl," was born Doris Mary Ann Von Kappelhoff on April 3, 1924, in Evanston, Ohio, a suburb of Cincinnati. As a young girl, Day had aspirations to be a dancer, but her dreams were shattered by an automobile accident that severely injured her right leg. She turned then to the development of her voice with coach Grace Raine. Raine arranged for her to appear on Cincinnati radio station WLW on an amateur showcase, which earned her a featured spot on the station. For the competition, she sang Howard Dietz and Arthur Schwartz's "Day after Day," the song that would ultimately be the source of her stage name. In 1939, she began singing with the Bob Crosby band (led by Bing's brother) before moving on in 1940 to sing for the next six years with the Les Brown band, with which she made her first recordings.

Day's movie career began in 1948 with *Romance on the High Seas,* which placed her on a dual career track as singer and movie star. She enjoyed box office success with films such as *Calamity Jane* (1953), *The Man Who Knew Too Much* (1956), *Pillow Talk* (1959), *Please Don't Eat the Daisies* (1960), *Midnight Lace* (1960), and many others, demonstrating her talents for both comedy and drama. Simultaneously, Day became a best-selling recording star, turning many of the songs from her movies into some of the most popular songs of the day. After the death of her husband/manager in 1968, Day stopped making movies, focusing instead on a top-ranking television show, *The Doris Day Show* (1968–73).

Since the late 1970s, Day has directed much of her energy to animal rights issues. She established her first nonprofit organization in 1977, and today heads the Doris Day Animal League and Doris Day Animal Foundation, through which she has brought attention to the inhumane use of animals in laboratory testing, rescued thousands of dogs and cats from the streets and placed them in caring homes, and provided referral services for pet owners.

Courtesy of Doris Day

OHIO
WOMEN'S
HALL OF
FAME

Profiles of Two Hundred Ohio Women

Ruby DEE

1924–

CUYAHOGA COUNTY

R<small>UBY</small> D<small>EE</small>, born Ruby Ann Wallace in Cleveland, Ohio, moved to New York with her family when she was a baby. She graduated in 1945 from Hunter College with a bachelor of arts degree in French and Spanish and worked briefly as a translator. Her career choice, however, was actress. She began acting with the American Negro Theatre when she was a college student. Her Broadway debut was a walk-on part in *South Pacific* in 1943. In 1946, she appeared in *Jeb* opposite Ossie Davis (whom she married in 1948), and in the 1946–47 season, she received national recognition for her title role in *Anna Lucasta*. Dee was well on her way to establishing herself as a world famous actress, writer, and producer.

Dee has performed in innumerable stage productions, most notably *Raisin in the Sun* (1959), *Purlie Victorious* (1961), and *Boesman and Lena* (1970), for which she won an Obie Award (1971). In 1965 her roles in *The Taming of the Shrew* and *King Lear* established her as the first African American woman to play major parts in the American Shakespeare Festival in Stratford, Connecticut. She also received a Drama Desk Award for her performance in *Wedding Band* and an Ace Award for *Long Day's Journey into Night*. In the movies, Dee attracted national attention in 1950 for her performance in *The Jackie Robinson Story* and subsequently appeared in more than twenty films. On television, she has an extensive list of guest appearances and has been nominated seven times for Emmy Awards, winning in 1991 for *Decoration Day*. As a writer, she has received a Literary Guild Award (1989) for her plays, poems, and children's stories. She was inducted into the Black Filmmakers Hall of Fame (1975) and the Theater Hall of Fame (1988). In 1995, Dee and her husband were celebrated as "national treasures" when they were awarded the National Medal of Arts, and in 2000 they received the Screen Actors Guild Life Achievement Award.

Dee and Davis are also well known for their social activism. They were close friends and supporters of Martin Luther King Jr., serving as masters of ceremonies for the historic 1963 March on Washington, and they have been involved in many demonstrations for justice, equality, and empowerment.

Stage and Screen Performance

Phyllis DILLER

1917–

ALLEN COUNTY

PHYLLIS DILLER, born Phyllis Driver in Lima, Ohio, on July 17, 1917, graduated from Central High School in 1935. She studied at Sherwood Music Conservatory in Chicago for three years and continued at Bluffton College in Bluffton, Ohio, where she met her husband, Sherwood Diller. At the age of thirty-seven, Diller was working as a newspaper writer, columnist, and publicist for radio station KSFO in San Francisco and raising five children. With the encouragement of her husband, she prepared a nightclub act that was booked into San Francisco's Purple Onion in 1955, for two weeks. She was so successful that she continued to perform there for almost two years. From this striking beginning, Diller established herself through live performances, television, and movies as an outrageous comic with a distinctive and irrepressible laugh.

Diller has appeared in innumerable venues around the world, drawing capacity crowds at supper clubs and concert halls from Carnegie Hall in New York to Caesar's Palace in Las Vegas and touring Canada, England, Bermuda, Monte Carlo, and Australia. In 1966, she accompanied Bob Hope on his tour of South Vietnam, and she appeared on twenty-two of his television specials. Diller's list of television appearances includes regular stints on *The Tonight Show* and guest spots on several other programs. Her movie credits include three films with longtime friend Bob Hope (e.g., *Boy! Did I Get a Wrong Number*) and dozens of others, most notably Elmer Rice's prize-winning satire *The Adding Machine,* in which she had a dramatic role. Diller has appeared also in Broadway and other stage productions, including a performance as the Wicked Witch in a St. Louis production of *The Wizard of Oz* (1992). She has written four best-selling books. Diller has also displayed her musical talents, appearing as a piano soloist with more than a hundred symphony orchestras in the United States and Canada and receiving acclaim as piano virtuoso Dame Illya Dillya.

Diller has received a broad range of honors and awards: the AMC Cancer Research Center Humanitarian Award (1981), Celebrity Businesswoman of the Year by the National Association of Women Business Owners (1990), Lifetime Humor Award from the National Humor Institute (1993), a star on the Hollywood Walk of Fame, and an award from the American Academy of Cosmetic Surgery.

222

OHIO
WOMEN'S
HALL OF
FAME

Suzanne FARRELL

1945 –

HAMILTON COUNTY

Courtesy of the Kennedy Center; Paul Kolnik, photographer

Suzanne Farrell, born Roberta Sue Flicker in Cincinnati, Ohio, on August 16, 1945, became the youngest ballerina in the history of the New York City Ballet when she joined the corps de ballet of the company at sixteen years of age in the 1961–62 season. The path to such a distinctive achievement, however, was not one easily predicted. She did not grow up expecting a career in dance. She was tall, fidgety, tomboyish, and not interested in dancing. She began studying dance at the age of eight with her sisters when her parents decided that dance classes might make her more ladylike. Initially, she preferred tap and acrobatics to ballet, but by the age of twelve she was working diligently, practicing and rehearsing at the Cincinnati Conservatory of Music. In 1959, Farrell was selected to audition for the legendary choreographer George Balanchine, and with the support of a Ford Foundation Scholarship she moved to New York to attend his school. Her life was changed forever.

By the summer of 1963, Farrell was dancing featured roles with the New York City Ballet, appearing in a role in *Arcade,* created for her by choreographer John Taras, and in leading roles in *Agon, Orpheus, Liebeslieder Walzer, Don Quixote,* and many other ballets. After touring Europe and the Middle East, Farrell was named principal dancer, and in 1966 she undertook the lead role of the Swan Queen in Balanchine's version of Tchaikovsky's *Swan Lake,* performing to much critical praise. After her marriage to fellow dancer Paul Mejia, Farrell left the company and began dancing with Ballets of the Twentieth Century, a Brussels-based company. Later, she returned to the New York City Ballet and other United States–based companies, retiring from the stage in 1989, but continuing to teach Balanchine ballets to new generations of dancers worldwide and serving as an advisor to the Fort Worth Dallas Ballet. In 2000, she launched the Suzanne Farrell Ballet in partnership with the Kennedy Center for the Performing Arts in Washington, D.C.

Farrell has received numerous awards, including honorary doctorates from universities such as Yale and Georgetown, and an Emmy Award in 1985 for her performance in *Eight by Alder,* choreography by Mejia.

223

Stage and Screen Performance

Lillian GISH

1893–1993

STARK COUNTY

Courtesy of the Stark County, Ohio, Bicentennial Committee

L ILLIAN GISH was born Lillian Diana de Guiche on October 14, 1893, in Springfield, Ohio; her sister, Dorothy (1898–1968), was born in Dayton. Both attended school in Massillon, Ohio. All of the Gish women—Lillian, Dorothy, and their mother, Mary—were talented actors, but Lillian excelled both in front of the camera and behind it, with a career stretching from 1902, when she debuted at The Little Red School House in Rising Sun, Ohio, through 1988, when she made her 106th feature film, *The Whales of August,* at the age of ninety-two.

In 1912, Gish went to New York with her mother and sister to visit their friend Mary Pickford, who introduced them to silent filmmaker D. W. Griffith. Griffith gave all of them parts in *An Unseen Enemy.* This collaboration was the first of forty films that Gish would do with Griffith, including the highly controversial *Birth of a Nation* (1915). Through their thirteen-year alliance, Gish established herself as the quintessential silent film heroine—beautiful, frail, innocent, virginal—an image in stark contrast to the highly confident professional pioneer in filmmaking that she actually was.

Gish made her debut as the first female film director in 1920 with *Remodeling Her Husband,* starring her sister Dorothy. In 1922, Lillian Gish started making movies at MGM, where she gained the distinctive privilege of artistic control over her films. She made her first sound movie, *One Romantic Night,* in 1930. Shortly thereafter, she returned to the Broadway stage, where she spent most of the remainder of her career, returning periodically to do films, such as *Duel in the Sun* (1946), *Portrait of Jennie* (1948), *The Comedians* (1967), *Twin Detectives* (1976), *Hobson's Choice* (1983), and *Adventures of Huckleberry Finn* (1985), and occasionally television programs as well. The Academy of Motion Picture Arts and Sciences presented Gish with an honorary Oscar in 1971, and in 1984 the American Film Institute awarded her its Life Achievement Award.

Massillon dedicated a street, Lillian Gish Boulevard, in her honor, and Bowling Green State University honored both Gish sisters in naming the Gish Film Theater and Gallery. Lillian Gish died on February 27, 1993, in New York; Dorothy Gish died in 1968.

Elsie JANIS (Bierbower)

1889–1956

FRANKLIN COUNTY

Courtesy of the Elsie Janis Collection of the Laura M. Mueller British and American Theatre and Film Collection, the Jerome Lawrence and Robert E. Lee Theatre Research Institute, The Ohio State University Libraries

Elsie Janis (Bierbower), born in Columbus, Ohio, on March 6, 1889, began performing at the age of six with an imitation of Anna Held, a popular performer of the era, singing "Won't You Come Play with Me." Her professional career as a child began in a Neal and Griffin Stock Company production of *East Lynne.* By age fourteen, she was earning a salary of twenty dollars a week at the Great Southern Theatre. She left Columbus for New York with her mother, Josephine Janis Bierbower, who guided Elsie's career until 1930. Janis was an immediate success in New York, soon receiving an invitation to sing before President William McKinley in the White House. Using the name Elsie Janis, she excelled as a mimic, singer-comedienne, and actress, and for the first thirty years of her fifty-year career, she was known as the queen of vaudeville comedy.

A succession of hits established Janis's reputation as a star in both the United States and London, where she made her debut in 1914 in *The Passing Show.* During World War I, she was the only woman entertainer permitted at the front. She entertained troops throughout war-torn areas and was credited with more than six hundred performances. She was known as the "Sweetheart of the AEF" (American and European forces) and received several honorary decorations. After the war, Janis returned to the United States and headed her own troupe, "Elsie Janis and Her Gang." Eventually, she moved to Hollywood, writing screenplays, story lines, dialogue, and songs, and appearing in several movies, including *Close Harmony; Dark Victory,* for which she cowrote one of the songs; and *Women in War,* her last movie before retirement in 1940. During World War II, she came out of retirement to repeat her services as an entertainer for the troops. Janis died on February 26, 1956, in Beverly Hills, two days before her sixty-seventh birthday.

225

Stage and Screen Performance

Maidie NORMAN

1912–1998

MAIDIE NORMAN, born Maidie Ruth Gamble on October 16, 1912, in Villa Rica, Georgia, spent most of her childhood in Lima, Ohio. By the time she was ten, she was studying drama and performing in Shakespearean plays. She graduated from Central High School in 1930; went to Bennett College, receiving a B.A. in 1934; earned an M.A. in theater from Columbia University in 1937; and trained at the Actors Laboratory in Hollywood from 1946 to 1949. Norman made her film debut in *The Burning Cross* in 1948 and her stage debut in *Deep Are the Roots* in Los Angeles in 1949. Norman appeared in more than thirty-five feature films, numerous stage productions, and a wide range of television programs, miniseries, and television commercials.

When Norman, a talented actor, dancer, and singer, came to Hollywood in 1945, she found few outlets for African American women beyond stereotypical servant roles. Over the years, while she did indeed play many servant roles, she was an outspoken critic of such limited and limiting representations, and she was persistent in portraying her characters with dignity and pride. Her most recognizable movie titles include *Whatever Happened to Baby Jane?* (1962), *Written on the Wind* (1975), and *Airport 77* (1977). She appeared in numerous popular television shows, such as *Marcus Welby, MD, Barnaby Jones, Ironside, The Incredible Hulk, Little House on the Prairie,* and many others.

During the 1950s, Norman also lectured at colleges throughout the nation, sharing her knowledge of African American theater and literature. In 1955 and 1956, she taught at Texas State College in Tyler; she was artist in residence at Stanford University, 1968–69; and in 1970 she was asked to develop a course at UCLA on the history of black theater, which was one of the first African American studies courses offered at UCLA. Norman taught at UCLA until her retirement in 1977.

Norman received many awards and honors over her career, including the Black Filmmakers Hall of Fame Award (1977); the Maidie Norman Research Award, established by UCLA in her name in 1982; and an honorary doctorate from Bennett College (1992). She died on May 2, 1998.

Courtesy of the Ohioana Library Association

226

Josephine Lindeman SCHWARZ

MONTGOMERY COUNTY

Josephine Lindeman Schwarz was born in Dayton, Ohio, on April 8, 1908. She began taking ballet lessons as a young child, studying in Chicago and New York during school vacations. She started dancing professionally while she was still in high school and ultimately performed nationally and internationally, including in New York, Austria, and Germany. In 1927, Schwarz and her sister Hermene (1902–1986) founded the Schwarz School for Dance in Dayton. Hermene taught at the school, while Schwarz continued to dance in New York. In 1937, however, Schwarz sustained a knee injury that ended her performance career, and she returned to Dayton to devote her talents and energy to choreography and the development of the school.

In 1937, Schwarz took the seven most advanced dancers at the Schwarz School to form the Experimental Group for Young Dancers. This group, renamed the Dayton Theater Dance Group in 1941 and the Dayton Ballet Theater in 1957, evolved into the Dayton Ballet Company (renamed in 1988), the second oldest regional company in the United States. In 1971, the Dayton Ballet was designated a major company by the National Association of Regional Ballets. Other major landmarks were the company's first touring season in 1974 and its first performance in New York (1983). In 1987, the Dayton Ballet was selected to perform at the opening ceremonies of the Pan-American Games. The 1987–88 season marked the company's fiftieth anniversary. The Dayton Ballet has built a national reputation for excellence both in its dancers and choreographers (for example, Joseph and Dan Duell and Donna Wood) and in its productions (such as the first full-length production of *Sleeping Beauty,* the first *Swan Lake* to be choreographed for a company of fifteen, and its trademark *Fast Company*).

Schwarz served as program director, teacher, and choreographer. She choreographed more than sixty major works and numerous dances for plays, operas, and special events. Most noted among her pieces are *Escapes* and *I Watched Myself Grow Up.* Schwarz also served on several national boards, including the National Endowment for the Arts, and many regional advisory groups as well, including the Ohio Arts Council. Josephine Schwarz remains an inspiration for dance in Dayton and throughout the state of Ohio.

OHIO WOMEN'S HALL OF FAME

VISUAL ARTS

THIS COLLECTION OF PROFILES WOULD NOT BE complete without a chronicle of the achievements of Ohio women in the visual arts. These women have demonstrated a capacity not only to see the world as a place filled with beauty and curiosities, but also to represent magnificently what they see. These artists have been photographers, painters, textile artists, multimedia artists, architects, designers, and sculptors in marble, ceramics, and other materials. They have helped those around them see and re-see both ourselves and the environments in which we live. They have been trailblazers in their own media in much the same way that others have been pioneers on the land, such that collectively they have created legacies for the eye, the heart, and the soul.

BERENICE ABBOTT

HARRIET JACOBY ANDERSON

NANCY FORD CONES

MARY E. COOK

ANN HAMILTON

BERNICE KOCHAN

(MARY) EDMONIA LEWIS

MAYA LIN

JANE REECE

ALICE SCHILLE

Berenice ABBOTT

1898–1991

CLARK COUNTY

*Courtesy of the Museum of the City of New York;
Kay Simmon Blumberg, photographer*

BERENICE ABBOTT, an internationally recognized photographer, was born in Springfield, Ohio, on July 17, 1898. She attended public schools in Columbus and Cleveland and attended the Ohio State University for a short time before moving in 1918 to New York, where she intended to study journalism at Columbia University, but soon switched to sculpture. After 1921 she divided her time between Paris and Berlin. In Paris, after working as a darkroom assistant for American photographer Man Ray from 1923 to 1925, she set up her own studio, photographing well-known Parisian expatriates, artists, writers, and aristocrats, and built a reputation for portraiture, as demonstrated by her first one-person show, *Portraits photographiques,* in 1926.

During this period Abbott became aware of the photographic work of Eugène Atget, who later in 1927 came to her studio to be photographed, shortly before his death. When his collection of photographs became available for sale, Abbott, who much admired them, purchased the entire collection. She cared for Atget's work for the next forty years, and through her publication in 1930 of *Atget, photographe de Paris,* she brought him critical and popular attention.

By 1929, despite her great success in Paris, Abbott returned to the United States, making New York City her home. There she developed a passion for the city itself. In addition to her ongoing work as a portrait photographer and a new interest in photographing scientific subjects and physical phenomena, Abbott's activities now included documenting images of the city. Funded by the Federal Art Project from 1935 to 1939, Abbott produced *Changing New York,* with text by Elizabeth McCausland.

Abbott exhibited her work almost continuously in the United States throughout her long and successful career. She wrote seventeen books, received four U.S. patents for inventions related to her profession, and taught photography at the New School for Social Research in New York City from 1934 to 1958.

In 1954, while photographing the Atlantic Coast, Abbott first experienced the attractions of the state of Maine. In 1956 she bought a home in Monson, Maine, which she moved into permanently by 1968. Abbott died in her home in Monson in 1991.

231

Visual Arts

OHIO
WOMEN'S
HALL OF
FAME

Harriet Jacoby ANDERSON

1913–1980

ATHENS COUNTY

"The architects' artist."

—*Ohio Architects*, 1968

Harriet Jacoby Anderson, a painter and textile artist, received an M.A. in fine arts from Ohio University in 1933. She spent the following years raising a family, and in 1961 she returned to school to study techniques of modern art at the Ohio State University. Beginning a career as an artist, Anderson developed an unusual style of collage using acrylic paints, natural (or "found") materials, and Japanese papers. In 1967, she began to work in wool and fiber tapestries as well. Anderson has been honored with numerous one-person shows, and her pieces are in local and national collections, including the David Rockefeller Collection in New York City, the Union Gallery at the Ohio State University, and the Huntington Trust Gallery.

Anderson is also acknowledged as a devoted patron of the arts. She was a volunteer for the Columbus Gallery of Fine Arts. She served as president of Columbus Beaux Arts, chairperson of the Designer Craftsmen Show, member of the Women's Board of Columbus Gallery of Fine Arts, and member of its board of trustees. Moving to Athens, Ohio, in 1973, she founded the Friends of Trisolini Gallery at Ohio University and started a gallery shop to provide an outlet for local craftsmen. In addition, she was a trustee of the Hocking Valley Arts Council, chaired the Visual Arts Committee for the Ohio Arts Council, and served on the board of the Ohio Foundation of the Arts, the Trisolini Gallery Board, and the Public Broadcasting Advisory Board for Ohio University.

Anderson's advocacy is perhaps best exemplified by her efforts to establish the Dairy Barn as a center for crafts and arts in Southeast Ohio. Slated for demolition in 1977, the sixty-three-year-old barn seemed to Anderson a perfect home for a cultural arts center. Her campaign to accomplish this goal was successful, and the Dairy Barn is now listed on the National Register of Historic Places. Anderson had both an architectural and an artistic vision that was essential in the preservation of cultural possibility in this area.

Courtesy of Dr. Ora E. Andersen

232

OHIO WOMEN'S HALL OF FAME

Nancy Ford CONES

1869–1962

WARREN COUNTY

Courtesy of Dr. Randle H. Egbert, Jr.

Nancy Ford Cones, born in Milan, Ohio, was an internationally known photographer who considered herself an amateur despite the fact that she received more than fifty-four awards in national photographic competitions from 1902 through 1916. Living in Covington, Kentucky, after her marriage to James Cones (a painter, self-taught photographer, and innovative expert in film processing), Cones and her husband had a photography studio until 1905 when they moved to Loveland, Ohio. There Cones documented images of Ohio country life. She photographed work in farm fields as well as in farm homes, creating images that projected a romantic aura for such tasks during an era of rapid industrialization when audiences were finding provincial views of life and work satisfying and compelling.

Cones was an active member of the Cincinnati Photographic Club and became well known during these years for her portraits of prominent Cincinnati residents, including President William Howard Taft and artist Henry Farny. Cones also worked with Bausch and Lomb and Ansco Corporation and received lucrative advertising contracts with Eastman Kodak. All three manufacturers purchased, used, and exhibited her work and helped to establish her as one of a very few photographers, especially women, who were able to make a significant income in this field. Her photographs were deemed valuable not only for their commercial marketability, but also for their artistic merit.

Among Cones's awards was second prize (among 28,000 entries) for a competition sponsored in 1905 by the Eastman Kodak Company. Her photographs have been exhibited in galleries and museums across the country and in London, England. They are included in many prestigious collections, such as the Cincinnati Art Museum, the George Eastman House, the Chicago Art Institute, the University of Iowa Museum of Art, the Metropolitan Museum of Art, and the Smithsonian's National Portrait Gallery. They have been featured in several magazines, including *Country Life in America, Woman's Home Companion, Browning's Magazine, Photo-Era Magazine,* and *American Photography.*

233

Visual Arts

Mary E. COOK

1864-1951

FRANKLIN COUNTY

Mary E. Cook, born in 1864 in Chillicothe, Ohio, was the first woman to enroll in ceramic engineering at the Ohio State University. Leaving the university in 1911 without completing the program, she went on to study in New York and Paris, where she became a student of the famous American sculptor Paul Wayland Bartlett. In 1912 and 1913, she had her own studio in Paris, and exhibited there, including a piece considered to be one of her best, "Joyeuse Rencontre" or "A Happy Meeting." When Cook returned from Paris, she also exhibited in New York, Philadephia, Chicago, and Toledo.

Following World War I, Cook put her talents as a sculptor and student of human anatomy to practical and humane use. Appointed to keep records of plastic surgery in France, Belgium, Italy, and England for the medical museums and to help inform the government about what was being done for soldiers disabled in the war, she had not yet begun work when the armistice agreement was signed. In 1919 she was reassigned to Fort McHenry, near Baltimore, to assist surgeons in reconstructing the faces of wounded soldiers. Her responsibility was to make masks from the soldiers' faces to be copied by the surgeons in rebuilding their destroyed features. After Fort McHenry, Cook was sent to the Fort Hayes Hospital in Columbus, with forty-six of the worst cases. Ultimately, she spent a total of three years working with more than five hundred maxillo-facial cases.

With Cook's return to Columbus, she was once again able to use her talents to create sculptures. She set up a studio that was visited by other famous sculptors, including internationally renowned Gutzon Borglum, who praised her work. She received commissions from churches, individual patrons, and community and civic organizations, including the Ohio State University. In addition, she was commissioned to prepare seven panels in marble for the new Woman's Building at the corner of Front and Town Streets. Cook died in 1951 after a prolonged effort to recover from an accident in which a large sculpture fell on her at her studio.

Courtesy of the Ohio Historical Society

Profiles of Two Hundred Ohio Women

Ann HAMILTON

1956–

FRANKLIN COUNTY

ANN HAMILTON was born in Lima, Ohio, on June 22, 1956, and grew up in Columbus. From 1974 to 1976, she attended St. Lawrence University, where she studied liberal arts. She graduated from the University of Kansas in 1979 with a B.F.A. in textile design and received an M.F.A. in sculpture from Yale University in 1985. She has taught at the University of California at Santa Barbara and is currently on the faculty of the Ohio State University.

Hamilton is known for large installation pieces that combine her interests in textiles and sculpture and include a wide variety of materials—flowers, feathers, textiles, animal hair, and so on—in order to create complex and evocative layers of meaning for her audiences. Since her debut in 1981, she has participated in more than sixty solo and group exhibitions in cities nationally and internationally, including, among others, Pittsburgh, Cleveland, Chicago, Santa Fe, New York, Los Angeles, Philadelphia, Houston, Miami, Columbus, São Paulo, Sydney, Montreal, London, Lyon, Dublin, and Knislinge, Sweden.

In 1999 Hamilton represented the United States at the forty-eighth Venice Biennale and presented a work entitled "Myein," a Greek root of the word mystery, which refers both to an abnormal contraction of the eye's pupil and a rite of initiation. According to Judith H. Dobrzynski of the *New York Times,* this installation "deals with how we know what we know and what we blind ourselves to, how the invisible affects us and how the visible can be veiled, how we learn from seeing and from touching. . . . [I]t is about looking very hard at the things we as humans do to other people."

Hamilton has received many prestigious awards, including a Guggenheim Fellowship, a Louis Comfort Tiffany Award, the Larry Aldrich Foundation Award, a National Endowment for the Arts fellowship, and in 1993 the coveted MacArthur Foundation Fellowship.

235

Visual Arts

Bernice KOCHAN

1926–

CUYAHOGA COUNTY

Bernice Kochan was born in Cleveland, Ohio, on August 30, 1926. She graduated from West Technical High School and studied at the Cleveland Institute of Art. Kochan set a remarkable pace as a philatelic artist whose designs are among the most reproduced in the nation. In 1969, she designed the tuberculosis Christmas seals. In that same year, two United States postage stamps of her design were issued—the six-cent W. C. Handy and Alabama statehood stamps—thus making her the second woman in postal history to have designed two stamps and the only woman to have designed two commemoratives in one year. The two stamps were reproduced 130 million times each and the Christmas seals 8 billion times.

As an artist, Kochan has also been a major contributor to the Cleveland community. Working in her studio in the historical Cleveland Arcade, she designed the symbol used for Cleveland's Super-Sesquicentennial Celebration in 1971 and the variation of this symbol used as the logo for the Greater Cleveland Bicentennial Commission. For seven years, she designed Christmas cards for the Heart Association of Northeast Ohio, Inc., and she has designed logos and other art for the City Club, the Cleveland Zoological Society, the inaugural issue of the Cleveland Zoo local post stamps, the Cleveland National Air Races, and many public relations agencies.

Now retired, Kochan has created art for a variety of organizations, including the American Chemical Society, the Rubber City Stamp Club in their tribute to Judith Resnik (also featured in this collection), and the Danbury Mint Postal Commemorative Society in their tribute to classic movies.

(Mary) Edmonia LEWIS

C. 1843 OR 1844

LORAIN COUNTY

Courtesy of the Massachusetts Historical Society

(M̲ary) E̲dmonia L̲ewis, the first Ojibwa (Chippewa)–African American sculptor to achieve international distinction, often listed her birthplace as Greenhigh, Ohio, but verification has not been found, since her birthplace is also variously listed as New York and New Jersey. Born in the early 1840s, Lewis (known among her Indian family as Wildfire) grew up as an orphan among a group of Missisaugas who fished and hunted along the northern shore of Lake Ontario. Eventually, her older brother Samuel (Sunrise) enrolled her in preparatory school at New York Central College in McGrawville, New York, where she studied with three leading African American intellectuals of the day, Charles Reason, George Vashon, and William Allen. In 1859, Lewis enrolled at Oberlin College, studying successfully there until apparently racially motivated accusations of thefts and a brutal beating of her by parties unnamed caused her to leave for Boston in 1863 without being allowed to graduate.

With the help of Boston's abolitionist community, Lewis apprenticed to sculptor Edward Brackett and began her career by creating terra-cotta medallions of champions of liberation (e.g., John Brown and Wendell Phillips) and terra-cotta busts of others, most notably Colonel Robert Gould Shaw (the white leader of the African American Fifty-fourth Massachusetts Infantry). Financed by sales of copies and photographs of her bust of Shaw, Lewis moved to Rome in 1865. There she became a member of an expatriate group of U.S. artists and writers that included several women sculptors. In Rome, she continued to study and refine her art, working more in marble and establishing herself as a master of the neoclassical style. Among her most famous works are *Forever Free* (1867–68); *The Old Indian Arrowmaker and His Daughter* (1872); *Asleep* (1874); *Awake* (1874); *Abraham Lincoln* (1874); *Hagar* (1875); and *The Death of Cleopatra* (1876). These pieces are currently displayed at the Smithsonian's National Museum of American Art, the Howard University Art Gallery, and the San Jose Public Library.

Although Lewis's fame was greater in Europe than in the United States, she received commissions from both sides of the Atlantic and was invited to major exhibitions: the Philadelphia Centennial Exhibition (1876), and the Chicago Interstate Exposition (1878). Lewis died, presumably in Rome, on a date unknown after 1909.

237

Maya LIN

ATHENS COUNTY

She created what is arguably the most moving architectural touchstone of her generation.
—*New York Times*, 1998

Maya Lin was born in Athens, Ohio, on October 5, 1959, into a family of talented artists, poets, and literary scholars. Upon graduation from Athens High School in 1977, Lin enrolled at Yale University, where she received undergraduate and graduate degrees in architecture in 1981 and 1986 respectively. In 1981, when Lin was still an undergraduate, her design for a Vietnam veterans' memorial was selected from more than 1,400 competition entries, bringing her national and international recognition in the world of art, architecture, and design. Over the years, the Vietnam Veterans Memorial, sited among other treasured monuments in Washington, D.C., has served the nation well. It draws more than four million visitors each year, and in its simplicity, it succeeds in both memorializing the dead and giving solace and inspiration to the living.

In 1987, Lin opened her own studio in New York, where she now lives. Her works include other large-scale sculptures, among them the Civil Rights Memorial (1989) at the Southern Poverty Law Center in Montgomery, Alabama; *Groundswell* (1993) at the Wexner Center for the Arts at the Ohio State University in Columbus; *Women's Table* (1993) at Yale University; and *Reading a Garden* (1998) at the Cleveland Public Library in Cleveland, Ohio. She has also created studio sculptures, furniture, and building designs.

238

Lin's awards are many, including the Henry Bacon Medal for Memorial Architecture, a prestigious award named for the designer of the Lincoln Memorial, granted in 1984 for the Vietnam Veterans Memorial; the architecture prize from the American Academy of Arts and Letters; the Presidential Design Award; and the American Institute of Architects Honor Award. In 1995, a documentary about Lin and her work, *Maya Lin: A Strong Clear Vision*, won the 1995 Academy Award for Best Documentary, and her autobiography, *Boundaries* (2000), has been well received.

Profiles of Two Hundred Ohio Women

Jane REECE

1868-1961

MONTGOMERY COUNTY

JANE REECE was born in West Jefferson, Ohio, in 1868, and lived in Dayton from 1904 until her death at the age of ninety-two in 1961. One of Dayton's most famous artists, she was primarily a self-taught photographer who specialized in portraiture, or pictorialism. She saw photography as a form of visual poetry, and her desire was to use this form to bring out the true personality of her subjects and express the highest ideals of beauty.

Reece named her first studio "Rembrandt Studio," as she sought to create photographs that were mindful of the paintings of artists such as Rembrandt, Vermeer, Millet, and Hals. For example, she posed models in diaphanous gowns, used exotic costumes, and photographed them through diffusion lenses to soften the images, all in an effort to meet the ideals of the pre-Raphaelite painters and demonstrate that she was indeed a regional example of an international movement in her field.

Reece received her first major recognition in 1907 when the Photographers Association of America, convening in Dayton, honored her by naming her the first woman portraitist to be made a member. She exhibited in sixty-nine foreign and fifty-seven U.S. exhibitions and received fifteen honors and awards. She made what she labeled "Camera Cameos" of almost six hundred of the most respected citizens of Dayton. She had five studios in Dayton and made studio visits to Columbus, Akron, and Detroit for portrait sittings. As her eyesight declined, Reece created her last photograph in 1944.

In 1952, she presented her entire collection of almost four hundred prints and all her medals and awards from 1911 to 1951 to the Dayton Art Institute. Upon her death in 1961, nearly nine thousand negatives were added by bequest and are currently stored at the Wright State University Library Archives. In 1963, the Dayton Art Institute held a Jane Reece Memorial exhibit, *The Wonderful World of Photography*, and in 1997 the museum held another 250-print exhibition, *The Soul Unbound: Photographs by Jane Reece (1868–1961)*.

239

Visual Arts

Alice SCHILLE

1869–1955

FRANKLIN COUNTY

ALICE SCHILLE, one of the foremost American watercolorists of the early twentieth century, was born in Columbus in 1869, the daughter of a prosperous bottle and soda manufacturer. Graduating in 1893 from the Columbus Art School (which later became the Columbus College of Art and Design) at the top of her class, she continued her studies at the Art Students League, the New York School of Art, and William Merritt Chase's summer school at Shinnecock, Long Island, one of the earliest schools of outdoor painting in America. From 1903 to 1904, she attended the Acadème Colarossi in Paris. Schille traveled often in order to paint, going during the summer, for example, to England, Germany, France, Spain, Holland, Yugoslavia, Russia, North Africa, Mexico, Guatemala, Norway, Turkey, Greece, and Belgium. During these trips, she visited museums and observed other painters (such as John Singer Sargent, August Rodin, Henri Matisse, Paul Cézanne, Picasso, Diego Rivera, and Georgia O'Keeffe). Ultimately, Schille developed her own highly original, personal style. Schille returned in 1904 to Columbus, where for the next four decades she taught at the Columbus School of Art while continuing her travels.

Early in her career, Schille's paintings were included in exhibitions at the New York Water Color Club and the Société Nationale des Beaux-Arts. Subsequent to her return to Columbus, she exhibited frequently, not only in Columbus, but also in cities across the nation: Chicago, Cleveland, Cincinnati, Detroit, Philadelphia, New York, and Washington, D.C. She received numerous honors and awards, including the Philadelphia Water Color Club Prize (1915) and first prize at the Panama-Pacific International Exposition (1915).

Schille retired in 1948 from the Columbus School of Art and died in 1955. Her works have been displayed recently in Atlanta, New York, Columbus, Dallas, Chicago, and Washington, and two of her paintings have been on loan to the American Embassy in Bonn.

240

APPENDICES

APPENDIX 1

Ohio Women's Advisory Council of the Ohio Bicentennial Commission and the Staff of the Ohioana Library Association

OHIO WOMEN'S ADVISORY COUNCIL OF THE OHIO BICENTENNIAL COMMISSION

Ellen Nasner, public affairs manager, OhioReads, Department of Education, chair
Betty Barbe, Worthington, Ohio
Sally Farran Bulford, Mt. Sterling, Ohio
Carrie Diroll, student, Youth Council
Lana Eisenbraun, Harriet Taylor Upton Association
Louise Fisher, executive director, Ohio Women with Disabilities Network
Joy Gough, reenactor—Lucy Ware Webb Hayes
Mariwyn Heath, Heath Associates
Linda Hengst, director, Ohioana Library Association
Judy Logan, curator, Garst Museum
Nancy Rose, Council of Ohio YWCAs
Imogene Davenport Trolander, posthumous member (1924–2000)
Anastasia K. Vargo, student, Youth Council
Charlene Ventura, executive director, YWCA—Greater Cincinnati

THE OHIOANA LIBRARY ASSOCIATION

Linda R. Hengst, director
Barbara Meister, librarian
Cynthia Sweet Bard, administrative assistant
Kathleen Hipes, library assistant
Kate Templeton Fox, editor, *Ohioana Quarterly*

APPENDIX 2

Profiles by Region

CENTRAL OHIO

Fairfield

Georgia Griffith

Franklin

Sandra Shank Beckwith
Tina (Marie) Bischoff
Bunny Cowan Clark
Mary E. Cook
Dorothy Alice Cornelius
Eva Mae (Parker) Crosby
Ellen Walker Craig-Jones
Jo Ann Davidson
Gertrude W. Donahey
Jessie Stephens Glover
Ann Hamilton
Kathleen V. Harrison
Stephanie Hightower
Rebecca D. Jackson
Elsie Janis (Bierbower)

Carol S. Kelly
Cheryl Krueger-Horn
Farah B. Moavenzadeh Majidzadeh
Ada M. Howe Martin
Mary Andrew Matesich
(Elizabeth) Anne O'Hare McCormick
Florence Spurgeon Zacks Melton
Harriet Hyman Parker
Helen Hoff Peterson
Emma Phaler
Benvin Sansbury
Alice Schille
Grayce Edwards Williams

Licking

Cora Bell Clark
(Geraldine) Jerrie L. Fredritz Mock
Victoria Claflin Woodhull

EAST CENTRAL OHIO

Belmont

Betty Zane

Coshocton

G. Maxine Haxton Carnahan

Harrison

Mary Leonore Jobe Akeley

Muskingum

Tami Longaberger
Lorle Porter
Margaret Diane Quinn

NORTHERN OHIO

Cuyahoga

Florence Ellinwood Allen
Mary Beaumont
Halle Berry
Patricia Ann Blackmon
Frances Payne (Bingham) Bolton
Mary O. Boyle
Jeanette Gecsy Grasselli Brown
Patricia M. Byrne
Jean Murrell Capers
Tracy Chapman
Ruby Dee
Dorothy (Dora Schnell) Fuldheim
Sara J. Harper
Donna L. Hawk
Bernadine Healy
Adella Prentiss Hughes
Jane Edna Harris Hunter
Stephanie Tubbs Jones
Rosabeth Moss Kanter
Dorothy L. Kazel
Bernice Kochan
Blanche E. Krupansky

Maggie (Margaret) Eliza Kuhn
Carol Hilkirk Latham
Fannie M. Scott Lewis
Irene Duhart Long
Ruth Reeves Lyons
Andre Norton
Karen Nussbaum
Nancy C. Reynolds Oakley
Darlene M. Owens
Yvonne Pointer (Triplett)
Muriel Siebert
Farah Moavenzadeh Walters
Georgeta Blebea Washington
Margaret W. Wong

Lake

Frances Jennings Casement

Lorain

Frances Marion (Fanny) Jackson Coppin
(Mary) Edmonia Lewis
Toni Morrison
Helen Steiner Rice

NORTH CENTRAL OHIO

Ashland

Lucille G. Ford

Huron

Ethel G. Swanbeck

Knox

Mary Ann Ball Bickerdyke
Helen Grace McClelland
Helen E. Weiner Zelkowitz

Marion

Mary Ellen Withrow

Morrow

Rae Natalie Prosser de Goodall

NORTHEAST OHIO

Ashtabula

Betsy Mix Cowles
Eleanor Cutri Smeal

Mahoning

Antoinette Parisi Eaton
Elizabeth McMichael Powell

Trumbull

Zell Patti Smith Hart Deming
Elizabeth J. Hauser
Marie Barrett Marsh
Phebe Temperance Sutliff

NORTHEAST CENTRAL OHIO

Portage

Carol A. Cartwright
Hattie Lena Gadd Larlham
Harriet Taylor Upton

Stark

Lillian Gish
Sharon Lane
Norma Snipes Marcere
Renee Powell
Margaret Arline Webb Pratt

Summit

Rita Dove
Carole Garrison
Mary Ignatia Gavin, C.S.A.
Carol Heiss (Jenkins)
Dorothy O. Jackson
Sylvia Lewis
Paige Palmer-Ashbaugh
Willa B. Player
Judith A. Resnik
Ludel Boden Sauvageot
Henrietta Buckler Seiberling
Julia Curry Montgomery Walsh

Wayne

Maria Sexton

NORTHWEST OHIO

Defiance

Daeida Hartell Wilcox Beveridge
Amelia Swilley Bingham

Erie

Christine M. Cook
Nancy Linenkugel, O.S.G.
Audrey Mackiewicz
Jacquelyn J. Mayer (Townsend)

Henry

Marjorie M. Whiteman

Lucas

Mildred Wirt Benson
Norma B. Craden

Ruth L. Davis
Aurora Gonzalez
Bettye Ruth Bryan Kay
Martha J. Pituch
Alice Robie Resnick
Ella Nora Phillips Myers Stewart

Sandusky

Ivy S. Gunter

Wood

Mildred Mason Bayer
Christine Brennan
Sarah M. Deal
Betty D. Montgomery
Gloria Steinem

SOUTHERN OHIO

Gallia

Marian Regelia Alexander Spencer

Lawrence

Nannie (Scott Honshell) Kelly Wright

Ross

Sarah Jane Woodson Early
Esther M. Greisheimer
Lucy Ware Webb Hayes
Cindy Noble (Hauserman)
Emma Ann Reynolds
Nancy Wilson

Scioto

Kathleen Battle

Vinton

Maude Charles Collins

247

SOUTHEAST OHIO

Athens

Harriet Jacoby Anderson
Eusebia Simpson Hunkins
Maya Lin
Barbara Ross-Lee

Washington

Frances Dana Gage
Nancy P. Hollister

SOUTHWEST OHIO

Butler

Mary L. Bowermaster
Louella Thompson

Hamilton

Elizabeth Blackwell
Emma Lucy Braun
Rosemary Clooney
Martha Kinney Cooper
Doris Day
Suzanne Farrell
Marilyn Hughes Gaston
Nikki Giovanni
Janet Kalven
Dorothy Kamenshek
Beatrice Lampkin
Jennie Mannheimer
Marjorie B. Parham
Jennie Davis Porter
Helen Rankin
Margaret Unnewehr Schott
Harriet Beecher Stowe
Lillian D. Wald

Shelby

Farida Anna Wiley

Warren

Nancy Ford Cones

SOUTHWEST CENTRAL OHIO

Clark

Berenice Abbott

Clinton

Louise McCarren Herring

Darke

Susan F. Gutermuth Gray
Annie Oakley

Greene

Hallie Quinn Brown
Jewel Freeman Graham
Virginia Esther Hamilton
Zoe Dell Lantis Nutter
Imogen Davenport Trolander

Miami

Joan C. Heidelberg

Montgomery

Margaret J. Andrew
Erma Fiste Bombeck
Electra Collins Doren
Charity Edna Adams Earley
Cathy Guisewite
Mariwyn Dwyer Heath
Jane Reece
Josephine Lindeman Schwarz
Virginia MacMillan Varga
Faye Wattleton
Clara E. Weisenborn

WEST CENTRAL OHIO

Allen

Phyllis Diller
Maidie Norman

Auglaize

Nanette Davis Ferrall

Mercer

V. Lanna Samaniego

Putnam

Lauretta Schimmoler

249

APPENDIX 3

Profiles by Century

Eighteenth Century

Betty Zane

Nineteenth Century

Mary Leonore Jobe Akeley
Florence Ellinwood Allen
Mary Beaumont
Daeida Hartell Wilcox
    Beveridge
Mary Ann Ball Bickerdyke
Amelia Swilley Bingham
Elizabeth Blackwell
Frances Payne (Bingham)
    Bolton
Emma Lucy Braun
Hallie Quinn Brown
Frances Jennings Casement
Cora Bell Clark
Maude Charles Collins
Nancy Ford Cones
Mary E. Cook
Martha Kinney Cooper
Frances Marion (Fanny)
    Jackson Coppin
Betsy Mix Cowles
Norma B. Craden
Zell Patti Smith Hart
    Deming
Electra Collins Doren
Sarah Jane Woodson Early
Frances Dana Gage
Jessie Stephens Glover
Esther M. Greisheimer

Elizabeth J. Hauser
Lucy Ware Webb Hayes
Adella Prentiss Hughes
Jane Edna Harris Hunter
Elsie Janis (Bierbower)
Mary Edmonia Lewis
Jennie Mannheimer
Helen Grace McClelland
(Elizabeth) Anne O'Hare
    McCormick
Annie Oakley
Emma Phaler
Margaret Arline Webb Pratt
Jane Reece
Emma Ann Reynolds
Benvin Sansbury
Alice Schille
Henrietta Buckler Seiberling
Ella Nora Phillips Myers
    Stewart
Harriet Beecher Stowe
Phebe Temperance Sutliff
Ethel G. Swanbeck
Harriet Taylor Upton
Lillian D. Wald
Farida Anna Wiley
Victoria Claflin Woodhull
Nannie (Scott Honshell)
    Kelly Wright

Twentieth Century

Berenice Abbott
Harriet Jacoby Anderson
Margaret J. Andrew

Kathleen Battle
Mildred Mason Bayer
Sandra Shank Beckwith
Mildred Wirt Benson
Halle Berry
Tina (Marie) Bischoff
Patricia Ann Blackmon
Erma Fiste Bombeck
Mary L. Bowermaster
Mary O. Boyle
Christine Brennan
Jeanette Gecsy Grasselli
    Brown
Patricia M. Byrne
Jean Murrell Capers
G. Maxine Haxton
    Carnahan
Carol A. Cartwright
Tracy Chapman
Bunny Cowan Clark
Rosemary Clooney
Christine M. Cook
Dorothy Alice Cornelius
Ellen Walker Craig-Jones
Eva Mae (Parker) Crosby
Jo Ann Davidson
Ruth L. Davis
Doris Day
Sarah M. Deal
Ruby Dee
Phyllis Diller
Gertrude W. Donahey
Rita Dove
Charity Edna Adams Earley

Antoinette Parisi Eaton
Suzanne Farrell
Nanette Davis Ferrall
Lucille G. Ford
Dorothy (Dora Schnell) Fuldheim
Carole Garrison
Marilyn Hughes Gaston
Mary Ignatia Gavin
Nikki Giovanni
Lillian Gish
Aurora Gonzalez
Rae Natalie Prosser de Goodall
Jewel Freeman Graham
Susan F. Gutermuth Gray
Georgia Griffith
Cathy Guisewite
Ivy S. Gunter
Ann Hamilton
Virginia Esther Hamilton
Sara J. Harper
Kathleen V. Harrison
Donna L. Hawk
Bernadine Healy
Mariwyn Dwyer Heath
Joan C. Heidelberg
Carol Heiss (Jenkins)
Louise McCarren Herring
Stephanie Hightower
Nancy P. Hollister
Eusebia Simpson Hunkins
Dorothy O. Jackson
Rebecca D. Jackson
Stephanie Tubbs Jones
Janet Kalven
Dorothy Kamenshek
Rosabeth Moss Kanter
Bettye Ruth Bryan Kay
Dorothy L. Kazel
Carol S. Kelly
Bernice Kochan

Cheryl Krueger-Horn
Blanche E. Krupansky
Maggie (Margaret) Eliza Kuhn
Beatrice Lampkin
Sharon Lane
Hattie Lena Gadd Larlham
Carol Hilkirk Latham
Fannie M. Scott Lewis
Sylvia Lewis
Maya Lin
Nancy Linenkugel
Irene Duhart Long
Tami Longaberger
Ruth Reeves Lyons
Audrey Mackiewicz
Farah B. Moavenzadeh Majidzadeh
Norma Snipes Marcere
Marie Barrett Marsh
Ada M. Howe Martin
Mary Andrew Matesich
Jacquelyn J. Mayer (Townsend)
Florence Spurgeon Zacks Melton
(Geraldine) Jerrie L. Fredritz Mock
Betty D. Montgomery
Toni Morrison
Cindy Noble (Hauserman)
Maidie Norman
Andre Norton
Karen Nussbaum
Zoe Dell Lantis Nutter
Nancy C. Reynolds Oakley
Darlene M. Owens
Paige Palmer-Ashbaugh
Marjorie B. Parham
Harriet Hyman Parker
Helen Hoff Peterson
Martha J. Pituch

Willa B. Player
Yvonne Pointer (Triplett)
Jennie Davis Porter
Lorle Porter
Elizabeth McMichael Powell
Renee Powell
Margaret Diane Quinn
Helen Rankin
Alice Robie Resnick
Judith A. Resnik
Helen Steiner Rice
Barbara Ross-Lee
V. Lanna Samaniego
Ludel Boden Sauvageot
Lauretta Schimmoler
Margaret Unnewehr Schott
Josephine Lindeman Schwarz
Maria Sexton
Muriel Siebert
Eleanor Cutri Smeal
Marian Regelia Alexander Spencer
Gloria Steinem
Louella Thompson
Imogen Davenport Trolander
Virginia MacMillan Varga
Julia Curry Montgomery Walsh
Farah Moavenzadeh Walters
Georgeta Blebea Washington
Faye Wattleton
Clara E. Weisenborn
Marjorie M. Whiteman
Grayce Edwards Williams
Nancy Wilson
Mary Ellen Withrow
Margaret W. Wong
Helen E. Weiner Zelkowitz

251

APPENDIX 4

Other Notable Women

This collection profiles two hundred women, but the list of women nominated was far longer. Their names are chronicled below as further evidence of how richly and variously Ohio women have contributed to their communities, the state, the nation, and the world. This list is composed of people whose achievements have been documented in some way—by their nomination for this publication, by their inclusion in the Ohio Women's Hall of Fame, by their records as local, state, and national office holders, and so on. There are legions of other women, however, whose stories are essentially unknown, except perhaps by family, friends, or local associates, and whose achievements are not publicly documented. This publication, therefore, is just a beginning in the long-overdue effort to acknowledge and celebrate the invaluable work of women throughout the history of this state and across all walks of life.

WOMEN NOMINATED FOR THIS PUBLICATION

Aull, Marie
Badger, Earladeen
Bacon, Delia Salter
Baldwin, Lillian
Ball, Carol L.
Bampton, Rose
Barber, Kathleen L.
Barnes, Helen F.
Bauer, Clara
Behrensmeyer, Mary Jo
Berlin, Grace F.
Bettelini, Carrie Steineman
Biggins, Anna Ash
Biggs, Ione M.
Biles, Fay R.
Bingham, Eula
Black, Helen Chatfield
Blubaugh, Artha
Boardman, Mabel T.

Bolte, Ann
Boreczky, Rebecca S.
Boyd, A. Margaret
Boyer, Elizabeth
Boyer, Ida
Bracken, Harriet
Braig, Donna Fisher
Braun, Annette
Brown, Laura
Bulford, Sally Farran
Byers, Marilyn
Cadaract, Victoria
Campbell, Edith
Campbell, Elizabeth
Campbell, Marianne Boggs
Campbell, Mary
Cauffman, Joy Garrison
Clarke, Marie
Cleveland, Beatrice J.

Clonch, Patricia L.
Coffey, Virginia J.
Colombi, Viola Famiano
Conover, Charlotte Reeve
Cook, Lois Anna Barr
Cooper, Sally J.
Costilla, Alvina
Cotner, Mercedes
Coulton, Claudia J.
Cratty, Mabel
Crawford, Ruth Porter
Cronise, Florence
Cronise, Nettie
Crumbley, Katherine Nameth
Dambrot, Faye H.
Danziger, Margaret
Darst, Lily
Davies, Lois
DeLeon, Margarita
Diaz-Sprague, Raquel
Dorsey, Martha
Doulton, Diane
Dow, Cora
Drake, Grace L.
Drennan, Cynthia
Drury, Harriet Maltby
Duerk, Alene
Dumont, Julia L.
Durnell, Hazel
Dyer, Elizabeth
Easterling, Barbara J.
Eastman, Linda
Eberling, Lena
Eddy, Mary
Edwards, Mary
Eriksson, Ann
Ernst, Phyllis A.
Evans, Elizabeth
Evans, Naomi J.
Everhard, Caroline McCullogh
Ewing, Catherine Fay

Farians, Elizabeth
Farris, Lillie
Fasset, Josephine
Fast, Louisa K.
Faust, Grace Fern
Fenberg, Matilda
Fernandez-Mott, Alicia
Fletcher, Patricia Louise
Flowers, Daisy M.
Foley, Bernice W.
Ford, Constance Elaine
Frankenberg, Caroline Luisa
Fredericka, Theresa
Gallager, Ursula M.
Garfield, Eliza Ballow
Gauchat, Dorothy
Gazelle, Ann
George, Zelma Watson
Gillmor, Karen
Gish, Elizabeth
Glendinning, Hooker
Glenn, Annie
Goldsmith, Elizabeth
Goode, Ida
Goodman, Kathryn
Gossett, Lillian Brown
Gould-Hochman, Elizabeth
Graves, Michelle Y.
Greer, Agnes Reeves
Griesse, Jill Harms
Griffin, Velma Shotwell
Hagler, Katherine
Hall, Bobbie M.
Harrington, Sister Jean Patrice
Harris, Sarah E.
Harshman, Florence
Hawver, Dr. Mary E.
Hayner, Mary Jane
Heckewelder, Sara Ohneberg
Henry, Nea
Herbert, Clarice Gamble

253

Hiatt, Marjorie
Hintz, Joy Alice
Hoffman, Shirley G.
Hollenback, Maude
Holley, June A.
Hoover, Carole F.
Hopkins, Edna Bel Boies
Hovorka, Dorothy Humel
Huang, Jennie
Irwin, Josephine
Izant, Grace Goulder
Jackson, Luella Talmadge
Jammal, Eleanor
Janis, Barbara
Janis, Lillian
Jensen, Geraldine
Jermain, Frances D.
Jones, Gertrude Ward
Kakiris, Barbara
Kane, Beatrice
Kane, Carol
Kapossy-Palasics, Kathy
Kaptur, Marcy
Kaukonen, Amy
Keeler, Harriet L.
Keller, Edith M.
Kelly, Lorana
Kennedy, Cornelia
Kingsley, Florence Morse
Kirkham, Jane
Kitchen, Tella
Klemack, Maria Cadiz
Kline, M. Consolata
Knittle, Rhea
Kunkle, Virginia Lloyd
Lake, Sarah
Lamson, Joan E.
Larsen, Bea V.
Law, Mary
Laws, Annie
Lazarus, Mary K.

Leedy, Emily L.
Leimbach, Patricia Lenton
Lenski, Lois
Lev, Alice Raful
Leveque, Katherine S.
Levin, Maxine Goodman
Libbey, Florence
Longman, Evelyn B.
Luebke, Grace
MacCracken, Eliza Daugherty
MacDonell, Martha Shorts
Macelwane, Geraldine
Macko, Manne Variano
Maher, Amy
Mahoney, Carolyn
Mahoney, Margaret A.
Mandel, Barbara A.
Manning, Helen Taft
Mayer, Beverlie Buck
McCullogh, Rubie J.
McHamm, Deborah
McKell, Estelle
McKelvey, Dorothy
McQuate, Maud
McQueen, Joanne
Merritt, Agnes S.
Middleton, Lucille Gregg
Miller, Belle
Miller, Louise Klein
Miller, Ruth R.
Moon, Donna
Moore, Martha C.
Morgan, Violet
Mulholland, Helen Warner
Murphy, Gratia
Myers, Linda James
Nagle, Nadine
Nava, Amelia
Nemeth, Mary Louise
Nielsen, Mary
Nuppert, Louise

Nussdorfer, Lucille
Oakar, Mary Rose
Olshansky, Rena J.
O'Rourke, Ann L.
Papier, Rose L.
Parsley, Leann
Perry, Doris
Peters, Jean
Peterson, Virgene
Pfeiffer, Marie
Pincham, Edna D.
Pinkerton, Catherine
Player, Minnie R.
Plummer, Maxine
Porter, Susan L.
Poulton, Diane W.
Prentiss, C. J.
Pryce, Deborah
Przelomski, Anastasia
Purdy, Virginia Milner
Rajadhyaksha, Kasturi
Randolph, Lottie
Redinger, Rachel Blair
Reed, Allene
Regula, Mary A.
Reilly, Jean Waid
Riel, Pauline
Rocker, Linda
Rogers, Carole
Rothschild, Beryl E.
Rubin, Lee (Lenore)
Ruehlmann, Virginia J.
Sandoe, Mildred
Sandusky, Mother Mary
Santmyer, Helen Hooven
Scott, Barbara
Scott, Carol
Scott, Evlyn
Shackelford, Thekla R.
Sherwood, Kate Brownlee
Shur, Fanchon

Smith, Mildred
Spain, Jayne Baker
Spence, Paula A.
Sprague, Kate Chase
Spretnak, Charlene
Steinbrenner, Mary Jen
Steinem, Pauline Perlmutter
Sterne, Bobbie
Stewart, Eliza Daniel
Storer, Maria Longworth
Strickland, Marcy
Strother, Sarah A. B. Merriam
Sullivan, Kathryn
Taft, Annie Sinton
Taylor, Mary Emily
Thoburn, Isabella
Thomas, Edith M.
Thompson, Eliza
Thornton, Jerry Sue
Timken, Suzanne P.
Tribe, Deanna L.
Trimble, Marian
Untermeyer, Jean Starr
Utz, Carolyn
Vaglia, Marilyn
Valiquette, Marigene
Van Ho, Kay Frances
Ventura, Charlene
Vereeke-Hutt, June
Vesey, Kim
Vetrone, Nancy
Walker, Ann B.
Walker, Selma Lois
Walker-Taylor, Yvonne
Walsh, Stella
Weber, Doris M.
Weishaupt, Clara
Welch, Odella
Weller, Ida
Wells, Marion S.
Wells, Sarah E.

255

Whitman, Ann

Williams, Maude

Winning, Freda Gerwin

Wintermute, Martha

Wolcott, Mary

Wolcott, Rachel

Wollenberg, Joyce

Woods, Jacqueline

Woodward, Alice

Yost, Pauline

Young, Mary Miller

Zannoni, Stella Marie

Zeisberger, Susan Lecron

Zimpher, Nancy Lusk

WOMEN WHO HAVE SERVED AS FIRST LADIES

Listed below are the names of all of the women who served as first ladies of the state of Ohio and Ohio women who have served as first ladies of the United States. Over the course of their political careers, in partnership with their husbands, they contributed substantially to their communities. This collection has highlighted Lucy Ware Webb Hayes and Martha Kinney Cooper as women representative of this group. Hayes served both as the first lady of Ohio (twice) and as the first lady of the nation; Cooper founded the Ohioana Library Association and, in doing so, helped to make this volume possible.

Ohio First Ladies

Mary Worthington Tiffin, 1803–7

Sarah Smith Kirker, 1807–8

Hannah Huntington, 1808–10

Sophia Wright Meigs, 1810–14

Pamela Clark Looker, 1814

Eleanor Swearingen Worthington, 1814–18

Rachel Woodrow Trimble, 1822, 1826–30

Mary Parkhill Morrow, 1822–26

Nancy McDonald McArthur, 1830–32

Friendly Sumner Lucas, 1832–36

Mary Lemon Vance, 1836–38

Sarah Obsun Shannon, 1838–40, 1842–44

Sarah Ross Corwin, 1840–42

Julia Larwill Bartley, 1844

Elizabeth Welles Bartley, 1844–46

Sarah Shuck Bebb, 1846–49

Harriet Cook Ford, 1849–50

Mary Rice Wood, 1850–53

Catherine Jane Chase, 1856–60

Anne Neil Dennison, 1860–62

Maria Smith Tod, 1862–64

Caroline Nelson Brough, 1864–65

Eliza Brown Anderson, 1865–66

Helen Finney Cox, 1866–68

Lucy Ware Webb Hayes, 1868–72, 1876–77

Margaretta Proctor Noyes, 1872–74

S. Agnes Riddle Young, 1877–78

Mary Threlkild Bishop, 1878–80

Ann Olmsted Foster, 1880–84

Mary Perry Hoadly, 1884–86

Julia Bundy Foraker, 1886–90

M. Elizabeth Owens Campbell, 1890–92

Ida Saxton McKinley, 1892–96

Ellen Ludlow Bushnell, 1896–1900

Carolyn Parmely Herrick, 1904–6

Anna Williams Pattison, 1906

Caroline Conger Harris, 1906–9

Olivia Scobey Harmon, 1909–13

Allie Dustin Willis, 1915–17

Margaretta Blair Cox, 1917–21

Lucy Fegan Davis, 1921–23

Mary Harvey Donahey, 1923–29

Martha Kinney Cooper, 1929–31

Mary White, 1931–35

Berenice Chrisman Davey, 1935–39

Harriet Day Bricker, 1939–45

Jane Sheal Lausche, 1945–47, 1949–57

Metta Herbert Stevers (Hostess), 1947–48

Mildred Stevenson Herbert, 1948–49

Violet Helman Brown, 1957

Betty Hewson O'Neill, 1957–59

Myrtle England DiSalle, 1959–63

Helen Rawlins Rhodes, 1963–71, 1975–83

Mary Kathryn Dixon Gilligan, 1971–75

Dagmar Braun Celeste, 1983–91

Janet Voinovich, 1991–99

Hope Taft, 1999–

First Ladies of the United States

Anna Tuthill Symmes Harrison, 1841

Lucy Ware Webb Hayes, 1877–81

Lucretia Rudolph Garfield, 1881

Caroline Lavinia Scott Harrison, 1889–92

Ida Saxton McKinley, 1897–1901

Helen Herron Taft, 1909–13

Florence Kling Harding, 1921–23

Other Notable Women

BIBLIOGRAPHY

Blatt, Martin H., Thomas J. Brown, and Donald Yacovone, eds. *Hope and Glory: Essays on the Legacy of the Fifty-fourth Massachusetts Regiment.* Boston: University of Massachusetts Press, 2001.

Glavac, Cynthia, O.S.U. *In the Fullness of Life: A Biography of Dorothy Kazel, O.S.U.* Denville, N.J.: Dimension Books, 1996.

Hine, Darlene Clark, ed. *Black Women in America: An Historical Encyclopedia.* Vols. I and II. Brooklyn: Carlson Publishing, 1993.

Hood, Marilyn G., ed. *The First Ladies of Ohio and the Executive Mansions.* Columbus: The Ohio Historical Society, 1970.

Jones, Adrienne Lash. *Jane Edna Hunter: A Case Study of Black Leadership, 1910–1950. Black Women in United States History.* Brooklyn: Carlson Publishing, Inc., 1990.

Kates, Susan. *Activist Rhetorics and American Higher Education, 1885–1937.* Carbondale: Southern Illinois University Press, 2001.

Kuhn, Maggie, et al. *No Stone Unturned: The Life and Times of Maggie Kuhn.* New York: Ballantine Books, 1991.

Lawson, Ellen Nickenzie. *The Three Sarahs: Documents of Antebellum Black College Women. Studies in Women and Religion.* Vol. 13. New York: The Edwin Mellen Press, 1984.

Nasner, Ellen Susanna. *Clearview: America's Course.* Haslett, Mich.: Foxsong Publishing, 2000.

Ohio Women's Hall of Fame Archives, Ohio Department of Job and Family Services, Columbus, Ohio.

Ohio Women's Policy and Research Commission. *Women of the Ohio General Assembly: 1922–1996.* Columbus: Ohio Women's Policy and Research Commission, 1996.

Ohioana Library Association Archives, Columbus, Ohio.

Smith, Jessie Carney, ed. *Powerful Black Women.* Detroit: Visible Ink, 1996.

Women's History Committee, Gen. Ed. *In Search of Our Past: Women of Northwest Ohio.* 7 vols. Toledo: Women Alive! Coalition, 1987–2003 to date.

Selected Internet Resources

About Tracy Chapman. http://www.about-tracy-chapman.net. (2003).

Academy of American Poets, Find a Poet. http://www.poets.org/poets. (2003).

Andre Norton. http://www.andre-norton.org. (2003).

Africana: Gateway to the Black World. http://www.africana.com. (2003).

Alcoholics Anonymous. http://www.alcoholics-anonymous.org. (2003).

"Biography of Kathleen Battle." Bach Cantatas. http://www.bach-cantatas.com/Bio/Battle-Kathleen.htm. (2003).

Biographical Directory of the United States Congress, 1774–Present. http://bioguide.congress.gov. (2003).

The Black Family Network. http://blackfamilynet.net. (2003).

"Cessna 180: Spirit of Columbus." Smithsonian National Air and Space Museum. http://www.nasm.si.edu/nasm/aero/aircraft/cessna180.htm. (2003).

Columbus Dispatch. http://www.cd.columbus.oh.us. Columbus, Ohio. (2003).

"Eleanor Smeal." Feminist Majority Foundation Online. http://www.feminist.org/welcome/esbio.html. (2003).

Encyclopedia of Cleveland History. http://ech.cwru.edu. (2003).

Enquirer. http://cincnnati.com/. Cincinnati, Ohio. (2003).

"Farah B. Majidzadeh." Ellis Island Medal of Honor. http://www.neco.org/awards/recipients/fbmajid.html. (2003).

First Ladies' Gallery. The White House. http://www.whitehouse.gov/history/firstladies/index.html. (2003).

Heiss, Carol. U.S. Figure Skating Association. http://www.usfsa.org/about/worldskatingmuseum/index.htm. (2003).

"For Those Interested in Alcoholics Anonymous History." Welcome to Silkworth. http://silkworth.net. (2003).

Horizons. University of Cincinnati. http://www.horizons.uc.edu. (2003).

"Irene Duhart Long, M.D." Kennedy Space Center. http://www-pao.ksc.nasa.gov/bios/long.htm. (2003).

Justices of the Supreme Court of Ohio. http://www.sconet.state.oh.us/Justices. (2003).

Latham, Carol. Thermagon, Inc. http://www.thermagon.com. (2003).

"Margaret Wong." Margaret Wong & Associates Co., LPA. http://www.imwong.com. (2003).

"Marilyn Hughes Gaston, MD." Rural Health Conference. The University of Alabama. http://rhc.ua.edu/gaston.html. (2003).

"Sister Mary Ignatia Gavin, CSA." Angel of Hope. http://www.srsofcharity.org/aa.html. (2003).

MSN Entertainment. http://entertainment.msn.com. (2003).

Miss Nancy Wilson. http://www.missnancywilson.com. (2003).

National First Ladies' Library. http://www.firstladies.org. (2003).

National Organization for Women. http://www.now.org. (2003).

National Public Radio. Audio Archives. http://www.npr.org. (2003).

National Women's Hall of Fame. http://www.greatwomen.org. (2003).

Ohio Dominican University. http://www.ohiodominican.edu. (2003).

The Ohio State University. http://www.ohio-state.edu. (2003).

Ohio University. http://www.ohiou.edu. (2003).

Ohio Women's Hall of Fame. http://www.state.oh.us/odjfs/women/Halloffame. (2003).

PBS American Masters. http://www.pbs.org/wnet/americanmasters/database. (2003).

Painted Voices: Rita Dove. *Black Collegian* http://www.black-collegian.com/african/painted-voices. (2003).

Post. http://cincnnati.com/. Cincinnati, Ohio. (2003).

"Rita Dove." Gale. http://www.gale.com/free_resources/poets/bio/dove_r.htm. (2003).

The Rosemary Clooney Palladium. http://www.rosemaryclooney.com. (2003).

"Tami Longaberger Biography." Chief Executive—Nota Bene. http://www.chiefexec.net/depts/notabene/156tami.htm. (2003).

260

"Toni Morrison." Empire: ZINE. http://www.empirezine.com/spotlight/toni-morrison/
  toni-morrison.htm. (2003).

Verison Millrose Games. http://www.millrosegames.com. (2003).

Victoria Woodhull: The Spirit to Run the White House. http://www.victoria-woodhull.com.
  (2003).

Walters, Farah M. *Ellis Island Medal of Honor Recipients.* http://www.neco.org/awards/recipients/
  index2.html#w. (2003).

Women in American History. Encyclopedia Britannica. http://www.search.eb.com/women. (2003).

Women's History. The History Net. What You Need to Know About.
  http://womenshistory.about.com. (2003).

261

INDEX